D0231482

700040028635

GOLDFISH, CATERPILLARS & GUINEA PIGS

GOLDFISH, CATERPILLARS & GUINEA PIGS

ACCOUNTS OF PILOTS AND AIR CREWS
FROM THE SECOND WORLD WAR

COLIN PATEMAN

FONTHILL

This book is dedicated to all men who took to the air within the allied and Commonwealth air forces during the Second World War.

'Courage is rightly esteemed the first of human qualities, because it is the quality which guarantees all others.' Winston Churchill

Fonthill Media Limited
www.fonthillmedia.com
office@fonthillmedia.com

First published in the UK and USA 2012

British Library Cataloguing in Publication Data:
A catalogue record for this book is available from the British Library

Copyright © Colin Pateman, 2012

ISBN 978-1-78155-078-6 (print)
ISBN 978-1-78155-093-9 (e-book)

The right of Colin Pateman to be identified as the author of this work has been asserted by him in accordance with the Copyright, Designs and Patents Act 1988.

All rights reserved. No part of this publication may be reproduced, stored in a retrieval system or transmitted in any form or by any means, electronic, mechanical, photocopying, recording or otherwise, without prior permission in writing from Fonthill Media Limited

Typeset in 10/14 Sabon
Printed and bound in England.

CONTENTS

Acknowledgements

It is to be noted that the research undertaken on this publication has taken place over many years. Several of the contributors have sadly since passed away. I respectfully include their names below alongside other valued contributors and, in addition, thank all individuals not mentioned for the many letters and other forms of correspondence.

S. McQuillan – 196 Squadron, C. Stone DFM – 72 Squadron, Alex Campbell – 514 Squadron, E. Trotter DFC DFM – 156 Squadron, Gp Capt. Randle CBE AFC DFM, D. Morgan – RAF Escaping Society, B. Morgan – RAF Escaping Society, P. Pipkin, D. Felton, L. Zwingli, J. Caws, W. Willemsen – Dutch Association of Allied Aircrew Helpers, Guy de Win – Historical Document Centre Belgian Armed Forces, RAF Air Historical Branch, P. Baillie, Imperial War Museum, D. Farnsworth – Historic Flying Co., Simon Muggleton, Mrs Robertson – Goldfish Club, R. Graham – Goldfish Club, J. Adams – Caterpillar Club, J. Toper – Guinea Pig Club, R. Marchant – Guinea Pig Club, M. Quayle – Spinks, D. Erskine-Hill – Dix Noonan and Webb, Oliver Clutton-Brock, Rick Jones, Martyn Ford-Jones, Phillip Kaufmann – Lancashire Aircraft Investigation Team, Michael Dilts – Switlik Parachute Co., James Caws.

Where possible I have credited photographic images. The majority originate from my collection. Every care has been taken to trace copyright holders, however if I have omitted anyone, I apologise and will, if advised, make corrections to any future edition. Special thanks to David Farnsworth for his superb images to support the appendices, and to Mark Quayle and David Erskine-Hill for the use of their respective auction house photographic archives.

It would be remiss of me not to mention my wife Sarah-Jane, who constantly answered my information technology problem-solving questions with great patience and ability.

Foreword

An entire generation of young men fought for our country's freedom. In the air, at sea, or on land, the fight for survival became a daily battle. For airmen, it was their duty to do whatever it took to defend the skies and ward off the enemy over Europe and other areas of conflict during the Second World War. The Royal Air Force, together with her Commonwealth counterparts, comprised of young men from all walks of life: academics, tradesmen, and those who volunteered direct from schooling. The common denominators between them were the determination, personal strength, and willingness to fight for freedom. These young men were prepared to accept many challenges. The academics honed their skills as navigators and pilots; engineers developed their skills to ensure the aircraft remained in the air, whilst others were trained in the skills required for air gunnery, bomb aiming, and wireless operators. Many of the young men were volunteers trained in weekend camps facilitated by the Royal Air Force. Significant numbers of young men consistently and willingly followed others who were lost in the trade of war.

Through the research undertaken and evidence gathered in the writing of this book, I have been able to provide detailed accounts of aircrew who, despite the odds stacked against them, fought to survive, escaping death by the use of parachutes, rubber inflation devices in the sea, or – through sheer determination and will power – walked back to freedom through enemy territory. Also the young men, who were so terribly burned in aerial combat and from crash landings, but through the expertise of an incredible and pioneering surgeon, were given a second chance. The spirit of survival was celebrated across the entire air force in the guise of unofficial clubs, which grew and became widely respected during the Second World War, continuing into peacetime.

The Second World War comprised of 2,074 days and nights between 3 September 1939 and 8 May 1945. It must be remembered that, whilst film and prints have immortalised the pilots who fought in the Battle of Britain in the famous Spitfires and Hurricanes, many men took part in Bomber Command operations, which had grown from what was considered in the early part of the war to be an ineffective force, to one of immense capability, designed for the specific purpose of winning the war. The destruction of Germany's highly effective war machine engaged endless young crews in bomber aircraft high above occupied Europe and other areas of conflict. Those aircraft with iconic names like the Lancaster and Halifax became replacements for the early light bombers that took such heavy losses during the initial conflict.

Approximately 125,000 aircrew served Bomber Command, and 55,573 became fatal casualties. The Commonwealth War Graves Commission maintains a significantly large proportion of those casualties' graves to this day. The Reichswald Cemetery near Cleves contains 3,971 RAF casualties alone, more than any other of the thirteen cemeteries within Germany. The Berlin cemetery itself reflects the many aircrew casualties lost in the Battle of Berlin campaign undertaken by Bomber Command between August 1943 and March 1944. The Commonwealth War Graves Commission has registered 347,151 recovered casualties from all services in the Second World War, with all graves commemorated and cared for in perpetuity.

There remains an additional 232,931 personnel who are registered as missing. These casualties are commemorated by individually inscribed names upon many memorials across the world. The principle air force memorials recording these losses are at Alamein, Singapore, Malta, and the large Runnymede Memorial in Surrey, south-east England. The essential criteria in deciding where an airman was to be commemorated depended on where he was based, and not necessarily the area in which he was presumed lost. The Runnymede Memorial itself commemorates 20,000 airmen and women of the Commonwealth Air Forces who died over north-western and central Europe, the British Isles, and the eastern Atlantic and who have no known grave.

I am full of respect and admiration for these young men, many of whom were inexperienced in life, yet did more than anyone could have asked of them. The stories I have told within this book are those that had a chance to cling to life, and as such are forever members of the Guinea Pig, Goldfish, Caterpillar, or Late Arrival clubs.

Colin Pateman

Introduction

There were a number of clubs during the Second World War that a serving member of the Royal Air Force or Commonwealth aircrew could join. One of the first was the Malcolm Club, formed by the air officer commander-in-chief, Air Chief Mar. Sir Arthur Tedder (later Lord Tedder). Sir Arthur was anxious to provide for members of the RAF in Algiers, North Africa. The Malcolm Club was named after RAF Wg Cdr Hugh Malcolm, the first recipient in the Royal Air Force to be awarded the Victoria Cross in North Africa in the Second World War, who lost his life aged twenty-five. Alongside the Malcolm Club, which grew across the entire network of both overseas- and UK-based stations, were other clubs and organisations, including the NAFFI, the navy, army, and air force institutes – the latter being created by the British government during the interwar period. These clubs provided recreational and retail establishments for the British armed forces.

Not so easy to join were a number of exclusive and unofficial clubs where eligibility was determined by the need to satisfy certain conditions upon application. Those that sought membership could claim that it was most definitely earned through experiencing some of the more dramatic situations that an airman could encounter through flying, both in training and in operational deployments across all commands within the allied air forces.

The Caterpillar Club and the Goldfish Club were formed as a result of airmen using equipment designed and manufactured specifically to save lives. The Late Arrivals Club was through the sheer determination on the part of the airman to return back to allied lines in the western desert. Eligibility for the Guinea Pig Club was the most exclusive due to an airman having had to be operated on by the legendary plastic surgeon Archibald McIndoe. These were the four main 'unofficial' clubs, and whilst achieving membership status was not on an airman's wish list, those that were eligible

The Malcolm Club.

were acknowledged by others to be worthy of respect and admiration for surviving despite all the odds.

There were individuals that achieved eligibility to several of the clubs through one incident alone, such as an airman who used a parachute to save his life from a burning aircraft and who then received medical treatment by Archibald McIndoe. This made him a recipient of both the Caterpillar and Guinea Pig Clubs.

In addition to the then well-known Irvin Air Chute Co., there were many manufacturers engaged in the production of equipment that was constructed and designed to save the lives of aircrew. PAK Parachutes in Mitcham, Surrey, was a smaller company that had patents upon their own parachutes. They made and supplied many chutes under licence to other parachute manufacturers. Stoke Road in Guildford, Surrey, was home to many factories including RFD Co.,[1] who produced parachute harnesses as well as Youngman auto-inflating survival dinghies, and the GQ Parachute Co. who designed and produced their own parachutes. James Gregory and Raymond Quilter, the partners in GQ Parachute Co. saw massive expansion in orders from the Air Ministry. Remaining in Surrey, they expanded into larger premises becoming a significant rival to Irvin's. These were by no

Air crew wearing early flying suits and parachute harnesses celebrating their return from bombing the German fleet on 18 December 1939.

means the only companies engaged in the production of such equipment; they are, however, some of the more significant of that time.

Each company provided the Air Ministry with their respective orders, with safety and quality control being of paramount importance during the entire manufacture and production process. Each item was given a unique serial number, enabling every Mae West life jacket, parachute, harness, or dinghy to be identifiable. In respect of parachutes, the Royal Air Force issued record cards; a form 1507 that would show the store's reference number, the contract number, supplier's reference, the parachutes personal identification number, the type of parachute, and any modifications undertaken to the parachute. An inspection date, noted against the authorising officer's signature, confirmed and recorded that the item was serviceable. Having been issued and deployed operationally, the parachute section would recall the parachute after several months' service. Form 1507 would be amended to reflect the re-examination of the parachute and any repairs undertaken. Prior to repacking, the parachute would be aired to ensure complete dryness. The parachute would then be reissued to another member of aircrew.

Much the same procedure was followed with Mae Wests, but several officers, particularly within Fighter Command, personalised them with painted charms or mascot images. These no doubt were regarded as personal issue by those pilots, treating them in the same way as their own flying helmets and oxygen masks, where personal responsibility was undertaken. The survival items would travel with each officer or NCO on postings or movements within the Royal Air Force.

The Caterpillar Club: Irvin Air Chute Co.

The Caterpillar Club was founded by Leslie Irvin of the Irvin Air Chute Co. of Canada in 1922. Around 1920, Leslie was a twenty-four-year-old stunt man from California, who demonstrated the first 'free drop' parachute – having made the chute himself on a borrowed sewing machine. Flying safety experts were so impressed that the American Air Force and British RAF promptly adopted the parachute as standard equipment.

Irvin then opened production factories in the USA and England. An early brochure of the Irvin Parachute Co. acknowledges a William O'Connor, who, on the 24 August 1920 at McCook Field Flying Station near Dayton, Ohio, became the first person to be saved by an Irvin parachute. On 20 October 1922, Lt Harold R. Harris, chief test pilot in the engineering division at Dayton jumped from a failing monoplane fighter. Shortly after, two reporters from the Dayton Herald, realising that there would be more jumps in future, suggested that a club should be formed. Harris became the first member, and from that time forward any person who jumped from a disabled aircraft with a parachute became a member of the Caterpillar Club.

The name 'Caterpillar Club' simply makes reference to the silk threads that made the original parachutes, thus recognising the debt owed to the silk worm.[2] Later in the war, the switch to nylon occurred. The caterpillar is symbolic of the silk worm, which lets it descend gently to earth from a height by spinning a silky thread upon which to hang. Another metaphor is that caterpillars have to climb out of their cocoons to escape. 'Life depends on a silken thread' is the club's motto.

In 1922, Leslie Irvin agreed to give a gold pin to every person whose life was saved by one of his parachutes. The Irvin Golden Caterpillar has amethyst eyes. Several stories have circulated in relation to differing coloured eyes on the caterpillar pins, but only the amethyst exist in the original issue pins. In order to gain membership to the Caterpillar Club, prospective members produced documentation of a life saving incident to the parachute manufacturer. In many applications the parachutes were identified by serial

Caterpillar Club Pin.

numbers and types. Those details were frequently checked against the factories production information. Letters to Irvin's were in some instances very detailed. The requirements for receiving a gold pin and membership were stringent, with all personnel applying to the club needing to evidence that their life had been saved by the parachute.

PO C. Penfold became the first RAF pilot to apply for membership into the Caterpillar Club. Having evidenced his account on the 17 June 1926, when his Avro developed aileron control difficulties which forced him to bail out over a golf course, Leslie Irvin enrolled Penfold as his first Royal Air Force officer into the club. Penfold was acknowledged as the thirty-first member. Within a matter of weeks, two flight sergeants, H. Steanes and W. Frost, were to have the honour of becoming the first NCOs to be accepted. On the 20 July 1926, both pilots collided in their Fairey Fox aircraft over Andover. Steanes and Frost jumped from the aircraft and made safe descents; both aircraft were destroyed. Between June 1926 and June 1930 the Caterpillar Club enrolled a total of forty-seven Royal Air Force applicants.

At the end of the Second World War, the number of members with Irvin pins had grown to over 34,000, though the total of people saved by Irvin parachutes was estimated to be 100,000. There were other parachute manufacturers who issued an insignia for successful jumps. GQ Parachutes Co. formed their Gold Club in 1940 and issued a lapel pin. The Switlik Parachute Co. of Trenton, New Jersey, issued both gold and silver caterpillar pins, and the Pioneer Parachute Co. in Skokie, Illinois, presented plaques to people who had packed the parachutes that were known to have saved lives.

In addition to saving lives through the use of a parachute, many men had to evade enemy-occupied territory and then became members of the Royal Air Forces Escaping Society.[3] Each recipient of the caterpillar pin is living testimony to the lifesaving ability of the Irvin-type air chute. In addition to

Congratulations . . .

It is indeed a pleasure to welcome you as a member of the Caterpillar Club.

As is customary, we have had the official insignia of the Club made and engraved especially for you, which you will find attached, together with your membership certificate.

We have pleasure in sending these to you with our compliments and best wishes, in recognition of the emergency parachute jump which you made.

CATERPILLAR CLUB.

Caterpillar Club Congratulations Card.

the membership pin, Irvin issued a membership card. At least two variants exist; one of these is the European Division, which has an illustration of a large caterpillar upon the card. The more commonly seen membership card depicts two parachutes. Both variants were hand signed by Leslie Irvin and heat sealed within plastic. Some examples exist where Mrs Leslie Irvin applied the signature, instead of her husband.

Applications to join the Caterpillar Club consistently increased throughout the Second World War. The membership statistics are:

1944:
July   9,783
October   12,409
November   13,075

1945:
January   14,528
April   17,862

May	20,952
June	22,618
July	23,034
August	23,505
September	23,797
October	30,000

Many applications originated from RAF prisoners of war. Germany operated approximately fifty-four prisoner of war camps, identified as Oflag,[4] Stalag,[5] and Stalag Luft.[6] The majority of allied airmen captured across Europe were imprisoned in the Stalag Luft camps. Stalag Luft III Sagan was made famous for the great escape tunnels in March 1944.[7] In early 1945, the combined-camp registration undertaken by the Germans indicated that approximately 169,000 officers and men of the British dominion, and other allied forces, were imprisoned across these European camps.[8]

Leslie Irvin became proficient at processing the applications received from the prison camps. Most were received via the *Kriegsgefangenenpost* prisoner of war postal system, either on flimsy air mail letters or the *Kriegsgefangenenlager* postcards. This censored mail was always replied to by Leslie, his wife, or a member of his staff, and frequent instructions were received from the airmen to send the membership card and caterpillar pin to a wife or family member. In 1944, the club was forced to write to new members advising that the membership cards had been forwarded as requested, but it was proving impossible to keep up with the supply of the gold caterpillar pins. Many applicants from the 1944-45 periods never received their membership pin until well after the war.

During the Second World War – although unofficial – eligible aircrew would wear the tiny caterpillar on their uniform. Frequently now seen in period photographs, the pin would generally be attached to any medal ribbons if so awarded to the recipient, typically the Distinguished Flying Cross, or the Distinguished Flying Medal. The pins were frequently lost, and post-war years saw many requests to the club for replacements. As a service to members who had experienced the loss of their original gold pin, Irvin supplied replacement silver pins. For this reason, variations of the pins exist. Early issue pins were engraved 'Pres [presented] by Irvin', with the recipients rank and name below. Later issue pins included only the recipient details. The minute chisel engraving is masterful in detail.

In February 1945, Irvin Air Chutes published a special request to all of its members:

The Caterpillar Club is a properly constituted organisation open to all who save their lives in emergency with an airchute of Irvin design, regardless of the manufacture. There is no entrance fee or charge of any kind. Those who qualify are enrolled as soon as authenticated applications have been scrutinised. A membership card is sent immediately to a newly elected member and, shortly afterwards, follows the Club badge, the little golden caterpillar, with his name engraved on the back. This genuine gold pin is the only approved badge of the Club. Members are particularly asked not to wear any other unofficial insignia and to discourage others from purchasing or wearing any imitation or unapproved substitute such as the embroidered fabric badges which are being sold by apparently misguided traders.

The Caterpillar Club: Switlik

Two civilian members of the military parachute unit at McCook Field,[9] United States Army Air Corp, Dayton, Ohio – Mr Mumma and Mr St Clair – became involved in the investigation of the aircraft accident in which the former USAAC pilot, Harold Harris, jumped to safety by the use of his parachute in late 1922.

Sometime later, St Clair suggested the parachute escape should herald the start of an exclusive club. Various names, including the Skyhookers Club, were suggested, however the Caterpillar Club was eventually settled upon. Both Caterpillar clubs originated within close proximity to each other, following the incident in 1922 involving Harold Harris.

In 1925 Mr Walter Lees of the Packard Motor Car Co. suggested some sort of an emblem for the Switlik Caterpillar members; he had a vested interest in the club as he had recently become a founder member.[10] A pin in the shape of a caterpillar worm, with the words 'Caterpillar Club' emblazoned across its back, was designed by St Clair. This was very different from the subtle and small gold pin created by Irvin.

At that time there was no formal connection to any parachute manufacturer. Any person whose life was saved by the use of a parachute in an emergency jump from an aeroplane was eligible for membership in the Caterpillar Club. The Caterpillar Club name and badge design was technically held under the control of St Clair, who left the USAAC engineering division and gained employment with the Switlik Parachute Co.

Stanley Switlik,[11] a Polish immigrant, had been responsible for the development of the company that carried his name. He began manufacturing

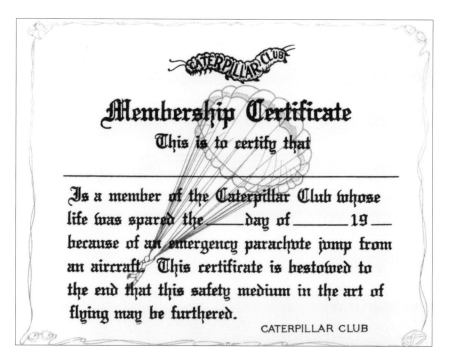

Membership Certificate
This is to certify that

_____

**Is a member of the Caterpillar Club whose
life was spared the ____day of _____ 19 ___
because of an emergency parachute jump from
an aircraft. This certificate is bestowed to
the end that this safety medium in the art of
flying may be furthered.**

CATERPILLAR CLUB

Switlik membership certificate.

parachutes in the 1930s as a result of the boom in aviation. In 1941 Switlik parachutes were directed by the War Department to increase production on a massive scale. This they achieved, becoming one of America's most efficient and effective suppliers of parachutes during the Second World War. St Clair was an engineer with Switlik Parachute Co. for a period of over twenty years. On the 18 June 1943, St Clair sold the Caterpillar name and design to Switlik Parachute Co. for just $1.

To this day, the Switlik Caterpillar Club has a very large membership, but surprisingly, only twenty-five members of the Royal Canadian Air Force and the Royal Air Force satisfied the stringent requirements to gain membership during the Second World War.[12] Many Commonwealth pilots and aircrew were trained in airfields across both Canada and the United States, and therefore the twenty-five Switlik Caterpillar Club members most probably joined as a result of training incidents involving emergency escapes.

It is of note that membership of this club was accepted from applicants who had saved their lives by the use of any manufactured parachute. Switlik Parachute Co. embraced the Caterpillar Club and supported it in every aspect. The company continues to develop and manufacture survival equipment to the military and civil aviation industry today. The Caterpillar Club archives are held within the company's repository, and amongst them are the rather exclusive twenty-five members from the RCAF and RAF of the Second World War.

The Roo Club: Dominion Parachute Co.

Light Aircraft Pty Ltd, Sydney, Australia, was a significant manufacturer of parachutes to the allied Far East campaign during the Second World War. Their parachutes carried the identification label 'Dominion Parachute' with the company logo of a kangaroo depicted descending upon an inflated chute. The factory commenced major production in early 1941, and the design was primarily to the standard set by Irvin parachutes. As with Irvin, the company decided to allow the dominion parachute users, whose lives had been saved, membership to a club administered from the factory. The Roo Club was represented by the parachuting kangaroo.

The events over Buckingham Palace at 11.10 a.m. on Friday 13 September 1940 provided the inspiration to present a special seat-pack assembly dominion parachute to the Royal Air Force, and in particular to the 501 Squadron Hurricane pilot responsible for shooting down the Buckingham Palace bomber. A single Luftwaffe bomber[13] had dropped several high explosive bombs that fell into the quadrangle and forecourt of the palace. Three staff and a warden were slightly injured as a result of the attack. The damage was not particularly bad but media interest was high. Photographs of the bomb damage to the iron railings, breaching the security to the palace, created a strong physical image in the newspapers. The King and Queen were resident in the palace at the time of the raid.

The Blitz Then and Now, published by After the Battle, provides the following quote from His Majesty King George VI:

> We went to London from Windsor and found an air raid in progress. The day was very cloudy and it was raining hard. The Queen and I went upstairs to a small sitting room overlooking the quadrangle. All of a sudden we heard the zooming noise of a diving aircraft getting louder, and louder, and then saw two bombs falling past the opposite side of Buckingham Palace into the quadrangle. We saw the flashes and heard the detonations as they burst about eighty yards away. The blast blew in the windows opposite to us, and two great craters had appeared in the quadrangle. From one of these craters water

from a burst main was pouring out and flowing into the passage through the broken windows. The whole thing happened in a matter of seconds, and we were very quickly out into the passage.

In all five bombs had been dropped. Two fell within the central quadrangle of the palace, two outside at the front, one of which was a delayed action bomb with an unknown timed fuse, and the last bomb landed in the palace's chapel. The bombing did not end until 8.40 a.m. the following morning, when the delayed-action bomb that was lying between the forecourt gates and the Victoria Memorial finally detonated. Although bomb disposal units had been given ample time to build 6-foot-high sandbag walls around the bomb, the explosion destroyed much of the forecourt fencing around the south gate and left a large crater.

The Luftwaffe bomber thought to have been responsible was located by the now famous pilot Ginger Lacey, operating with 501 Squadron from RAF Kenley. At that time he was a sergeant pilot, and was vectored into an area of sky covered in deep cloud in terribly difficult flying conditions. Managing to maintain contact, Lacey engaged his guns in an attempt to shoot down the bomber. His Hurricane was in turn struck by the bombers defensive guns, resulting in a fire from the Hurricane's engine. Undeterred, Lacey continued to fire at the bomber. He managed to inflict the utmost-possible damage, with both engines of the bomber erupting in flames. Lacey needed to escape from his cockpit, as the flames had entered the footwell and his trousers were now burning. The experience of bailing out and parachuting to safety was about to be undertaken by Lacey for the first time. Floating down under his canopy, Lacey saw his Hurricane P2793 plunge into the ground near Maidstone, Kent. It appears that the German bomber did in fact manage to cross the English Channel, but eventually crashed, killing all on board.

The special parachute was referred to as the 'royal parachute' due to the connection with the Buckingham Palace raid. The metal quick release box was engraved:

> For Gallant Service Over Buckingham Palace
> Presented by Staff of Light Aircraft Pty Ltd
> Sydney Australia

Just two days later on the 15 September, Lacey was to claim three enemy aircraft shot down during aerial combat and a further aircraft damaged in combat over Kent. On the 17 September he himself was shot down, and once more forced to take to the silk, his parachute thankfully saving his life once more.

Air Vice-Mar. Sir Quintin Brand KBE DSO MC, air officer commanding 10 Group RAF, presented Ginger Lacey with the specially made royal parachute at RAF Chilbolton in July 1941. It became a treasured possession for Lacey, who had been rewarded with the Distinguished Flying Medal and bar whilst in the non-commissioned ranks. Later commissioned and promoted, he is regarded as one of the great Battle of France and Battle of Britain 'ace' pilots. At the end of the war he had accumulated a total of twenty-eight enemy aircraft destroyed, five probably destroyed, and nine others damaged.[14] Ginger Lacey died in 1989 and the presentation dominion parachute that he had kept and treasured was later handed over to the care of 501 Squadron. It is now regarded as a most important piece of history for this famous Battle of Britain fighter squadron.

During the Blitz, Buckingham Palace and its grounds were bombed on sixteen separate occasions. The palace forecourt, inner quadrangle, and both north and south wings were all struck by high explosive and delayed-action bombs. The specific targeting of Buckingham Palace by the Luftwaffe resulted in only partial success. Physical damage was limited and there were no mass casualties. It is of note, however, that a police officer was killed by a single bomb that was dropped on 8 March 1941, and several staff sustained injuries during the bombing of Buckingham Palace during the Second World War.

The Goldfish Club

The Goldfish Club was formed in November 1942 by Charles A. Robertson. He was the chief draftsman at P. B. Cow & Co.,[15] who were at that time one of the world's largest manufacturers of air-sea rescue equipment. After hearing of the experiences of airmen who had survived a ditching at sea, Charles decided to form an exclusive club for the pilots and aircrews who owed their lives to their life jackets and dinghies. The Air Ministry had previously vetoed an earlier attempt by a Reginald Foster Dagnall, RFD Ltd, to create a similar club under the title of the Silverfish Club. At that time his company was actively engaged in manufacturing rubber life rafts of similar design to those of P. B. Cow. An interesting point to note is that the Goldfish Club was created in the month that Reginal Dagnall died.

With P. B. Cow & Co.'s backing, and tacit consent from the Air Ministry, the club was duly named the Goldfish Club: gold for the value of life, and fish for the water. RAF and allied airmen who escaped from their distressed aircraft over the sea and used an emergency dinghy were invited to become life members of the club. Each member was presented with a heat-sealed waterproof membership card (an innovative concept for that period in time), and an embroidered badge, with a bar to the badge for those who used an emergency dinghy for a second time. News of the club spread rapidly, and in January 1943, the BBC broadcast an interview by Wynford Vaughan-Thomas[16] with Charles and two members who had qualified on their first operational flight.

Charles Robertson's original badge design consisted of bound wire thread, to make it hardwearing, upon a dark cloth background. There were problems in obtaining the required wire in sufficient quantity. In fact, due to wartime regulations, the production of metallic-embroidered badges was prohibited and all cloth severely rationed. These problems were overcome with silk embroidery substituted for wire upon black cloth. The obstacle as to the requirement of coupons for the supply of cloth needed a solution, however. Colleagues of Charles working in the drawing office of P. B. Cow resolved this issue by volunteering to surrender their dress suits. The material was subsequently used for the initial badges. An additional appeal by columnist William Hickey of the *London Daily Express* resulted in a substantial amount of old evening-dress suits being sent in to Charles by readers. From that point onwards the production of 'goldfish badges' had been secured.

Official uniform dress regulations prohibited the wearing of the Goldfish Club badge on British and American uniforms. Naval aircrew[17] generally wore it on their Mae Wests, whereas many RAF aircrews wore the badge under the flap of their left hand uniform pocket. The goldfish badge was also frequently sewn on the central pleat of battledress jackets. Although it was an unofficial award, it was respected by the senior ranks and allowed to be worn openly in many instances.

In April 1943, the correspondence section within the popular publication *Flight* carried an article:

'The Goldfish Club'. Membership conditions too narrow.

Some publicity has been given to the formation of the Goldfish Club open to those who have saved their lives by using their rubber dinghies. So far as I can see no provision has been made for those who avoided a watery end by other means. Sometimes, for various reasons, the dinghy didn't work and the crews did it the hard way, hanging on to a piece of aircraft that might sink at any moment. My crew had nearly an hour of this tingling expectancy before the Navy turned up. Fortunately a cruiser saw us go in. The Goldfish Club, if open to only dinghy users in its present form, is not representative of those who have ditched. Per Ardua Ad Mare.

Charles Robertson replied to the letter:

May 6th 1943

The letter from 'Per Ardua ad Mare' (Anonymous) expresses the opinion that the qualification necessary to join the Goldfish Club are too limited. Since I have from time to time received letters from airmen with similar views, it may be of interest generally to explain that the club was originally formed to grant recognition to those airmen who had been through the ordeal of using an emergency dinghy, and thereby saving their lives. The policy of the club was mainly dominated by letters received from aircrews that were exceedingly enthusiastic concerning the formation of a club of this nature. Thus it will be appreciated that the club qualifications dependence on the use of an emergency dinghy was introduced by popular consent, and confirmed during the clubs inauguration by broadcast in 1942. I do occasionally receive letters from airmen who have saved their lives by the use of a Mae West life jacket, or even by clinging onto aircraft wreckage and on these occasions membership is invariably granted, the membership card being endorsed to cover this in an appropriate manner. It should be emphasised that a life saved is the main factor and it is this we really wish to commemorate. While I have the opportunity, I feel sure members will be interested to know that the club badge and illustrated membership card have been accepted as official exhibits in the Imperial War Museum.

C. A. Robertson. Hon Secretary. Goldfish Club.

Charles designed the Goldfish Club membership card himself. His skills as an architect are reflected in the quality of the design, with his own artwork used on the reverse of the card. Examination of a card reveals that the design has stood the test of time as a contemporary piece of art, combining the elements of not only the dinghy produced by P. B. Cow, but the impressive illustrations of aircraft, pilots, and pertinent elements relative to the club, are all present. The front of the cards recorded the incident date. All membership cards were personally signed by Charles, and identified to the recipient.

By the end of the Second World War, the club had 9,000 members from all branches of the allied forces. Charles attempted to end the granting of membership at the end of the war, but with applications continuing to arrive, membership had to continue as well. Charles resigned from P. B. Cow in 1947. However he continued to act as the membership secretary, retaining the club records and operating it at his own expense.

An article in the Royal Air Force Association journal *Airmail*, in January 1951, brought renewed interest in the Goldfish Club, and following a successful and well attended reunion dinner, the club was reorganised on a formal basis in March 1953 – but this time becoming subscription based. Members were required to rejoin on that basis, providing basic details of their ditching and submitting a fee of 5s a year. Reunions have been held annually ever since at various venues with many distinguished guests. In response to a message of greetings sent to her, Mae West[18] made it clear that she took great pride in the fact that members of the RAF had adopted her name for their life jackets. Aircrew who joined the Goldfish Club, having had their life saved by the use of a Mae West, had the membership card with 'Endorsed Membership' typed in red, advising that it was as a result of the Mae West. The newly formed subscription-based Goldfish Club made it clear that members were required to renew membership on an annual basis.

Charles Robertson eventually settled in the market town of Hailsham, East Sussex, where he ran a successful toy shop business for many years. The author had the privilege to meet with his family during the attempt to locate and secure any Goldfish Club records of administration. Due to the passing years, and with no reason to think otherwise, the original Goldfish Club records regarded as personal to Charles were destroyed, hence no longer in existence.

Members of the Goldfish Club have included airmen who qualified in the First World War, more than twenty years before the club was formed. A large number of those who joined during the Second World War rejoined on learning of the club's continued existence. Interestingly, the only German member to qualify was ejected from his F104G jet aircraft as part of the NATO forces in 1971. Many of the older club members have passed on, but new members continue to keep the club in existence. Helicopter crews predominate these days, since ditchings are rare among combat aircraft.

The Late Arrivals Club

The Desert Air Force formed the Late Arrivals Club in June 1941. Membership was exclusive for those personnel who, following the need to abandon their aircraft as a result of enemy action, or mechanical failures, successfully returned to allied lines, having eluded the enemy and survived the harsh and inhospitable desert conditions.

The Late Arrivals Club was unofficial, however a certificate was issued with a badge that stated, 'The member is permitted to wear the Emblem of the Winged Boot on the left breast of his flying suit.' The badge, made in the shape of a winged desert flying boot, was originally sand, cast in silver, and made by local jewellers and silversmiths in Egypt. The boot signified those members of the club who had walked back from behind enemy lines. The certificate also stated, 'This airman when obliged to abandon his aircraft on the ground or in the air as the result of unfriendly action by the enemy, succeeded in returning to his Squadron on foot or by other means long after his estimated time of arrival. It's never too late to come back.' It became an accepted requirement for those applying for membership to have taken longer than 48 hours to evade the enemy to walk to the safety of their own lines.

One of the first members of the Late Arrivals Club was a young pilot from 80 Squadron, FO Peter Wykeham-Barnes. On 4 August 1940, during the squadron's first serious aerial battle over Bir Taieb el Esem, Peter engaged Italian aircraft in his Gladiator aircraft.[19] Peter shot down two enemy aircraft, but was himself shot down and walked back towards the Egyptian border where he was picked up by a British army patrol. Although this action took place in 1940, prior to the club being formed, Peter was welcomed as a founder member in early 1941. Peter had joined the Royal Air Force as an aircraft apprentice in 1932 and three years later took a cadetship to the RAF college at Cranwell. Graduating in 1937 as a pilot to 80 Fighter Squadron, Peter was awarded the DFC in November 1940 and a bar to that medal in 1941. A DSO followed in 1943 for leading offensive operations in the Italian theatre, and he later took command of 140 Mosquito Wing in 2 Group, where he led the legendary Mosquito raid on the Gestapo headquarters at Aarhus in Denmark – for which was awarded a bar to his DSO. Peter continued to serve post war within the RAF and reached the rank of air vice-marshal, probably the highest ranking member of the Royal Air Force to have worn the 'winged boot'.

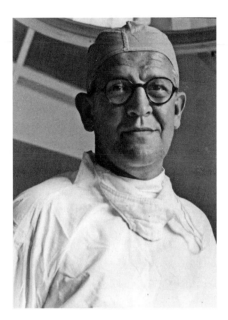

Guinea Pig Surgeon Archie McIndoe.

The Guinea Pig Club

The Guinea Pig Club was founded by thirty-nine medical patients in 1941. Each patient had been a member of the Royal Air Force, or one of its Commonwealth air forces, and had been subjected to reconstructive plastic surgery at the Queen Victoria Hospital in East Grinstead. These RAF aviators had been operated upon by the New Zealand surgeon, Archibald McIndoe. McIndoe arrived in London in 1930 when he took up an appointment as clinical assistant in the department of plastic surgery at St Bartholomew's Hospital. Soon afterwards, he received his first permanent appointment as a general surgeon and lecturer at the Hospital for Tropical Diseases and the London School of Hygiene and Tropical Medicine. In 1934, he obtained the fellowship of the American College of Surgeons. McIndoe held this appointment until 1939, when he became a consulting plastic surgeon to the Royal North Stafford Infirmary and to Croydon General Hospital. McIndoe had trained with his cousin Harold Gillies,[20] who stimulated his lifelong passion for reconstructive surgery. McIndoe later became the consultant surgeon to the Royal Air Force, specialising in plastic surgery. Although plastic surgery was established during the First World War, McIndoe was one of only three experienced plastic surgeons in Britain when war was declared against Germany in 1939.

Archibald McIndoe went on to achieve critical acclaim during the Second World War for his pioneering work at Queen Victoria Hospital.[21] He carried out ground breaking reconstructive surgery techniques on pilots and aircrew who had suffered serious burns or significant disfigurement from across the Commonwealth air forces. This was a time of great technical developments and inspiring work by McIndoe. It was, however, membership to the exclusive Guinea Pig Club that provided the most significant medication: the psychological reconstruction of its members. This proved fundamental to the process of keeping up morale, and he saw no reason to exclude beer from the wards. Established in 1941 – first as a drinking club – the Guinea Pig Club ensured that the men did not feel isolated whilst undergoing treatment at the hospital. The beer was on tap and became an all-important part of recovery.

The term 'guinea pig' indicated the experimental nature of the reconstructive work carried out on the club's members, and the new equipment and procedures designed specifically to treat these terrible injuries. In the early days of plastic surgery for burns, there was little emphasis on reintegration of patients into normal life after treatment. The Guinea Pig Club was the result of McIndoe's efforts to make life in the hospital easy for his patients and to begin to rebuild them psychologically in preparation for life outside the hospital. Full membership was open to all allied air forces servicemen who had suffered injuries – primarily as a result of fire, but other facial injuries were included. Inevitably aircrews suffered considerably from explosions and fire eruptions when involved in crashes, however ground crew personnel often risked their lives in rescue attempts, resulting in similar injuries. Reconstructive surgery operations at East Grinstead conducted by McIndoe automatically entitled the patient to Guinea Pig Club membership. The types of injuries requiring his attention frequently entailed significant numbers of operations, the piece by piece rebuilding of damaged skin tissue over weeks, months, and years. Unlike many military hospitals at the time or since, patients were encouraged to lead as normal a life as possible. They could wear their usual clothes or service uniforms instead of 'convalescent blues', and were able to leave the hospital at will. Despite the pain and seriousness of their injuries, the patients never lost their sense of humour, hence the name, the 'Guinea Pig Club', and this was reflected in the way the club was run with humour working its way into the club's committee selections. Archibald McIndoe became president of the club and it was decided that the first secretary had to be a patient with badly burned fingers, which meant he was excused from writing many letters; meeting notes could be short and therefore easy to read. The first treasurer had to be a member whose legs were burned, as this ensured he could not abscond with the funds. The emblem of the club became a guinea pig with RAF wings, to signify they were McIndoe's Guinea Pigs. If patients had fractures or lacerations they were referred to as 'mashed', and if they had severe burns they were 'fried' or 'hash-browned'. The Guinea Pigs had their own particular style of black humour.

One of the reasons that pilots and aircrews suffered so seriously came about from the new high-octane fuels used within aircraft from all commands of the RAF. Aircraft fuel tanks frequently ignited when struck by enemy anti-aircraft fire. In addition, the entire fuel system operated by the flight engineers within Bomber Command represented vulnerable areas to damage and subsequent eruption of fire. The aircraft designers continued to develop self-sealing fuel tanks[22] in an effort to combat that serious threat. The early Battle of Britain fighter pilots suffered deep tissue burns, the like of which surgeons had not encountered previously. In many instances, the fuel system feeding the engine, which was no more than a few feet away from the pilot's cockpit, forced the flames directly back onto the pilot. In the process of escaping the cockpit, the pilot was subjected to the full force of the fire being fanned back onto his face.

None of the patients came direct to the Queen Victoria Hospital, but were sent to general air force hospitals first. McIndoe then handpicked a selection of cases, by referral or personal intervention, from across the country. Most were British but representatives from the Commonwealth included Canadians, Australians, New Zealanders, and by the end of the war, Americans, French, Russians, Czechs, and Poles. During the Battle of Britain, most of the patients were fighter pilots, but by end of the war, a total of around 80 per cent of the club members were from crews of Bomber Command. It became noticeable that the burns injuries of pilots who ditched in the sea healed differently. These Goldfish Club members inspired McIndoe to introduced saline baths. Guinea Pigs responded well to this system, an interesting development as a result of nothing more than pure observation. There were long gaps between operations, and convalescent homes provided a change of venue to the Guinea Pigs, however a return to ward three in East Grinstead was always welcomed, with members referring to the ward as the 'sty'. The additional operations always progressed the healing, but it was in some cases a very long route to the end result. By 1942 a large number of Canadian airmen were also being treated at the hospital, and around that time, a Canadian surgeon named Ross Tilley joined McIndoe's

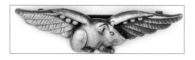

Left: First type Guinea Pig badge.
Below: Second type Guinea Pig badge.

team. There were now so many patients at the hospital that they were in danger of running out of space. Tilley took it upon himself to appeal to the Canadian government, who built a separate wing for the Canadian airmen that opened in 1944.

Many of McIndoe's patients returned to service on an interim basis between operations, usually in RAF operations control rooms and occasionally as pilots. Those unable to serve in any capacity received full pay until their final surgical operation had taken place, and only then were they invalided out of the service. McIndoe also provided some personal financial support to his patients for their subsequent entry to civilian life. In 1945 the Canadian government presented the Canadian wing of the hospital as a gift to the residents of East Grinstead, as a thank you for the kindness and compassion they had shown towards the Guinea Pigs.

In 1947 the Guinea Pig Club strengthened its support to members, creating a new post, organising secretary, which was undertaken by Bernard Arch of Chase Road, London. One of the key tasks of this post was the distribution of the membership badges, of which two types were produced. A 1-inch-wide blazer badge finished in a silver metal, and a larger 2-inch-wide, hollow-backed, impressed metal badge, finished in silver metal. From

Guinea Pig 50th Anniversary gold wash badge.

records available, it was a Guinea Pig Club member, the late Henry Standen, who designed the badge. To celebrate the fiftieth anniversary of the club,[23] a specially commissioned 2-inch badge was produced for each surviving member. The badge was solid in construction, numbered on the back and finished in gold gilt, identical to Henry's initial design depicting the winged guinea pig.

Henry Standen had served in 83 Squadron. It was during the last few weeks of 1941 when his Hampden[24] aircraft suffered from an unexplained set of circumstances that resulted in a serious fire. Within the bomb bay of his aircraft was a large sea mine; the aircraft had not taken off but had been preparing to do so, and the mine was to have been dropped in the entrance to Brest harbour. The Hampden rapidly erupted into an inferno, exploding whilst Henry was escaping from the aircraft, with both the explosion and flames inflicting terrible injuries upon his body. Having joined the Guinea Pigs in East Grinstead, Henry instantly realised that his right hand was most unlikely to create the drawings and painting he had loved to do. By determination and patience, he re-created his ability to draw with the use of his left hand. It is most appropriate that this gifted artist, who enrolled into the Guinea Pig Club, should have been responsible for the design of the club's badge. Interestingly, a few of the early club members possessed Guinea Pig Club membership cards; a simple design with little more than the hospital name with the members details below. Unlike the Goldfish and Caterpillar Clubs, the Guinea Pig Club saw no need to develop the idea further. The primary identity of club membership became the club badge and tie, which carried the emblem of the badge in its weave. At a later date an additional badge was commissioned from the company Fattorini and Sons in Birmingham. Incorporating the winged guinea pig badge within its design, underneath sat the initials F.G.P.C. ('Friends of the Guinea Pig Club') within a blue enamel half circle, enclosed by laurel leaves. This badge allowed the club to recognise and award those that endeavoured by to support the Guinea Pigs by extraordinary means.

Another key individual within the club was the holder of the post of resettlement secretary, J. E. Blacksell – known to all as 'Blackie'. He had originally been posted by the Air Ministry to East Grinstead Hospital as an RAF physical training instructor, but was suddenly exposed to hospital patients with very differing needs in that department. Blackie acted as facilitator in the necessary communication between the ministry and McIndoe's team. Post-war, he returned to his home in Abbey Road, Barnstable, Devon, where he continued to engage with the many aspects of resettlement for all the club's members. Blackie was always to be seen wearing the club's tie displaying the RAF colours and the winged guinea pig motif. In the 1950s, Blackie suffered a serious motor car crash, with the injuries he sustained requiring plastic surgery that was undertaken at Oldstock Hospital in Salisbury.

After the war, many honours were bestowed upon McIndoe. He was appointed CBE in 1944,[25] knighted in '47, and received numerous foreign decorations. At the Royal College of Surgeons, he became a member of the council in 1946, and vice-president in 1958. He helped to set up the British Association of Plastic Surgeons (BAPS), and was its third president.

The Guinea Pig Club

THE QUEEN VICTORIA HOSPITAL
EAST GRINSTEAD, SUSSEX
Phone—East Grinstead 987

Resettlement Secretary
J. E. BLACKSELL
31 Abbey Road
Barnstaple, Devon
Telephone—Barnstaple 3321

Organising Secretary
BERNARD F. ARCH
45 Gwalior House
Chase Road, London, N.14
Telephone—Palmers Green 2115

June 11, 1947.

Dear Wing Commander,

    I have heard about you from Blackie, and perhaps you have heard about me too. I have not sent your Membership Card ere this, because I was hoping to be able to include a Badge with it; unfortunately these latter will not be available until the day of the Dinner — July 19th., but I have a most solemn promise from the makers that they will be delivered in time for this function.

    You are quite near me at my Office; perhaps if there is any point you would like to take up in connection with the Guinea Pig Club you might like to give me a ring. My business card is attached.

    Great news about the Boss, isn't it? I don't know how all the boys will react to "Sir Archibald" instead of "Mac"!

    Looking forward to meeting you,

                Yours sincerely,

Wing Commander R.C.Wright,
68 Chester Square,
London SW1.

Guinea Pig letter and miniature lapel badge.

McIndoe's contributions to plastic surgery were both significant and numerous. At the Queen Victoria Hospital, he built up a centre that rapidly became a model for the rest of the country. He died in his sleep on the night of 11 April 1960. Archibald McIndoe's ashes were buried in the Royal Air Force church of St Clement Danes, a most fitting tribute to this amazing man who was responsible for saving so many airmen's lives during the Second World War.

His life continues to be celebrated: the Blond-McIndoe Research Unit was opened in his memory by the minister of health at the Queen Victoria Hospital on 22 March 1961.

In 1998, the Guinea Pig Club statistics, provided by the late Jack Toper,[26] advised the author that the original membership of 650 had dwindled to 109, age having taken its inevitable toll. At that time, the youngest guinea pig was seventy-one, and the oldest ninety-three. With no new membership possible, the club had few years left, and so it was, in 2007, the Guinea Pig Club held its sixty-sixth and final annual dinner at the Felbridge Hotel, East Grinstead. At that time only ninety-seven members were remaining across the world. One member was a great personality and friend to the author, Sidney McQuillan – his story is to be read within this publication. Sadly, on the 28 December 2008, Sidney himself passed away.

The Guinea Pig Club must be regarded as the most exclusive club of the Second World War.

CHAPTER 1

Taking to the Sea

The Royal Air Force and her Commonwealth companions were ill prepared for many aspects of the Second World War. As an island, during offensive operations the sea required crossing by aircraft on both departure and return to the respective airfields of Bomber Command, Fighter Command, and Coastal Command. For any aircraft forced to ditch into the sea, the chances of survival were not high, and aircrews were inadequately trained in the processes of surviving such traumatic events. The air-sea rescue service, who were responsible for rescuing aircrews, were lacking in sufficient launches to be in any way effective. The Royal National Lifeboat Institute was deployed within its own command structure in an attempt to support the rescue service. The Air Ministry recognised the urgent need to provide a robust infrastructure to recover airmen from the sea and improve training and equipment across the entire service.

As a result of an emergency meeting chaired by Arthur Harris,[27] and acting on the instructions from their chief of the air staff, Air Chief Mar. Sir Charles Portal, the Directorate of Air Sea Rescue was formed in February 1941. Incredibly at this time, the losses of trained aircrews were reaching an average of 200 each month. It was agreed that the rescue of RAF personnel from the sea had become of such importance that it required the full-time attention of an air commodore as director, and a naval officer as deputy director. This inter-service cooperation was a key element in achieving a successful service overall. Despite the important function of the new directorate, at that time there were no aircraft or dedicated aircrews provided for rescue purposes. The British Isles were divided into four geographic areas that coincided with the regions of responsibility within the Coastal Command structure. The Directorate of Air Sea Rescue was required to be in a position to provide the coordination of all sea rescue operations for aircraft and aircrews, the provision of rescue equipment to be dropped by aircraft at the scene of distress, and the provision of adequate marine craft. The directorate was also responsible for the development and introduction of all life-saving equipment and safety devices for aircraft that might be forced to ditch at sea. They immediately put in place an infrastructure of lectures and formal training for all operational aircrew. Posters were put up on crew room walls emphasising the importance of sea survival, and in 1942, the directorate proposed the position of every airfield having an appointed air-sea rescue officer; that newly created post being responsible for the entire issue of survival after a ditching. This also included the distress procedures, which had been inadequate – a key element to subsequent search-planning and to the safe location of any survivors. The station's leading radio operator and the air-sea rescue officer collaborated in order to educate the wireless operators in the drill required to achieve a successful SOS procedure. The most important aid to location was the dinghy-based wireless set, but the carrying of caged homing pigeons that could be released with position report messages were equally as important to ditched crews.

It was soon realised that aircrew personnel, who had survived a ditching or evaded capture, could be utilised to help in the education process. Operational aircrews, when addressed by such 'survivors', were attentive and receptive, not only listening but also engaging through many questions. This proved to be a powerful way to educate the men within the allied air forces. Survivors' talks were adopted and promoted by the station rescue officers; a policy that continued and developed throughout the entire war. It became common place for survivors engaged in the touring of airfields to include visits to the manufacturing factories of parachutes and dinghies, the workforce gaining great satisfaction in knowing that they were indeed saving lives through their hard work.

When a critical situation left no other option to a pilot, the ditching of an aircraft in the sea was recognised as practical and successful in the saving of many lives. The practice of securing all lower-escape hatches to delay water entry into the fuselage, and opening all upper-exit positions, proved to be critically important to any ditching. Escaping from the aircraft as soon as possible was an obvious priority for the entire crew. Emersion switches operated the automatic release of dinghies, backed up by physical switches that were fail-safe measures designed to be operated by the crew if needed. Frequent drill procedures were put in place to remind the crews of these emergency procedures, as well as their own personal areas of responsibility designed to ensure vital equipment was not left behind when they left the aircraft.

Fighter pilots were initially advised to avoid a ditching if at all possible, as the smaller airframe was highly likely to tip over and trap the pilot within his cockpit. In the early years of the war the only equipment provided to assist survival in the sea for the fighter pilots was the personal issue of the Mae West life jacket. Pilots were advised to escape by parachute, and inevitably, the number of pilots who perished was high, particularly during the Battle of Britain. It was a key priority to provide a single man dinghy for these pilots. The k-type was designed and manufactured by P. B. Cow & Co. Such was the improvement in survival rates that Charles Robertson included the k-type dinghy upon the rear face of the Goldfish Club membership card. The new dinghy was contained in a pack that was worn underneath the parachute, combining to form the seat for the pilot. The pack opened and inflated automatically; a mast and sail were included. Printed on the sail were sailing instructions. The sail was optional, as the mast assembly also converted into two paddles. Charles Robertson had designed a hood on the stern that could be pulled forward, providing protection from the weather, as well as an apron in the bow that could be drawn forward to cover the pilot. Through combining both apron and hood, the only exposed area of the airman was the head. It is thought these factors alone were responsible for extending the survivability of airmen in the k-type dinghy. By keeping the water out, body heat was retained, lessoning one of the acute dangers of death by exposure. Attached to the dinghy after its inflation was the 'dinghy pack'. Charles Robertson, in collaboration with the directorate, had been responsible for providing capacity for eight essential items designed to assist the survivor:

- Collapsible water bailer
- Fluorescent sea colouring pack
- Drogue or anchor to keep the dinghy on course
- Set of leak stoppers
- Distress signals
- Heliograph reflector to signal aircraft by sunlight
- Navigation compass
- Rations

The air ministry ordered 12,000 dinghies. Modifications and developments became an on-going process imposed by the variants of single-seat aircraft being flown by these pilots. The heavy bombers' h- and j-type dinghies were also subject to modification and development works. Valuable information secured from rescued aircrews was analysed and fed back to the air ministry, directorate, and the manufacturers of the survival equipment. This process ensured development and progression of sea survival equipment throughout the Second World War.

Without fresh water a man could be expected to survive no more than four to six days. The dinghy supplies were designed to support basic life expectancy, in the hope that during this period the air-sea rescue measures were being engaged to locate the ditched aircrew. For rescuers, aircrew within a dinghy would have been nothing more than an insignificant dot upon the massive expanse of sea making it a difficult task to locate them.

Several accounts exist where, despite the best efforts possible, survivors were not recovered within the critical life-expectancy periods involved. Many other incidents occurred where circumstances prevented the use of survival equipment. Any aircraft ditching into the sea was susceptible to serious damage. On 3 August 1943, Sgt McGarvey was flying a Stirling EF409 on an operation to Hamburg. His return from the target coincided with unexpected weather conditions that produced severe ice and electrical storms. The formation of ice on the aircraft created such difficulty that the crew abandoned the aircraft off Wilhemshaven. Sgt McGarvey, a Glaswegian policeman in civilian life, sustained injuries to both legs but escaped with his life. The only other crew member to survive was Sgt A. B. Grainger. Wilhemshaven was a heavily fortified port and the target of many allied bombing missions during the war. German forces had seen the plight of Stirling EF409, which took place within sight from the shore – the events are best described from the recommendation of the George Medal that was submitted after the repatriation of Sgt Grainger and Sgt McGarvey from prisoner of war camps in 1945 (*London Gazette*, 14 August 1945):

> On 2/3 August, 1943, this airman was pilot of an aircraft returning from an attack on Hamburg. His aircraft was hit by electrical storms and severe icing and became uncontrollable. At approximately 0200 hours he gave orders to abandon the aircraft off Wilhemshaven. He alighted in the sea near to his navigator, Sgt A B Grainger, who was a poor swimmer and had been wounded. Despite his own wounds, which rendered his legs almost useless, Warrant Officer McGarvey (who was a Sergeant at the time) swam towards the navigator, who was blowing his whistle.[28] Searchlights were being played on them and they tried to swim to the nearest shore position, Warrant Officer McGarvey towing the navigator who, after a time, could barely help himself along and relapsed into periods of unconsciousness. When dawn broke, they

set course for a light vessel which could be seen in the distance. The tide was, however, carrying them- away from the vessel. The navigator was only just conscious and Warrant Officer McGarvey, discarding his "Mae West," swam to the light vessel to obtain assistance. At 10.30 hours the navigator was rescued in an unconscious condition but recovered after artificial respiration had been applied. Warrant Officer McGarvey had assisted him for 8½ hours, eventually saving his life in most difficult and dangerous circumstances. Five other members of the crew were drowned.

The crew of Stirling Mark III EF409 consisted entirely of young sergeants; such a tragic loss of life is reflected by this example of five young men from 214 Squadron who died:

Sgt John Peter Taylor, 1434892, RAFVR KIA, 3 August 1943, aged twenty-one
Sgt Albert Samuel Biffin, 1313932, RAFVR KIA, 3 August 1943, aged twenty-one
Sgt Charles Dennis Curtis, 549252, RAF KIA, 3 August 1943, aged twenty-three
Sgt John James Evans, 619407, RAF KIA, 3 August 1943, age unknown
Sgt Gundon Dalton Loveridge, 1388965, RAFVR KIA, 3 August 1943, aged twenty-one
Sgt Alexander Alistair Robert McGarvey, 1345818, RAFVR, PoW no. 1325
Sgt A. B. Grainger, 1060146, RAFVR, PoW no. 222407

Bomber Command aircraft were equipped with additional dinghies in an effort to provide the best opportunities of crew survival after a ditching. The Stirling was constructed to store the large j-type dinghy, capable of holding the entire crew stowed in the port wing assembly. It was able to be deployed from that stowage by several methods, either hand-operated from within, outside of the fuselage, or by automatic flooding of the immersion switch (located in the nose section of the aircraft). In addition to the j-type, within the aircraft and stowed at various locations were several k-type individual dinghy packs. It was common practice for crew members to stow their personal parachute packs alongside the k-packs.

'Bomber Harris' continued to be troubled by the losses of aircrew in drowning incidents. Just three months after the previous account with Sgt McGarvey's crew, another 214 Squadron incident was to become of note within Bomber Command. Bomber Harris circulated to his command the

following report within the routine orders administration appendices, serial
nos A 212:

AIR CHIEF MARSHAL SIR A. T. HARRIS, O.B.E., A.F.C.

PART I – ADMINISTRATIVE

The Commander-in-Chief wishes to bring to the notice of all ranks in the
Command the fortitude, courage and perseverance of the under mentioned
N.C.Os. of No. 214 Squadron:

1485104 F/Sgt. G. A. Atkinson, Captain & Pilot. (missing).

1388280 Sgt. H. J. Friend, Bomb Aimer.

1807915 Sgt. D. C. Hughes, Flight Engineer.

1513213 Sgt. W. B. Edwards, Navigator.

1892607 Sgt. R. L. Bouttell, Mid Upper Gunner.

1368303 Sgt. J. C. Wilson, Wireless Operator.

R.79844 Sgt. W. Sweeney, Rear Gunner. (wounded & missing).

The above-named formed the crew of a Stirling aircraft (Stirling III, EF445,
BU-J) detailed to bomb Berlin on the night of 22-23 November 1943. Just
before they reached the target area the oil pressure on the port outer engine
began to drop and the captain noticed that the propeller was revolving at
excessive speed. He decided to complete the bombing run and the Bomb-Aimer
sighted and released the bombs correctly one minute after E.T.A. dangerously
low and the propeller was feathered to prevent a seizure with the result that
the aircraft was losing height. At 9,000 ft. it was dropping into icing cloud and
the pilot restarted the engine to gain more height for crossing a bad front. The
engine started but had to be stopped almost immediately to prevent it catching
fire and the propeller then failed to re-feather but continued to 'windmill'.
The aircraft lost height steadily until it was only 1500 ft. above ground at a
position given by the Navigator as 20 miles east of Hanover. Near this place,
the aircraft was engaged by anti-aircraft flak which wounded the Rear-Gunner
in the right leg but he refused to leave the turret.

The Wireless-Operator sent out an S.O.S. at about 21.45 hours and repeated
it until it was acknowledged. It was picked up at 22.30 as a very faint signal
and he was given a fix. From then onwards, although reception was very bad,
he maintained communication with the ground sending the height, speed,
course and D.R. position, obtained from Navigator, at intervals.

Near the Zuider Zee, the aircraft was picked up by the searchlights which
were attacked by the gunners and, crossing the island at about 50 ft. the

aircraft was again engaged by flak and searchlights; fifteen to twenty five of the latter were shot at by the gunners and doused. A F.W. 190 intercepted the Stirling but was shot down in flames by the Rear-Gunner.

When the Flight-Engineer reported there was only 10 minutes of fuel remaining, the captain ordered the crew to take up their ditching stations. Because of icing, a head wind and the wind-milling airscrew, the speed had been very low. Information of their plight was signalled to the ground station and the aircraft was fixed accurately as the Operator pressed his key down when the aircraft ditched halfway across the North Sea at 00.34 hours. Prior to ditching, the Captain called out the height of the aircraft as it approached the water and the Navigator gave him a surface report. The aircraft bounced off a swell and then made a very heavy impact with the water which caused the nose to sink in and the fuselage to break in half. The pilot was trapped in the nose and went under as the aircraft broke in two. The Navigator jumped into the dinghy and dragged in the Mid-Upper Gunner from the water. They heard the Wireless Operator calling, paddled up to him and helped him on board. The Rear-Gunner, who had been observed to jump into the sea, was also heard to call but they failed to find him and he was not picked up. After drifting for about an hour blowing their whistles, they heard an answering whistle, in the darkness, and eventually picked up the Flight Engineer from his 'K' type dinghy. When the Stirling hit the sea, the Bomb-Aimer got out of the astro hatch but was swept into the sea by the waves. The Flight Engineer passed him a 'K' dinghy which was swept away. The Bomb-Aimer re-entered the almost submerged fuselage, found another 'K' dinghy, held his breath and swam out again as the aircraft sank, three minutes after ditching. He inflated the dinghy and climbed in, but although he heard other members of the crew shouting and answered, he was too weak to paddle towards the sound and lost touch with them. After sunrise, he hoisted a red sail and fired a star cartridge when an Air-Sea Rescue Hudson approached.

The Hudson crew dropped smoke floats alongside and he was shortly after taken on board a high speed launch which continued the search and picked up the other four surviving members of the crew from the big dinghy about 40 minutes later. The Captain and Rear-Gunner could not be found.

This crew exercised very strong determination to inflict as much damage on the enemy as possible in spite of their difficulties and they showed an excellent team spirit. It was this good team work and initiative that made possible the long and difficult flight to the point when the aircraft finally ditched and the successful rescue of five members of the crew after attacking their target successfully.

BC/S.23054/B.

The number of airmen rescued, once the Directorate of Air Sea Rescue had formed, steadily increased throughout the war, reaching its busiest period during the D-Day month of June 1944, when around 400 rescues were recorded.

Figures vary, but by the end of the Second World War, over 13,000 lives had been saved from the seas around Great Britain. Of that total, 5,721 were aircrew, 4,665 non-aircrew, and 277 were enemy airmen.

The most highly decorated air-sea rescue pilot was Sgt Thomas Fletcher, who saved more people than any other airman in the Second World War. The recommendation for his Distinguished Flying Medal was endorsed with these words:

Thomas Fletcher 1003953 'C' Flight ASR Shoreham Sussex. 277 Squadron.

With reference to the attached recommendation, I am of the opinion that this pilot's action is worthy of consideration for an award of the Victoria Cross as indicated below. On the 2 October 1942, as pilot of an Air Sea Rescue Walrus, he volunteered the rescue of a pilot in a dingy which was on the edge of a mine field four miles from the coast of France and therefore within range of the enemy shore batteries. It was considered by the Royal Navy to be impossible to get a launch through this mine field in the state of the tides existing. The naval authorities at Dover considered that the mine field and these tides would be dangerous to a Walrus landing. Sgt Fletcher was fully aware of the risks when he volunteered to undertake the task. Sgt Fletcher landed his Walrus one hundred and fifty yards from the dingy and taxied to the fighter pilot in distress. The pilot on leaving his dingy failed to hold the Walrus boat hook but he was held above water by the rear gunner while the cockpit gunner came to assist. During the rescue, the Walrus was submitted to heavy shelling from shore batteries. Sgt Fletcher carried out the rescue with conspicuous gallantry whilst his air craft was being carried by strong winds and tide toward the mine field. He ignored all dangers and through coolness, considered judgment and skill succeeded in picking up the fighter pilot. The rescued craft had been carried to such a position that in taking off, it only just succeeded in clearing the mine field. This was the sixth successful rescue undertaken at sea by Sgt Fletcher. For this very gallant action, I strongly recommend that Sgt Fletcher be considered for the award of the Victoria Cross.

The air officer commander-in-chief authorised the immediate award of the Distinguished Flying Medal. Two months later, Sgt Fletcher performed an additional rescue for which he was again recommended for gallantry:

On the 14 December 1942, three or four men were sighted in a dingy eight to ten miles East of Dover. On arriving over the position, Sgt Fletcher saw six men on a raft and in spite of the fact that the sea was too rough to take off again, he immediately dropped a smoke float and landed with the intention of picking up the men and taxing back to the harbour. He taxied up to the raft. Flt Sgt Glew handed the boat hook to one of the men who were helped into the back hatch leaving the others on the raft. With difficulty, Sgt Fletcher taxied round and came back to the raft a second time but the men missed the rope and were knocked off the raft by the waves. They clambered back and the pilot taxied round again. This time, one of the men seized the rope and was pulled on board. The rest were knocked off the raft by a large wave and one was knocked unconscious by the hull of the Walrus. Two of the men in the water tried to swim towards the Walrus but owing to the rough sea, it was impossible to pick them up. Sgt Fletcher found the raft once more with one man aboard who was pulled unto the hatch by Sgt Glew. By this time it was completely dark and there was no sign of the men in the water. Sgt Fletcher therefore started to taxi back to Dover. The starboard windscreen on landing had been smashed in by the sea and water had been continuously shipped through the hatches, the waves breaking over Sgt Glew in the front hatch the whole time. A lot of water was being shipped through both hatches and the Radio transmitter failed. By the time the pilot started to return, there was eighteen inches of water in the Walrus which the gunners tried to bail out but the sea coming through the windscreen kept the level of the water up. Owing to these factors, it took Sgt Fletcher half an hour to turn his air craft onto the course for Dover and approximately one hour before he reached the mouth of the harbour. During the course of his journey home, Sgt Fletcher taxied through three mine fields. The three men rescued were Germans from a ship sunk as a result of naval action on the night of the 11 December. Sgt Fletcher carried out the rescue with conspicuous coolness and skill under extremely difficult conditions. This was the seventh successful rescue at sea undertaken by Sgt Fletcher in the course of which this pilot has directly contributed to the rescue of thirteen people.

The recommendation resulted in the immediate award of the bar to his Distinguished Flying Medal, as well as a commission in the field.

The Directorate of Air Sea Rescue was the predecessor to what is now the Search and Rescue Force of the Royal Air Force.

CHAPTER 2

Taking to the Silk

Falling from a stricken aircraft with nothing more than a billowing piece of silk cloth between you and almost certain death takes great courage. The word 'parachute' is formed from the French words '*para*', meaning 'shield' or 'guard against', and '*chute*', which equates to 'fall'. Thus parachute literally means, 'to defend from a fall'.

The early days of research and development led towards greater flight safety for all aircrews within the Royal Air Force. RAF Henlow has a direct connection to the development of silk technology. Parachutes have been tested there since 1925, when the Parachute Test Unit (RAFPTU) came to life. This was the same year in which the Irvin air chute became standard equipment deployed within the Royal Air Force.

The dangers of parachute experimentation were highlighted on the 9 March 1927, when Cpl East attempted to beat the then-world record 'delayed drop' of 4,300 feet. He dropped over 5,000 feet above Biggin Hill, but due to a significant drift – and with his parachute only half deployed – he made contact with some high ground and was killed. The Parachute Test Unit suffered a further fatal incident emphasising the dangers, but thankfully these were rare events.

Within the history of RAF parachute escapes, Sqn Ldr Warner DSO holds the record for being the first 'RAF padre' to escape a stricken aircraft and save his life by a parachute. On the 21 January 1930 he was being flown by Flt Lt Somerset-Thomas, of 4 Flight Training School, in a DH9A[29] over Abu Sueir, Egypt. This incident occurred en route to Cairo, when the engine came away from its mounting and caused the aircraft to go out of control and the men to parachute to safety. Unfortunately, because of a strong 30 mph wind, the padre was dragged along the ground for a quarter of a mile but suffered no lasting injuries. At the time of this escape, the Irvin Caterpillar

Club had a total membership of just 300. Somerset-Thomas and Warner had the honour of becoming the first live parachute escapers by RAF personnel to have taken place outside the UK. The Right Revd Warner resigned his permanent commission in 1933, but continued to practice his beliefs and supported the RAF during his lifetime.

Parachute safety was always a primary objective at RAF Henlow. During the Second World War, several aircraft types were on station and used to test the consistent parachute developments. It is thought that Irvin, the primary parachute manufacturers at that time, purposely based themselves at Letchworth, as it was in close proximity and readily accessible to Henlow.

Towards the end of 1940, Henlow employed between 250 and 300 men and women in the repair and packing sections, with over 200 parachutes being processed each week. The growth in parachute training saw the development of the Parachute Training School at RAF Ringway, in effect a further extension of the Parachute Test Unit that also included another unit called the Special Parachute Equipment Section. This had special responsibilities for the supply-dropping and for the Special Operations Executive.[30]

Many differing circumstances existed during the Second World War where pilots or aircrew leapt from an aircraft and entrusted their lives to the parachute. Before taking over as commander-in-chief within Bomber Command, Bomber Harris had voiced his concerns over the loss of aircrew and pilots in circumstances where it may well have been possible to escape from a stricken aircraft sooner. Harris took the view that the pilots and crews were far more valuable than the actual aircraft, and although the risk of an abandoned aircraft killing civilians was a concern, it was regarded as remote enough to be an acceptable risk. Harris put forward that pilots should assess a situation and not attempt to force the landing of an aircraft unless there was a 75 per cent chance of succeeding. In addition, the pilot should not retain his crew on board an aircraft unless it was assessed as being 99 per cent certain of being successful. Clearly this last statistic indicates that aircrew personnel were to be ordered to jump from the aircraft far more frequently than had been previously experienced.

There were two primary reasons to abandon an aircraft. Firstly, catastrophic circumstances as a consequence of flying over enemy-held territory with anti-aircraft gunfire (Flak), securing a hit that resulted in the inability for the aircraft to continue flying. Secondly, a culmination of events, possibly as a result of engine mechanical failures, fuel shortage, or battle damage, which then rendered the aircraft unsafe to attempt to return

An example of the billowing silk canopy which saved so many lives. Because of this, the Caterpillar Club was created.

back to base in England. In many instances the requirement to cross the North Sea brought forward a decision to use parachutes.

Pilots sat on their parachute when in the cockpit, and the harness, frequently referred to as 'the Sutton', strapped the pilot into his seat. The Sutton harness was fitted with a quick release buckle, which meant that in the event of an emergency the pilot would attempt to quickly negotiate his way from the seat whilst retaining the actual parachute and its own harness.

Aircrew personnel were issued with observer-type parachutes. These were stowed in the aircraft according to the position and duties of the individual crew members. The parachute harness was worn at all times, and if ordered by the pilot to 'prepare to abandon aircraft', the parachute was simply clipped on via two stout hooks situated at the front of the harness. The parachute itself rested on the chest of the wearer. Abandoning an aircraft was a well-practiced drill, additionally practiced in darkness, requiring the crew to locate and fit the parachute in replicated operational conditions. RAF bomber crews were primarily involved in night operations; in the event of needing to abandon an aircraft, the aircrew would await the order to 'jump', pull off their helmet with the attached oxygen mask and microphone leads, and then exit from the aircraft. All aircraft had different escape hatches to navigate. In some instances, the pilot may have been in a position to see the crew depart. Those with no line of sight to the pilot were expected to advise of their leaving. This enabled the pilot to manage his own escape once all crew had left. Many events could prevent the appropriate sequence of actions from taking place. Sudden catastrophic circumstances needed no such order from the pilot. Accounts exist where tail gunners, feeling that the aircraft was in imminent danger of destruction and with no ability to communicate to the pilot, escaped by parachute at a point unknown to any other crew member. In some circumstances, the pilot had only momentarily lost control, and once landed, he realised that the gunner had left the aircraft and hopefully deployed his parachute to safety.

Other events that took place within a stricken bomber could influence the decision-making process. An excellent example of a bomber crew changing circumstances just as they were about to abandon the aircraft can be found in the events that took place with a crew of 462 Squadron in 1944. The target was the oil plant of Sterkrade.[31] Cecil Baldwin, a bomb aimer on his eighteenth sortie, was flying in a Halifax aircraft that was hit by a flak shell[32] which started a major fire. This occurred just as they were on the immediate approach to the bombing run.[33] The pilot, FO Edward McGindle, ordered the crew to bail out. Three members of the aircrew dropped clear of the aircraft. A second flak shell struck, wounding Baldwin slightly and the navigator more seriously. Baldwin reported to McGindle that the navigator was too badly wounded to use his parachute. Baldwin then took the decision to cut up his own parachute to try and stem the flow of blood from the injuries to the navigator's abdomen and legs, as all the bandages from the first aid kit had been used. McGindle took the decision to try and reach Norfolk in the damaged aircraft, knowing that not everyone remaining in the aircraft now had a parachute. With the mid-upper and rear gunners having escaped by parachute upon the first order to bail out, only four parachutes remained in the aircraft, with five crew members still on board. The pilot ordered the wireless operator, Sgt Edward Whelan, to tackle the fire. Baldwin, who had had some elementary training as a navigator, took over the wounded man's station and was able to navigate the aircraft back cross the North Sea to England. The flight engineer, Sgt Stuart Soames, had meanwhile been trying to keep the damaged port inner engine going, but eventually had to switch it off. He later reported back that the tail control surfaces were badly shot about, and most of the fuselage skin burnt away. It was not until the aircraft crossed the coast that Baldwin told Soames that he had also been wounded, by which time he had lost so much blood that he passed out. The pilot managed to put the damaged bomber down safely at his home base.

Following this incident, the group captain who commanded RAF Driffield wrote:

> The devotion to duty and selflessness of F/Sgt Baldwin's actions in the above quoted incident cannot be too highly praised. These qualities in addition to the determination and fine spirit of comradeship displayed are thoroughly deserving of the immediate award of the Distinguished Flying Medal.

Air Chief Mar. Bomber Harris awarded the immediate DFM to Flt Sgt Baldwin on 31 October 1944.

Aircrews within Bomber Command endured treacherous sorties across occupied Europe. Many enemy hazards were encountered on the flight to reach their targets, but danger from the elements also lurked. Having escaped night fighter attacks and evaded searchlights, the crew then had to navigate back to England in sometimes impenetrable fog. Somewhere under the thick layer of fog would be the concrete runways and safety. These weather conditions became one of their worst enemies. The pilots would assess the situation and consider all options available. On many occasions, fuel became low and the orders were issued to bail out. At this point, the parachute was the only safety that they had. On other occasions, preparations to land were thwarted by the uncertainty of the landing gear being operational; the confirmation of locked landing gear being denied by the warning lights, presented the distinct possibility of crashing on the runway. Pilots had to make difficult, often life-threatening decisions.

The parachute was the saviour of countless lives without question, but it was not infallible. The device operated through a sequence of events that would normally led to the successful parachute deployment, however the inability to operate the ripcord as a result of injury or incapacity on the part of the wearer could have fatal results. Furthermore, the deployment of the parachute canopy in circumstances where the device was prevented from inflating properly by severely tangled lines was most likely to prove lethal, as were the circumstances where the canopy fabric was in flames, or badly damaged as a result of of fire within the aircraft. Unexplained circumstances also existed: PO Martyn A. King engaged the Luftwaffe over Southampton during the Battle of Britain, but was forced to bail out from his Hurricane P3616 as a result of damage inflicted during the air battle. The parachute inflated correctly but then collapsed during descent. PO King fell to his death at the age of just nineteen years old. A statement frequently seen upon archive documents, 'died as a result of a parachute malfunction', provides little explanation of the personal circumstances involved. Two 85 Squadron pilots engaged in the Battle of Britain on 1 September 1940 experienced differing events that led towards their respective deaths. Sgt Glendon B. Booth, piloting Hurricane L2071 over the skies of Tunbridge Wells, was forced to bail out at 2.15 p.m., when his aircraft caught on fire. Having been badly burned, his parachute opened correctly but was alight – although the parachute operated sufficiently to reduce his descent, as a result of his heavy landing and injuries sustained, he died several weeks later. Flying Hurricane P3150 over Kenley at the exact same time was FO Patrick P. Woods-Scawen. He was forced to bail out of his aircraft after an engagement with ME109s. His parachute failed and he fell to the ground. This pilot had previously been awarded the Distinguished Flying Cross, with the recommendation making reference to him having shot down six enemy aircraft during the Battle of France, and although wounded in action, he had escaped by parachute.

These are by no means exceptional examples, and unfortunately squadron diaries and official operational records – particularly within Fighter Command – hold many reports of similar incidents. Parachute failures after initial deployment were frequently referred to as 'Roman candles', a nickname that still exists. It is thought that the un-inflated silken canopy streaming in the air looked like a candle flame. The importance of parachute construction and its packing never left the minds of the WAAF staff employed within that department. Each parachute was packed and checked with the utmost care possible. It was then allocated to the crews, who frequently made quips about bringing it back if it did not work.

The account of Alex Campbell provides a graphic example of a bomber crew parachuting from a critically damaged bomber; his personal experience under the silk reveals a truly marvelous escape. It revolves around the day of 28 July 1944, when 514 Squadron were flying from RAF Waterbeach. It was the crew's twenty-fifth operation and the target was Stuttgart, Germany. A Junkers 88 night fighter, equipped with huge radar antennas, located the bomber stream and rounded upon Alex Campbell's Lancaster LL692:[34]

The JU88 came up from underneath and behind and started firing; he hit the cockpit, Bob [FO R. Griffin RCAF] was badly hit. I got some of the spray off of him bits of bone and shiny metal in the arm and face, it made it look like I was hit too, but I wasn't. How it missed Jock [Sgt W. Donaldson RAF] I don't

Alex Campbell RCAF.

know. He was standing right behind Bob. Judy [Flt Sgt E. Garland RCAF] was
out of his seat and sitting on the floor when those shells came through. He got
two of them in his leg injuring him badly. He was changing the tubes for the
GEE navigation system – as you get out of range of one set of operations, you
have to put in different tubes for different frequencies and ranges.

   Another attack put out one of our starboard engines, and I had to feather it,
but the one engine that was running on its own started to run away. The CSU
– Constant Speed Unit – packed up on it, and this let the propeller go into full
fine pitch, and it just screamed like a siren. I'd already given an order to the
crew to prepare to abandon the aircraft, I asked them to acknowledge. The
only one to not answer was the mid upper air gunner.[Flt Sgt E. Jones RAF] The
reason for him not answering was that some of the shells had burst his Perspex
canopy, pretty well blew off the mid upper turret, and cut off the oxygen and
microphone lines to his facemask. I told them all to jump, and you repeat
that word three times in the intercom – 'jump-jump-jump' to make sure there's
no misunderstanding. The bomb aimer was the first one out, he unlocked the
lower escape hatch which he normally lies on in his compartment. This hatch
is about two feet wide and about two and a half feet long.

Then the second pilot Bob Griffin, badly wounded but able to get out of his seat, went down the opening in front of him to the escape hatch, then a few seconds later he turned around and attempted to come back up. He had caught his rip-cord on something and his parachute had opened in the aircraft. That's a twenty-four foot silk parachute – quite a lot of silk packed in there, and it bounces and springs out when the tension is released. The cockpit and passageway was filled with silk and cord, blowing in the wind that was whistling through the broken windscreen. Bob was probably trying to get past us to get out of the way, so we could get out. But Jock, the flight engineer, managed to turn him around, and got him back down to the hole, bundled him up and shoved him out. Jock went out next of course, I remember he gave a little Winston Churchill 'V for victory' before he jumped.

I didn't realize at the time that Judy the navigator had been wounded. It was hard to tell if a person was walking normally in a Lancaster, it was rather awkward. But he came up to the front and went out there. Meanwhile, the wireless operator and the mid upper gunner had gone out the side door on the starboard side of the Lancaster, which is where you come in normally. All this time the plane is diving, and gaining speed, and on fire, we weren't very high – we started out at only about 7,000-8,000 feet. Not much air under you for a rapid descent like that.

Sam the rear gunner [Flt Sgt S. Harvey RCAF] had one working gun and he was still firing. I hollered at him to get the hell out of there. He was alone in his little compartment in his rear turret, with two sliding doors, which were directly behind him. He reached behind his back and grabbed the two doors, one slid to his right on a curved track, and the other to his left. He was then able, providing he was facing dead astern, to lean back into the aircraft, and on the starboard side of the aircraft was his parachute. Then he had to bring the parachute back into the gun turret and snap it on the two hooks on his chest. Then to get out, he swung the turret to the beam position, at right angles to the plane, pulled his knees up, and just rolled out backwards through the two open doors.

Fortunately Sam went out the starboard side, and I'm sure he must have realised that had he gone out the port side the flames would have just engulfed him immediately. I removed my helmet and intercom and let go of the control column. The Lancaster lurched down faster now, and I flew up in the air and landed in the passageway. Then the plane stabilised, I had to get back in my seat to get my seat pack and parachute back on properly because it was kind of tangled up. When I had bounced up, the dinghy I was sitting on had lodged between the seat and the throttle quadrant. So I had to get back in my seat, and get adjusted.

I stepped back out in the companionway, at the top of the stairs leading to the bomb aimer's compartment. The plane's nose was pointing downwards, and the floor was more or less behind me, I made one leap to go down in a hurry. As I pushed off, I got jabbed in the stomach, and just hung there. A telescoping pipe that pulls out in front of the flight engineer to rest his feet on had caught me, I was hanging on it. Then a big explosion occurred – I expect it could have been the port wing collapsing – and flung me against the starboard side of the fuselage. I hit the fuselage, and it unhooked me. Down I dropped on the glycol tank, which forms one of the two steps leading down into the bomb aimer's compartment, my head was about two feet away from the open escape hatch.

Gravity was still holding me to the floor, but it was a steep angle. So I bent my feet up behind me and pushed off against the glycol tank, towards the hole but the hatch had been sucked back and wedged into the escape hatch. Just barely out into the slipstream my shoulders and the rest of my body were inside, fortunately when my head had been out I was facing backwards or the air would have blown my eyeballs out. I was going about three hundred miles per hour, and you can't keep your eyes shut enough to keep the air out.

I thought that would be the end. Then I got mad and started thrashing and kicking and hollering. Well, I must have moved that wedged door just enough, because I finally wiggled out. I felt this rush of wind over my body, and both my flying boots were whisked off with the slipstream. This huge orange and black shape went whipping on past me. I knew I must be awfully close to the ground. I slapped my chest where my rip-cord should be and there was no D-ring there. No harness, nothing, no parachute on at all. Just about that time something attracted my attention above me – I was going down head-first. It was a chrome buckle on my parachute harness – one of the shoulder buckles or something, and it flashed above me. And sure enough there was my harness stretched out behind and above me, and the parachute pack wobbling and spiraling behind that again. I went to reach up, but bent my knees as I was reaching, and felt a tug at my ankles. Sure enough, it was the thigh straps, which had slipped down to my ankles and were still there. I hadn't realized it, but in my panic to squeeze and wriggle out of the escape hatch, my parachute harness had slipped right off my shoulders, and down my body and off my legs and caught around my ankles – which remember, no longer had any boots. I reached up and pulled the harness towards me hand over hand till I could reach the D-ring. Then I dug my fingers into the harness, and gave the D-ring a tremendous pull. All of a sudden that big chute just went whack, a big crack, and it opened – a beautiful canopy of white. It tore my fingers open, and cracked both my ankles together. Here I was hanging upside-down by my ankles. I guess I'd wound up my harness as I fell, because I saw the moon spiraling. Now that the chute had opened, the harness was unwinding. I was watching the moon go around, and saw a roof out of the corner of my eye I quickly grabbed for my ankles, because I didn't want to hit my head. I just got my head bent forward, when I hit the ground with the back of my head and shoulders at the same time, and crumpled up. If I hadn't realised the roof was there and prepared myself, I would have been just driven straight into the ground. You land in a twenty-four foot military chute at the same rate as if you were to jump from a ten foot wall onto the ground. That's why we never practiced parachute jumps. I landed on what turned out to be a stubble wheat field but I didn't know where I was. Normally to remove a parachute you turn a big circular button on the front of the harness, which releases the four clips, but I didn't need to worry about that because it was just lying in a heap beside me. I realised I'd probably be taken prisoner, but at least I knew I would be alive and able to see my twenty-first birthday next month.

Bob Griffin died as a result of his injuries. It is not known if his parachute worked effectively after its unintended release within the Lancaster. 'Judy' Garland was arrested and became a prisoner of war. The remaining six crew members all survived and successfully evaded capture, a completely different adventure for Alex Campbell RCAF after his amazing parachute escape.

Even with a fully functioning and correctly deployed parachute, safety was not guaranteed. Initially, fighter pilots engaged in combat with the aircraft as the sole target, however that philosophy changed and extended to the pilot who had managed to escape any destroyed aircraft. In frequent instances the parachute itself represented a large and relatively easy target to attack. PO Cedric Stone DFM provides a vivid account of his parachute descent over the desert within this book, where he was attacked whilst hanging – completely defenceless – below his silk parachute.

CHAPTER 3

Flt Lt Paul Libert, Spitfire pilot – Caterpillar Club

Paul Arthur Louis Ghislain Libert was born on 30 July 1918 in Godinne, a village in Namur, 40 miles south-east of Brussels, Belgium. At the age of seventeen, he commenced a voluntary engagement of four years with the Regiment de Forteresse de Namur. He was promoted twice between 1936 and '37, but reverted to the rank of private the following year at his own request. This may have been as a result of his intention to apply for a position as a student pilot at the Ecole de Pilotage in 1938, which he successfully attained the same year. He was awarded the *Brevet Elementaire*[35] on 30 January 1939, and the *Brevet Militaire* on 25 March 1939. He went on to join the 2eme Regiment Aeronautique (2nd Regiment, Belgium Air Force) on the 13 April 1939.

Having become a pilot within the Belgium Air Force, Paul flew in some of the very first Hurricane fighters that were delivered from the United Kingdom as part of his training. Stationed at Schaffen Airfield, 2 Squadron – part of the 1 Group within 2 Air Regiment – consisted of three fighter groups, each operating the most up-to-date combat aeroplanes available, Fiat CR 42s and Hawker Hurricanes.

On 3 September 1939, war was declared in Britain. Belgium called its men to arm, but they adopted the status of strict neutrality. The German aggression within Europe was also gathering pace, with the Luftwaffe flying many reconnaissance flights over Belgium, as indeed were France and Britain during a period known as the 'phoney war'. This was the period of time between September 1939 and April 1940, when seemingly nothing happened.

From early September 1939, Libert flew Hurricanes on general patrols, protecting the eastern borders of his home country. The aircraft he flew were unarmed, their objective to perform the primary role of directing intruding aircraft (by radio) to land at the nearest airfield. A great deal of activity and construction took place during this period of time. Across Belgium, some fifty airfields were in various stages of completion.

On the 2 March 1940 an event took place that ended the phoney war for the Belgium Air Force. Three Mk I Belgium Hurricanes approached a German aircraft trespassing over Belgium; they were about to radio a request to the intruding aircraft when the German crew fired upon the Hurricanes. One Belgium pilot was killed and another aircraft crash-landed. From that day onwards, the Belgium Air Force armed its intercepting aircraft. Libert was then flying a fully armed Hawker Hurricane.

On 10 May 1940, German Luftwaffe aircraft attacked the majority of operational airfields across Belgium, resulting in almost the entire Belgium Air Force being destroyed on the ground. The Luftwaffe attack upon Schaffen was of particular interest to the attacking force, as the Hawker Hurricanes were all placed in a line, which made them an easy target. Sgt Libert was on duty at Schaffen Airfield that day with his squadron. The alarm sounded around 4.20 a.m. and the pilots went to their aircraft thinking it was another exercise. At that moment fifty unidentified aircraft approached Schaffen Airfield. The Hurricanes started their engines but a few minutes later German bombers strafed the airfield and commenced bombing. The Belgium Hurricanes tried to take off but as they did so another stream of German aircraft attacked the airfield, leaving the Hurricanes to attempt to manoeuvre between the explosions and fires. Four Hurricanes were set alight and six others were badly damaged. The roof of the hanger fell in and all of the aircraft inside were destroyed.

Paul was badly burned when the fuel tank of his Hurricane exploded during the attack. He was lucky to survive with his life. Ironically, the 10 May date was to be significant in his life a few years later.

Paul had received serious burns to his face, neck, hands and right leg, as well as bullet wounds to the left – these wounds required significant medical treatment. The events of that day and the following weeks were traumatic for Paul and his country. The remaining operational aircraft were evacuated, but many had been lost and the men were forced to escape as best they could. Some made it to Great Britain, mostly those that had evaded through France, Spain and Gibraltar. The journey of Paul Libert was dictated by his medical condition;

10 May Hospital, Aarschot, Belgium
11 May Military hospital, Gent, Belgium
18 May Emergency hospital, Lauwe, Belgium

Notification of the formal award of his *Brevet Superieur*[36] took place on the 28 May 1940.

24 June Hospital, Loppem, Belgium
28 June Military hospital, Ukkel, Belgium

On the 20 May in the following year, records show Libert as receiving treatment at the military hospital in Namur, Belgium. In July 1941, with improved health, he was able to leave the care and control of the hospital; his military status was regarded as being on convalescence leave from service to his country. He was in occupied Belgium, not a safe place to be.

He set out to escape to Great Britain, where he hoped some of his friends were operating within the Royal Air Force. Over the next ten months he managed to establish contact with the underground escape network. On 21 May 1942, Paul left Belgium and entered France, where he was guided through the occupied country, crossing the Pyrenees Mountains, with the Comet Escape Line. He reached Gibraltar in July 1942.

From Gibraltar Paul departed on the steamship *Llanstephan Castle*, a troop carrier, which arrived at Greenock, Scotland, on 31 July 1942. This was an epic journey for Paul, after such injury and trauma. He was immediately taken into the Belgian forces, which led towards his integration into the Belgian section of the Royal Air Force. On 27 October 1942, Paul was posted to 17 Advanced Flying Unit, followed by a period of operational training at 61 OTU. In early 1943, with the rank of sergeant pilot, Paul was regarded as a fully qualified fighter pilot and authorised to fly operationally with the Belgium section of the Royal Air Force.

Paul Libert was very fortunate to have achieved this status. So many of his fellow countrymen were diverted from single-seat fighter status and – after less intense training – became navigators, air gunners, and general aircrew within the other commands.

In April 1943, along with two other Belgian pilots, POs Maskens and Evrard, Paul was posted into 610 Squadron at RAF Westhampnett, the satellite airfield to Tangmere, West Sussex.

Flying Spitfires, 610 Squadron was frequently scrambled in order to combat the German Luftwaffe, who flew fighter-bomber sorties on the south coast towns in England during 1943. These 'tip and run' operations were detrimental to the moral of the people and seen as a priority to combat, but it proved difficult for the RAF pilots to locate and destroy the Luftwaffe aircraft. With the arrival of the Belgian pilots on 13 April 1943, squadron records confirm that 610 Squadron were also flying many intruder sorties and escort missions over France.

Moving to RAF Parranporth in Cornwall, 610 Squadron's primary task was then to provide fighter escort to the Whirlwind[37] twin-engine fighter-bombers on raids upon the Cherbourg Peninsular areas. The operations undertaken by Paul were frequently coded 'ramrod', which related to bombing operations with a fighter escort, and 'Rodeo', which related to fighter sweeps.

On 13 June 1943, Sgt Paul Libert and FO Maskens were posted from 610 Squadron, moving into 349 Squadron (Belgium).[38] Sqn Ldr, I. G. du Monceau de Bergendal DFC, was the commanding officer, known to his pilots as 'the Duke'. He flew with Paul in B Flight on many sorties during the weeks ahead. As new pilots and ground crew arrived, the newly formed squadron became involved in army manoeuvres and training sorties. In August 1943, 349 Squadron moved from Kingscliffe, Northamptonshire, to Wellingore in Lincolnshire. On 17 August, Paul flew a sortie at dusk for the first time with his new squadron. In late August the squadron moved again, this time to Digby, Lincolnshire, and then onto Acklington, Cumbria. September 1943 saw the squadron involved in some engine conversions upon their Spitfires. The whole squadron were eagerly anticipating a move south into 11 Group in the hope of seeing action. A total of twenty new Mk VB Spitfires arrived on station during October. Great activity took place, with a further posting to Friston near Eastbourne, East Sussex, on 22 October 1943.

Now carrying the rank of pilot officer, Paul arrived on the open Sussex Downs Airfield, perched upon the cliff tops near Beachy Head. Exposed to the elements and living in tents overlooking the English Channel, it was about as close as possible he had come to seeing his home country. On 24 October 1943, 349 Squadron's first operational sortie took place. Paul was in one of twelve aircraft on a ramrod,[39] attacking Beauvais-Tille Airfield, 85 km north of Paris. This proved to be a simple duty as no enemy fighters or significant flak was encountered that day. November 1943 experienced terrible weather conditions; no doubt life on the exposed cliff top in Sussex was not well received by the squadron personnel. A few emergency sorties to search for bombers in distress, and attempts to escort them to safety, took place during the poor weather. Paul flew three consecutive escorts to bombers attacking Audinghen in the Pas-de-Calais, where German defences were constructed as part of their Atlantic wall.

Squadron records confirm that Paul flew several different Spitfire aircraft on operations; no allegiance to any particular airframe was indicated or

349 Squadron with Caterpillar recipient, Flt Lt Libert, standing fourth from left.

possibly allowed. As 1943 closed, Paul completed his flying logbook entries with a further four operational missions to Le Meillard, Sainte-Agathe-d'Aliermont, La Glacerie, and Plouy Ferme in northern France.

During January 1944, operations to escort daylight bombing attacks upon French targets continued. Frequently the squadron would form up with the light bombers over Beachy Head, Eastbourne, within line of sight of the landing ground at Friston. Towards the end of the month the pilots were delighted to receive free range offensive operations known as 'rhubarbs'. Released from the escorting protection duties, these were positively received but sadly few in number. Paul entered one rhubarb and seven ramrod codes into his logbook for that month. February brought another variant in operations: on the 12th, seven Spitfires from 349 Squadron acted as a fighter escort to six Mosquitos on a low-level bombing attack upon the Chateau de Bosmelet[40] in Normandy. A further twelve Mosquitoes conducted a similar raid upon Preval, attacking the V1 ramps. PO Croquet, who was with Libert's escort, was seen to crash at Epinay, northern France. Shrapnel from flak had hit the engine of his Spitfire and, having realising the damage to his aircraft was irreparable, he ventured to land his aircraft – the process of which twisted the fuselage and tore the wings off. The shock of the crash rendered him dazed in the wreckage. Luck was on his side however, and a local rescued him from the cockpit and hid him for several days so he could recover. PO Croquet successfully escaped through the Comète line and returned to 349 Squadron in September 1944, where he remained in service until after the war.

As the weather improved, 349 Squadron were posted to RAF Hornchurch in March 1944. Paul, having been promoted to the rank of flying officer, undertook two further escort operations to Holland and France before yet another squadron move, this time to Selsey, an advanced-type landing ground on the West Sussex coastline. Situated next to Pagham Harbour, it provided long and clear approach paths and a very flat surface to operate aircraft from. In fact, a pre-war private flying club had established itself at Selsey and built a fairly large hanger that proved useful to the squadron. This made the base ideal for both Typhoon[41] and Spitfire squadrons to operate from. The Air Ministry now saw it as an important provision for the protection of the planned D-Day beaches. It was a return to life in a tent for PO Libert. On 18 April, he took part in a sortie to attack Abbeville, northern France, with dive-bombing operations led by the commanding officer. Two days later, Libert was providing fighter cover duties over Dieppe, and subsequent ramrod escorts to further daylight-bombing operations in France. After completing his last sortie to the frequently visited French target of Abbeville on the last day of April, two senior Belgian officials arrived at Selsey – Mr Camille Gutt,[42] the finance minister, and Mr Steaerck of the Belgian War Office – and spent time talking with the squadron personnel.

As the build-up to D-Day progressed, 349 Squadron were called upon to continue the attack on V1 Rocket bases. These operations, coded as 'noball', presented very small targets that were difficult to locate. During the month of May, Paul flew a further nine operations, a heavy commitment as the squadron's strength of pilots was ten below its correct establishment of thirty-one. This created a heavy workload. The fourth anniversary of the day that caused him his serious burns was going to be a significant one for Paul. He was up early and records show that he was on his fortieth operational sortie with 349 Squadron, flying the normal fighter escort to Marauder Bombers of the USAAF, who were attacking Creil marshalling yards, just south of Compiegne in France.

Paul took off in Spitfire MK178 alongside ten others, and formed up to escort the bombers across the English Channel and over occupied France. Prior to reaching the target area, Paul experienced serious engine problems. Research has identified that his Spitfire developed an engine fault that resulted in complete loss of power, possibly caused by flak. Attempting to restart the engine caused it to burst into flames, at which time he was flying over Montdidier, northern France. Once again Paul suffered burns to his face, right ear, and temple. There was no greater danger than this to pilots escaping from a burning Spitfire, for the flames could so easily spread to the parachute, which was the only means of survival. A personal decision needed to be made in each individual instance, in respect of when to pull the handle to deploy the silk canopy parachute. The parachute used by Paul was an Irvin. Its deployment would have been of great relief to him when it functioned correctly, having sustained no damage, and more importantly, that the flames were no longer able to reach the fragile silk. The cold air on his descent would have no doubt provided some relief to the burn injuries sustained yet again on 10 May.

Having managed to escape from his aircraft and land by parachute, Paul had become eligible to join the Caterpillar Club. He was immediately arrested upon his landing and held in a local jail prior to being moved into Germany. Whilst held in Breteuil Prison,[43] Paul attempted an escape. The MI9 post-war questionnaire compiled by him quotes, 'One unsuccessful escape because of partial blindness due to wounds.' On 3 June 1944, he arrived at Dulag Luft,[44] the Luftwaffe's interrogation and reception camp for prisoners on the outskirts of Oberursel. Allied aircrew were informed of Dulag Luft during their escape and evasion lectures, and warned that should they be shot down and captured, they were to be very much on their guard. Interrogation and other means of milking any scrap of information were being deployed by the expert staff of Dulag Luft. Paul refused medical treatment for his wounds,[45] and upon being released from the interrogation camp, he was transferred to the prisoner of war camp at Stalag Luft III in Belaria. Life as a prisoner of war was to be endured from this moment onwards.

Stalag Luft III at Sagen, Germany, was built to accommodate RAF and allied flyers only. Situated close to a small town, the camp was surrounded by a forest of fir that ran unbroken towards the Czech frontier, its huts built on tree stumps. The camp compound was in the form of a square, nearly a mile in circumference, and housing fifteen barrack blocks. In March 1944 Stalag Luft III was made infamous by the great escape through the tunnels

POW photograph of Flt Lt
Libert with burn injuries.

dug under the wire. Of the seventy-six men who escaped, only three reached
England; the Gestapo shot fifty of the recaptured one by one with a single
bullet in the back.

On 15 May 1945 and in the rank of flight lieutenant, Paul was repatriated
to the United Kingdom, where he received treatment and care at the leave
centre in Goring, West Sussex. It was not until early in 1946 that he returned
to the Belgian section within the RAF, and after several short postings, he
was discharged from the RAF on 1 October 1946.

His family had been living at 129 Highbury Quadrant, London. It is not
known how his wife Mariette, and his son Jacques (born in August 1940),
escaped from Belgium. Sometime after leaving the service the family returned
to their mother country. Over the next few years Belgium was to honour her
pilots with a number of home-country awards. Paul was also honoured with
an Order of Chivalry by the king of England, as well as French awards for
his resistance work.

Flt Lt Libert's POW certificate.

Flt Lt Libert's POW registration.

Flt Lt P. A. L. G. Libert, Belgium Air Force, RAFVR 1939-47:

Authorised for two *chevrons de blessures* (two wound stripes)
Authorised to carry the badge 'Belgium Army' in United Kingdom
Officer de Lorder de Leopold II avec Palme
La Croix de Guerre 1940 avec Palme
Croix des Evades
Medaille Commemorative de la Guerre
Medaille de la Resistance
Medaille de la Combatant Militaire
Belgium Prisoner of War Medal
Honorary member of the Most Excellent Order of the British Empire
1939-45 Campaign Star
Air Crew Europe Campaign Star
Defence Medal
British War Medal

OBE Citation:

> A young courageous flying officer, already badly burnt on 10th May 1940 during the attack on the airfield at Schaffen, not having completely recovered from his burns, did not hesitate in leaving Belgium to re-join the Belgium Air force in England, where he arrived with his old wounds unhealed. After a long stay in Hospitals, he set out again in active service with the 610 and then the 349 Squadrons. He distinguished himself in the course of multiple actions and ground attacks, was shot down on the 10th May 1944, seriously injured again and taken prisoner.

Foreign Office despatch (T526/526/373) of 10 January 1948 reads:

> Flight Lieutenant Libert joined the Belgian Section of the Royal Air Force Volunteer Reserve in 1942 after having escaped from enemy occupied territory. He has endured many vicissitudes. In 1940 as a fighter pilot he was severely wounded and burned and while serving with No. 349 Squadron his aircraft was shot down over France and he was captured. He again sustained severe burns but with great courage and fortitude he refused treatment because he would not divulge information which might be useful to the enemy. As a prisoner of war Flight Lieutenant Libert has set an excellent example to all his fellow prisoners.

On 1 April 1948, Flt Lt Paul Libert was personally presented with his MBE at the Palais des Beaux. The chief of the imperial general staff, Field Mar. Lord Montgomery, was commanding. The pin of the Caterpillar Club was proudly worn by Paul just below his lower medal ribbon line. He remained in military service as a *lietenant aviateur* within the Belgium Air Force.

In January 1947 Paul retired from his military career and joined the Belgium national airline Sabena as a pilot. He went on to serve with them for six years, and finally retired from his flying career in 1973. Shortly before his retirement a Sabena Boeing 707 took off from Brussels to New York. Capt. P. Libert at the controls, his first officer, his son J. Libert, sitting next to him.

CHAPTER 4

PO William Fullerton DFM – Caterpillar Club

William Arthur Fullerton was born in St John's Wood, London, in 1916. Little is known of his employment following his London education, but he enlisted into the Royal Air Force Volunteer Reserve in 1938. Aged twenty-two, he embarked upon his initial training, and with the RAF gathering pace in aircrew recruitment, this was an ideal opportunity for him to volunteer for pilot duties.

Having achieved the required standard, William was awarded his flying wings and posted to 58 Squadron in Bomber Command. It was October 1940; the height of the Battle of Britain had passed, but the RAF was yet to have gathered pace and strength within its Bomber Command structure. As a novice pilot joining an operational squadron in 1940, William undertook several operations as the second pilot, prior to commanding his own aircraft. Equipped with Armstrong Whitley bombers, 58 Squadron operated from Linton-on-Ouse, Yorkshire.

The squadron had participated in the first operational penetration of German airspace in the Second World War, undertaking a nickel[46] or leaflet raid during the night of 3 of September 1939. Dropped from around 12,000 feet, the bundles of leaflets came loose and separated in the air, taking more than an hour to gently flutter to the ground and covering an immense area over Germany. William subsequently took part in twenty-one operational sorties, made up from the widest variety of targets possible. His squadron was selected for raids upon Cologne and Stetting, which William attacked in both instances. This was followed by the long transit to attack Turin, Italy, with events during this operation leading towards William's first emergency escape from an aircraft and subsequent membership to the Caterpillar Club. The squadron records show that fuel starvation created a situation where the entire crew abandoned the aircraft over Horsham St Faith; they all parachuted to safety.

Fullerton's leaflet drop issued by the Political Warfare Executive in the form of an oak leaf.

PO Fullerton's Irvin Caterpillar pins on his DFM medal.

Returning to operations, William was now operating as a first pilot and took part in attacks on Mannheim twice, with two further raids to the German capital of Berlin, and on four occasions to Brest, where the harbour held several major German naval units; 58 Squadron recorded what was thought to have been good bombing results on the night of 10 January 1941 there. An uneventful raid upon Dunkirk was followed by orders to attack Bremen on the night of 11 February 1941. Bomber Command detailed seventy-nine aircraft to participate. William Fullerton flew Whitley T4213, a relatively new aircraft that developed extractor[47] trouble after an hour in the air. Over the North Sea the aircraft was attacked by ME 109s. During a long engagement, the air gunners were successful in engaging with the fighters, forcing them to break off the sustained attack. Clearly the crew was very lucky to have survived such intense fighter activity; the aircraft was capable of returning back towards base despite being damaged – quite remarkable, as aircraft suffering with extractor problems were most likely unable to control the propellers pitch adjustments. Unbeknown to the crew, unexpected and severe fog had swept across the Midlands and the returning aircraft were forced to abandon any possibility of landing. Pilots gained height to enable the crews to escape by parachute once more. Twenty-two aircraft, from the strength of seventy-nine on the actual operation, failed to achieve a safe landing at their respective airfields. Bomber Command war diaries confirm that five men from those aircraft failed to make a safe parachute descent. William Fullerton and his crew of four all survived the parachute escape, their Whitley later crashing near Fulbeck, Lincolnshire. This was the second Caterpillar Club application for William. He received two pins from Irvin, both mounted on a gold brooch bar with safety chain, the reverse of the first engraved 'Sgt W. Fullerton', the second unnamed but the gold wearing bar inscribed, 'P.O. W.A. Fullerton, R.A.F.V.R.'.

William undertook three final operations with 58 Squadron; two upon Dusseldorf, and one against the U-boat pens at Lorient in March 1941. He was then posted to join 104 Squadron, who were equipped with Vickers Wellington aircraft, operating from RAF Driffield. The move to 104 Squadron enabled William to complete his full tour of operational sorties with raids to Ludwigshaven, Hannover, Kiel, Cologne, Bremen, and Wilhelmshaven. The dedication and leadership of having flown twenty-eight operations over occupied Europe was recognised by the award of the Distinguished Flying Medal to 741865 Sgt William Arthur Fullerton, Royal Air Force Volunteer Reserve, 104 Squadron.

The recommendation, dated 21 July 1941, states (*London Gazette*, 23 September 1941):

> This N.C.O., since joining No. 104 Squadron, has completed 7 operational trips. Prior to joining the squadron from No. 58 Squadron, he completed 9 trips as Captain and 12 as second pilot, a total of 28. He has shown great determination and energy and has proved himself to be an efficient Captain. On one occasion, in spite of the fact that his aircraft was hit and damaged by anti-aircraft fire near Ostend on 9th May, 1941, he continued his flight to Ludwigshaven and carried out a successful attack. He has set a splendid example to other members of his flight which has undoubtedly had some bearing on the success which this squadron has achieved. He is very strongly recommended for the award of the Distinguished Flying Medal.

Regarded as tour expired and rested from operations, William was posted to 22 Operational Training Unit, where he became a flying instructor. During May 1942, Bomber Command required units from within all elements of its command to advise upon the availability of operational crews in order to achieve the desired number of aircraft to partake in what was to be the

PO William Fullerton DFM.

largest bomber raid of the war. Code named 'Operation Millennium', this raid was the first of the British carpet-bombing raids against the Germans. It was a massive undertaking that included more than 1,000 bombers manned by more than 6,000 aircrew.

On 30 May 1942 William Fullerton piloted Wellington IC DV843, which took off at 10.44 p.m. from RAF Wellesbourne as part of the Millennium force. The target was Cologne. With so many aircraft over a target area, losses were likely to be high. Never before had so many bombers been dispatched to one target. Four of the Wellingtons flying from 22 Operational Training Unit failed to return. William's crew was one of those. His Wellington crashed at 11.40 p.m. at Dinteloord (Nord Brabant), Holland. The entire crew lost their lives. They were later buried in Bergen op Zoom War Cemetery. Ironically, they never reached the target area, where the expectations of collisions between aircraft had been so high. Bomber Command recorded a total of forty-one aircraft lost during Operation Millennium. It was, at that time, the highest recorded loss of men and aircraft during the war. The anticipated losses between collisions were unfounded, as only two aircraft suffered such a fate.

One of Britain's best-known pilots, Guy Gibson, later awarded the Victoria Cross for the 'Dam Buster' raids, also flew to Cologne as part of Operation Millennium. The then newly appointed commanding officer of 106 Squadron at Conningsby was flying with sixteen of his crews. He said:

> I for my part hate the feeling of standing around in the crew rooms, waiting to get into the vans that will take you out to the aircraft. It's a horrible business. Your stomach feels as though it wants to hit your backbone. You can't stand still. You laugh at small jokes, loudly and stupidly. You smoke far too many cigarettes, usually only half way through then throw them away. Sometimes you feel sick and want to go to the lavatory. The smallest of incidents annoy you and you flare up on the slightest provocation. When someone forgets his parachute, you call him names you would never use in the ordinary way. All this because you are frightened, scared stiff, I know because I have done all those things.[48]

Guy Gibson returned from Cologne; he later penned twenty-one personal letters to the families of those from his squadron who were lost on Operation Millennium. The officer commanding 22 Operational Training Unit posted a similar letter to the family of William Fullerton, along with an addition nineteen letters to the other men under his command who failed to return.

CHAPTER 5

Sqn Ldr Barcroft Mathers DFC, navigator – Caterpillar Club & PoW

Barcroft Malrose Mathers was an Australian, born on 31 January 1914 in the family home, 1 Kahibah Road, Mosman, New South Wales, Australia. Barcroft was employed in the commercial broadcasting industry, but both he and his brother James had a strong desire to fly within the military service. The brothers felt that opportunities to succeed in their joint ambition would be far improved by leaving Australia; they did so in 1937 and applied for a short-service commission within the Royal Air Force.

It was not uncommon for Australian applicants to be rejected for such commissions within the Royal Australian Air Force, only to succeed when applying for a similar commission in the Royal Air Force. There was a close relationship between the two forces, who were operating exchange schemes in the late 1930s. These schemes enabled officers to gain valuable experience, benefiting the individuals and respective services.

Barcroft was about to be rewarded for his enthusiasm and initiative in seeking his commission. His brother James was not so lucky, but he was to serve as a non-commissioned officer in the Royal Australian Air Force a couple of years later.

Barcroft received a letter on 4 January 1938 from the Air Ministry, Adastral House, Kingsway, London:

Sir,

I am commanded by the Air Council to inform you that they have approved your application for a short service commission in the Royal Air Force under the conditions of service detailed in the enclosed copy of Air Ministry pamphlet 13.

You will be required in the first instance to undergo a course of preliminary flying training at the civil flying school at White Waltham near Maidenhead, under the control of The De Havilland Aircraft Co Ltd and subject to your

Sqn Ldr Mathers.

satisfactory completion of that course you will be posted to the R.A.F. depot, Uxbridge, and will be appointed to a commission in the rank of acting Pilot Officer on probation with effect from the date on which you report there. You will undergo your advanced flying training at No. 8 Flying Training School, Montrose.

A copy of 'Instructions to candidates for short service commissions who are sent to a civil school for preliminary flying training' is enclosed and should be carefully read.

It is requested that you will notify this department as early as possible whether you desire to accept the commission offered under these conditions. If so, you should sign one copy of the undertaking referred to in paragraph 1(A) of the instructions and return it to this department with your reply.

Subject to your acceptance of these conditions you should report to the manager of the civil school before noon on Monday 17 January 1938 notifying him beforehand of the time of your arrival.

Candidates should also communicate beforehand with the manager of the school for information as regards accommodation.

I am to add that candidates are not entitled to the refund of expenses incurred on first joining the civil school.

I am Sir, your obedient servant.

Barcroft attended the preliminary flying training school with his hopes held high. Unfortunately he failed to achieve the required standard, and his ambition to becoming a pilot was dashed. He was assessed as having strong abilities in navigation, however, and was recommended to train as an air observer and navigator – all was not lost. Despite the massive disappointment, Barcroft knew that this next opportunity was likely to see him operational and fully qualified in a far shorter period of time, as the possibility of war with Germany was rapidly approaching. He was enlisted into the Royal Air Force on 19 March 1939.

Barcroft was issued with his Observer's Flying Logbook at the elementary flying training school, Perstwick. This was to record every hour and minute in the air, detailing his training and assessment as an observer. No longer under the short-service commission scheme, Barcroft commenced his training as Aircraftsman 580922 Mathers. Between 22 March and 20 May 1939, a total of 40 hours flying time had been recorded during his initial observer training.

In July of that year, the navigation skills were enhanced at the Air Observers School RAF North Coates. Barcroft gained experience in the Wallace aircraft,[49] bombing, and air firing exercises, which provided insight

Sqn Ldr Mathers' crew in front of a Whitley bomber.

towards operational offensive flying. August saw a temporary move to join
10 Squadron at RAF Dishforth, providing additional training for him in
the large Whitley bombers. Barcroft was on station at Dishforth when war
was declared on 3 September. The following month, he was posted to 1 War
Special Course at St Athen School of Air Navigation, which was the final
preparation to complete his training. He was promoted to the rank of leading
aircraftsman and added a further 40 hours flying into his logbook. The
majority of those hours were flown within the Anson aircraft, and navigation
principles were the same. The skill of navigation over occupied Europe, into
Germany, and returning, were ones that he would shortly demonstrate for
real. The course at St Athen concluded on 17 January 1940.

Barcroft returned to Dishforth and 10 Bomber Squadron in March. He
knew the station and the squadron's Whitley aircraft. Placed with B Flight,
he was keen to demonstrate his expertise. It was not long coming; new
crews were assigned nickel-dropping sorties, dropping propaganda leaflets
over specific locations across Germany. The operational record book for 10
squadron made on 22 March 1940 explains further:

> From the base to the Dutch Coast visibility and weather were bad but cleared
> over Germany. Owing to a navigational error this machine (Whitley K9033)
> turned south too soon i.e. before Borkum and violated North East Holland.
> However this error was discovered and the aircraft turned eastwards. At 20
> miles North of Frankfurt the nickels were dropped.

The first operation over Germany was completed by Barcroft and his crew;
it was an eventful exercise in his navigation skills.

Having been promoted to sergeant, Barcroft's next opportunity was to
fly over Germany carrying out a reconnaissance of canals and targets in
the Rhur on 6 April. This sortie was with a new captain and crew flying in
Whitley K9032. FO Prior lifted the aircraft off the runway at 8.50 p.m. The
navigational route was scheduled for Bramsche, Minden, Aurich, Emsweser
Canal, and Osnabruck. Anti-aircraft flak and searchlight opposition was met,
but no damage was sustained. Barcroft did an excellent job but the Whitley
suffered from the loss of its wireless receiver, removing the possibility of
obtaining any fixes to assist with navigation. The long sortie of over 9 hours
caused concern to the captain, and the fuel gauges were indicating very little
petrol. The decision was made to force a landing at Fairfield Spa Flow near
Grimsby, but unfortunately the aircraft struck a large tree and slewed round
upon hitting the ground at 5.44 a.m.

10 Squadron with Wing Commander Staton sitting central.

Thankfully no injuries were sustained; and the crew were picked up by another 10 Squadron Whitley at North Coates, before returned to Dishforth. Barcroft acted as second navigator and bomb aimer for his third operation on a night bombing raid on 16 April over Norway. The target was the airfield at Oslo. FO Prior acted as second pilot to the squadron commanding officer, Wg Cdr Staton. This may well have been as a result of the previous forced-landing experience by Prior. WC Staton was a First World War ace pilot, who wore the ribbons for the DSO, MC, and DFC gallantry awards. Bill Staton was known as 'King Kong' within 10 Squadron. He always had a dog by his side when on the station, and seized any opportunity to fly with the men under his command.

The imposing and vastly experienced Wg Cdr Staton continued to fly with Barcroft as his navigator for several sorties. The invasion of Belgium and France saw an increase in activity for 10 Squadron, with operations to Stravanger on 1 May, and Kleve on 12 May, where they bombed road and rail junctions. On 17 May Wg Cdr Staton flew the same crew to attack the oil plant at Bremen. This was to be a most eventful sortie for Barcroft Mathers; he was again acting as second navigator and bomb aimer. The

Mathers' Whitley being made ready for operations.

squadron records provide a well-written account of this operation, which led to the award of a bar to Wg Cdr Staton's DSO. The aircraft Whitley P4952 suffered great damage by flak and was to be featured in several war time publications.

In Australia, Mr and Mrs Mathers received an account of the raid written by Barcroft, and arranged for it to be published in their local newspaper. The news clipping recorded the action:

R.A.F. EXPLOIT SYDNEY MAN'S STORY

A graphic description of the ordeal of an RAF bomber during a raid has been sent to his family by a young Mosman man who was navigator in the crew.

The man's parents believe from information given in the letter that the commander of the bomber was probably a wing commander who has been awarded a bar to his D.S.O. for his part in an attack on the Bremen oil depot. The letter stated in part:

'The crash we had was nothing to our last raid. The barrage of fire of all descriptions light and heavy pom poms and flames was terrific, backed up by dozens of searchlights. The heavy stuff chunged and grinded as it burst just below us, and the other light fire made funny whining and swishing noises as it whistled past the cabin. We were in it for half an hour, and made several attempts to get through to the target before we succeeded, but we did, and we got our target, and then hell was turned loose on us. We felt the burst of our bombs, and could feel the bumps of their heavy anti-aircraft fire as it burst just below us.

'Then we were hit by a shell and thought our machine was on fire. It wasn't on fire but when we got home, how we did I don't know, we saw that half the starboard aileron was shot away and there was a hole 4ft 6in square in the starboard wing, beside shrapnel holes in various parts of the kite.

'I take my hat off to my captain, the wing commander to fly the machine into and through all that, and make the trip home with a badly hit aircraft some 450 miles 330 of them over the North Sea. Perhaps he does know fear, but he never shows it.

'We were standing by to jump at one stage. All that torn fabric fluttering in the slipstream illuminated by searchlights looked like we were on fire. We wouldn't land anywhere but our own base. I wouldn't give him a course for any other drome for I was keen to get back to our own as we had got so far. And so we made it and he put our machine safely on the deck.'

Wing Commander Staton's recommendation for the award of the bar to his DSO quotes:

> He led the attack on Bremen, when he dived and attacked from 1000 feet to ensure hitting the target. His aircraft was hit by six shells the last of which did considerable damage but he succeeded in reaching his home base.

Whitley P4952 had suffered serious damage, but still managed to drop two 500 lb bombs, six 250 lb bombs, and 120 4 lb incendiary bombs directly upon the oil plant. Several official publications illustrated the damage to P4952, confirming the sturdiness of British aircraft construction.

Only four nights later Barcroft climbed into another Whitley, this time serial number P4965. The operation was to Munchengladbach for the bombing of railways. The operation against these targets was designed to prevent supplies, material, and men from supporting the advancing German army that was surging through France. The very next night, 22 May 1940,

Sqn Ldr Mathers' crash landing on 6 April 1940.

Recovering the engine from Mather's crash landing on 6 April 1940.

Wg Cdr Staton returned as captain of Barcroft's aircraft to take part in another night of bombing against targets in the hope of stemming the German advances at Hirson. Wg Cdr Staton was forced to land at Tangmere on the return from France. The following morning he piloted the Whitley back to base. The base was to be the location of great celebration the following week, as Aircraftsman Oldridge, an air gunner of 10 Squadron, was believed to have been the first gunner to have shot down a German night fighter in the Second World War. On the night of 27 May he was flying on an operation to the Ruhr when the engagement took place close to Utrecht.

On 5 June, Whitley P4952 was taken on a test flight following the extensive repairs required after the raid upon Bremen. The airframe passed inspection and returned as operationally effective. Italy declared war upon France and Britain on 10 June. This was to have an immediate effect upon 10 Squadron. The next day Wg Cdr Staton – with what would appear to be his regular crew, including Barcroft as his navigator – took P4952 to the island of Guernsey. The Channel Islands were used as a refuelling point. The operation that night was an ambitious raid across the Alps to bomb Turin in Italy; a night bombing raid that Wg Cdr Staton once again commanded, and he deployed the very first marking of a target with flares himself – an idea conceived to improve upon the poor standard of bombing that was taking place during these early war operations. The process that developed into the 'path finder' in the later war years was developed by 10 Squadron.

Other operations to Chateau Thierry and Le Harve took place during June, but at the end of the month the term 'razzles'[50] started to appear in Barcroft's flying logbook. On 30 June at Hamm, razzle devices were dropped by Bomber Command in the hope of causing damage by fire to crops and woodlands.

The summer months of 1940 focused upon Fighter Command's defence of the sky, with the Battle of Britain escalating towards its peak. Luftwaffe bombers were constantly attacking Britain and the threat of invasion was always present. Bomber Command was trying to commit to strategic targets of importance, and 10 Squadron were heavily involved. Barcroft and his captain, FO Prior, bombed Kiel on 12 July, followed by Dusseldorf in the Ruhr on the 13th. The Dornier aircraft factory in Hamburg was the next target on the 20th, and finally the Focker Wolf aircraft factory at Bremen on the 22nd.

The personal objective of securing a commission was achieved by Barcroft in August, when he accepted the temporary position of pilot officer for the duration of hostilities.

Mathers' 149 Squadron Wellington R1593, flown by him on 30 March 1941 in the Scharnhorst Gneisenau attack.

Barcroft flew a few daylight training and photographic sorties during the first week of September. They was to be his final flights undertaken in the 10 Squadron Whitley aircraft. A new experience shortly presented itself, when Barcroft remained at RAF Leeming but moved squadron on 18 September, joining 7 Squadron. This was the very first squadron to receive the four-engined Stirling bomber, for which Barcroft took an instructor training role from September to December 1940. During this period, 7 Squadron was preparing itself to operate in this new mighty aircraft. The squadron moved to RAF Oakington in mid-November of that year.

At the close of 1940 Barcroft's flying hours had reached nearly 350, forty-nine of which had been within the Stirlings of 7 Squadron. The total number of operations flown was nineteen. It was expected that his tour of duty would continue within the Stirling bombers, but this was not to be. Barcroft received a posting that saw him move to RAF Mildenhall, where he was to return to two engines, this time fitted to the Vickers Wellington Bombers of 149 Squadron.

In early 1941, Barcroft undertook his first raid within a Wellington on 30 March; aircraft R1593 captained by Sqn Ldr Cookson. The targets were the German battleships *Scharnhorst* and *Gneisenau*, both docked at Brest. Many men within Bomber Command would write those two names within their flying logbooks, as a great many squadrons undertook attacks upon these important ships.

Barcroft was about to fly his first operation to the German capital city of Berlin. On 17 April he wrote in his logbook 'Berlin Blitz',[51] which proved to be an operation that passed without the need of further comment, as did entries relating to operations to Kiel, Essen, and Hamburg.

Barcroft was regarded as a most experienced observer navigator, with one tour of operational duty within Bomber Command completed. He was posted to NSTDU Woodley (Navigation Synthetic Training Development Unit) in July 1942, which had been formed in May 1941 and was situated in the Phillips and Powis works. The developments undertaken at Woodley were secret, involving important works designed to progress and improve the training of navigators. Barcroft's appointment at the Air Ministry to work at Woodley ran from 1 August 1941 to 31 January '43.

Barcroft's brother, James Bruce Mathers, had enlisted into the RAAF (Royal Australian Air Force) in Sydney. Employed as aircrew, he travelled to Great Britain to commence training. A common occurrence on the completion of training was to undertake an operation whilst still attached to the Operational Training Unit. On 25 June 1942, 27 Operational Training Unit despatched Wellington R1162 and her Australian crew, which was captained by a Canadian, to attack Bremen. Wellington R1162 failed to return; James and the entire crew perished. They are all remembered on the Runnymede Memorial; their remains were never found.

Promotion within the officers' ranks and the posting to development works within the RAF served Barcroft well. He was invited to become a temporary member of the Royal Automobile Club, based at Pall Mall, London, in December 1942, for the duration of his period of appointment at the Air Ministry. As an acting squadron leader, Barcroft attended the RAF Staff College at Gerrards Cross in Buckinghamshire between 1 February and 14 May 1943 with his posting distributed and published in the Air Ministry order (N)696.

Postings to the NTU (Navigation Training Unit) at RAF Upwood, and the BDU (Bomber Development Unit) at Feltwell and Newmarket, engaged Barcroft right through to late 1943. The development of path finder crews and target-marking procedures had utilised a lot of his time.

Remembering the early days with 10 Squadron, where simple flare marking was experimented upon, Sqn Ldr Mathers had seen, and been a part of, that entire developmental process. A further posting to 30 OTU (Operational Training Unit) at RAF Hixon in October 1943 endorsed his ability and knowledge in training night bombing crews within Bomber Command. It was the attached Navigation Training Unit at RAF Seighford, where Barcroft worked between November 1943 and January '44. During Barcroft's time at RAF Seighford, he was able to add to his sorties by flying on a leaflet drop on 30 December 1943. He was, however, about to leave his role of instructing and join a squadron for his second tour of operational duty. As an experienced navigator, and having been training crews for the path finders of 8 Group, it was clear where he was going to be of greatest value.

On 7 February 1944, Sqn Ldr Mathers joined 156 Squadron at RAF Warboys, commencing his second tour of operations within the path finder force of 8 Group RAF. His regular pilot at this time was WO Trotter. This team were soon to build a strong reputation of reliability and accuracy within the PFF.

'Al' Trotter DFM DFC explains:[52]

> When I commenced operations with 156 Squadron, it very quickly became obvious that our original navigator would not be able to carry out his duties because of proneness to air sickness and the squadron commanding officer recommended 'Bart' as a replacement. When we asked Bart if he would consider becoming our navigator it was at once obvious we had made a good choice, and one equally shared by Bart as well. Our new navigator had already completed one tour of 39 Ops, and wanted so badly to get back into the fray that he took a reduction in rank to do so. Despite his obvious experience he melted in with our whole crew quickly and enthusiastically, sharing his experience quietly and without any sense of being overbearing.

Barcroft and Al Trotter took part in many sorties marking the intended targets with the various flares and coloured incendiary bombs developed for use within the PFF of 8 Group. Accuracy was of utmost importance, and clearly Barcroft's role of navigation was a key role in providing success for the crew and squadron. His logbook records the technical factors of timing and the bomb loads carried in the Lancaster Mk III aircraft that equipped 156 Squadron:

21.1.44 Magdeburg Time over Target z was – 5 1 x 4,000 4 x 1,000 6 x 500
27.1.44 Berlin Time over Target zero 2030 actual 2028 z – 2 1 x 4,000 11 x 500

These details relate to 'z' hour being the predicted time over the target. In this case it was to be over Berlin at 8.28 p.m. They arrived 2 minutes prior and supported the path finder force by bombing with one 4,000 lb bomb and eleven 500 lb bombs:

28.1.44 Berlin Time over Target 0330 z – 2 Actual 03298.8 1 x 4,000 11 x 500

Barcroft's logbook entries explain how precise the navigation to targets was, with the average time to reach any target in the Rhur around 3 hours. The aircraft frequently reached the target within plus or minus a few seconds. On 3 February Trotter's crew were required to demonstrate a TI (Target Indicator) demonstration drop. Three days later they took part in a group exercise, where they were recorded as arriving on target just half a second late.

On 1 April 1944 Barcroft and his crew moved to RAF Little Staughton near St Neots, Huntingdonshire. They had been posted into the newly formed 582 Squadron within the path finder force. This squadron had been formed by detachments from 7 and 156 Squadrons, providing excellent credentials for a new path finder squadron. On 2 April Air Vice-Mar. Bennett, the officer in command of the path finder force, forwarded to Barcroft the authority to wear the path finder's badge. It was the tradition to attach the small letter slip signed by Bennett into the flying logbook:

Headquarters
Path Finder Force
Royal Air Force
To: Flight Lieutenant B. M. Mathers (44634)

AWARD OF PATH FINDER FORCE BADGE

You have today qualified for the award of the Path Finder Force Badge and are entitled to wear the badge as long as you remain in the Path Finder Force.

You will not be entitled to wear the badge after you leave the Path Finder Force without a further written authority from me entitling you to do so.

Air Vice Marshall Commanding Path Finder Force.

The path finder force eagle was instantly recognisable to all aircrews, and was normally worn within the pleat of the left breast pocket. A further two operations to Karlsruhe and Friedrichshaven in April were sandwiched between another crash-landing for Barcroft. His captain now promoted to pilot officer, Al Trotter sustained damage to the undercarriage of Lancaster F on 26 April as he took off from Digby on the return to Little Staughton.

Barcroft's second tour of operations continued into the following month, May 1944. Operations over Nantes, Louvain, Boulogne, Dortmund, and Rennes confirmed an increase in French targets during the build up towards D-Day.

Into June, 582 Squadron were tasked with supporting the allied bridgehead operations; marshalling yards and communication targets became a priority. Douai on the 14th proved to be a well-defended target, with the Luftwaffe managing to intercept the bombers and inflict serious losses that included the PFF master bomber. Al Trotter explains:

> On June 14 the target for our operation was the Douai Locomotive Works. My good friend, F/L J. H. Hewitt, DFC was designated the Master Bomber. We took off at 0021 and the Master Bomber followed three minutes later. Our crew was designated as the Illuminator for this raid. We identified the target using H2S and marked with green TIs. The weather was 6-8/10th cloud based at ten thousand feet and visibility was moderate and hazy. We attacked at 0156 hours from ten thousand feet. We dropped twenty four seven inch hooded yellow flares which really lit up the whole target area. At 0157hrs, we dropped our bombs. The green markers lay on track about five hundred yards apart and red TIs fell on top of each other midway between the greens. Bombing was concentrated on TIs as instructed by the Master Bomber. This was the last anyone heard from him. We were later told by the Squadron Commander, John's aircraft was intercepted by a night fighter over Douai and crashed killing all aboard.

This was the forty-third operation in which Barcroft had participated. The odds of successfully completing this number of operational missions within Bomber Command were very slim. He added to that number on 23 and 24 June, with raids to Coubronne and the V1 flying bomb site at Middel Straete, and another V1 site at Oisment on the 27th, followed by an operation to Blainville railway yards on the 28th. The next operation saw Barcroft's first green ink entry in the flying logbook.[53] The last day of June saw a daylight operation upon Hitler's Panzer Division at Villers Bocage.

On 27 June 1944, the award of the Distinguished Flying Cross to Acting Sqn Ldr Barcroft Melrose Mathers (44634) was announced and published

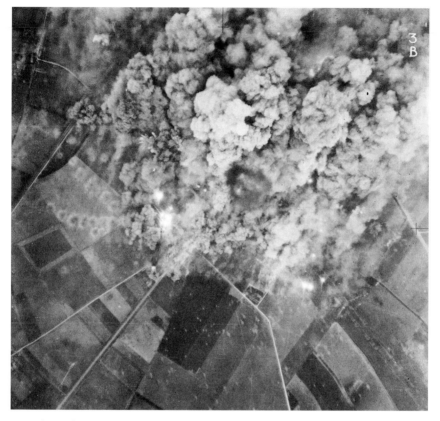

Sqn Ldr Mathers' daylight bombing raid on 18 July 1944 at 8,000 ft over Cagney.

in the *London Gazette*. The commanding officer of 156 PFF Squadron had recommended Barcroft for the non-immediate award of the DFC. It was duly endorsed and subsequently published, along with a large number of other Australian recipients.

In July 1944, 582 Squadron received orders to concentrate upon the previously visited V1 flying bomb sites across France. These small launching sites were difficult to locate and destroy. The terror, damage and death toll sustained by London and the home counties had reached massive proportions. Seventy to 100 flying bombs were now reaching their targets on a daily basis. On 30 June, one V1 landed at the Air Ministry building in Aldwych, killing forty-eight people. Between 2 and 15 July Barcroft and his crew attacked eight rocket facilities, some of which were underground storage sites. These daylight bombing raids had a direct impact upon reducing the numbers of V1 flying bombs being launched against London.

The allied push from Normandy had reached great difficulty around Caen at this time, and fortified villages and narrow roads presented the British second army with a problem that Bomber Command could help to resolve. Named as operation 'Goodwood', the requirement was for accurate and specific targets to be bombed during daylight. The path finder expertise was able to provide the answer. On 18 July Barcroft's Lancaster ND 969 F took off to bomb Cagney, Caen. The bomb load was 11 x 1,000 lb and 4 x 500 lb, and at a height of 8,000 feet the load was dropped. The aiming point photograph later identified this as having been a perfect result. On the same day, Al Trotter's crew were required to bomb the railway yards at Vaires. They were to act as the deputy master bomber crew, a positive recognition of the crew's credibility. The armament load consisted of four yellow target indicators and 6 x 1,000 lb bombs.

Reselected to act as deputy master bomber, Barcroft and his crew navigated a strong force of bombers to the V1 facility at Ferme Du Forestal on 20 July. Four yellow target indicators and 9 x 1,000 lb bomb loads were used. Once more the crew produced an aiming point photograph that provided evidence of an excellent result. A return to night operations on 10 August 1944 ensued with the railway junction and yards at Dijon the next objectives. The PFF led a force of 124 aircraft to attack what was described as an important communications target. Barcroft completed this operation, his sixtieth, and recorded within his flying logbook that the 7 x 1,000 lb bomb load and 6 x 4 inch by 7 inch flares had been dropped. In addition to this entry, Barcroft calculated that he had spent over 300 hours in the air whilst on operations. These combined statistics were far in excess of what was ever expected of aircrews during the Second World War.

Two days later the Opel motor works factory at Russelsheim was attacked by 297 Bomber Command aircraft. With proven path finder methods used as directed by the master and deputy bombers, Lancaster ND969 F in which Barcroft had already completed twenty operations, was once again deployed to carry his crew. The target was close to Frankfurt in Germany, and as expected, the flak over the target was fairly bad. Adding to that, enemy night fighters were sighted by several crews. Over the target, the directions to bomb on the various coloured flares were undertaken, and Al Trotter once again experienced the quality of navigation expected from Barcroft with timings over the target being perfect. Having completed their objectives, a course was set for the return to base. Suddenly, and without warning, their Lancaster was attacked from behind and below by an unknown Luftwaffe night fighter. The attack caused massive and immediate damage, and both starboard engines burst into flame. With the Lancaster rapidly reaching the stage of non-recovery, Barcroft and the surviving crew members responded to the call by the captain to abandon the aircraft. Al Trotter quotes:

> I had no elevator or rudder control and both starboard engines were on fire. Bart was the third member of the crew to pass me en-route to the forward escape hatch. I had no idea as to whether he and the others had been successful in their evacuation.

The reality of survival would now rest with the thin silk deployment of the Irvin parachute strapped to Barcroft's chest. On reaching the forward escape hatch, Barcroft found it difficult to extract himself due to the aircraft's uncontrolled and violent movements. Barcroft eventually managed to follow the flight engineer through the hatch:[54]

> Those first few seconds after I was flung through the escape hatch were a nightmare I shall never forget for as my chute was dragged from my arm I was certain it was not fixed to the harness clips. I certainly had not pulled the ripcord, but luck was with me as it opened. As I swung wildly in the air I saw Freddie (The Lancaster) burning furiously as she dived away in the distance on her last flight and thought then of how well she had served us to the end.

Lancaster ND969 F was one of thirteen Bomber Command aircraft that failed to return from that operation to the Opel motor works. ND969 F crashed near Papiermuhle (not far from Neumagen-Dhron), Germany, in the early hours of 13 August 1944. Flt Lt Elmer John Trotter, DFC DFM pilot, Sqn Ldr Barcroft Melrose Mathers DFC navigator, and Flt Sgt John Rawcliffe (flight engineer), successfully bailed out of the aircraft. The other four crew members all died that night and were later interred in the Rheinberg War Cemetery. The Luftwaffe pilot credited with the claim of having shot down Lancaster ND969 was FW Erwin Egelar of Stab IV/NJG1.[55]

On 13 August the commanding officer of 582 Squadron sent letters to the family of the entire crew immediately, as at that time no knowledge existed of their fate. Sqn Ldr Mathers DFC and his fellow crew members who survived were eligible to apply for membership to the Caterpillar Club, a fact that was probably far from his mind on the day his parents' letter had been dispatched from RAF Little Staughton. Al Trotter explains further:

I was captured the next night and lodged in a jail in Trier. Several hours later another person was thrown into my cell, and to my pleasant surprise it was Bart. The next morning our captors took us up to the local Military establishment where we were ushered into an office occupied by a German officer. He stood and gave the Nazi salute accompanied by the Heil Hitler. We both responded with our own military salute only to be met with loud shouting and obviously insisting on us responding by returning the Nazi salute which I refused with a Nein Nein. I received a punch which staggered me but recovered with a youthful reaction of responding. Bart grabbed me by the hair stating something like, 'You silly bugger that's what he wants.' I guess Bart more than likely saved my life with his quick reaction.

Barcroft Mathers remained a prisoner of war. It was while imprisoned in Stalag Luft III that he made written application to Leslie Irvin for his membership to the Caterpillar Club. Applications from allied prisoners of war were a regular occurrence, received from camps across the occupied countries. Membership cards were frequently posted to the camps directly. Several prisoners were lucky enough to receive a gift from the YMCA, a small wartime logbook. This personal item was equipped with pages for writing, painting, or drawing, and small envelopes designed for holding stamps or collectables. The personal letters received from the Caterpillar Club always received pride of place within these much-appreciated books. The Caterpillar Club meant a great deal more than just a membership card and a pin to these men.

Barcroft was held in Stalag Luft III, Sagan, Poland, until 27 January 1945, when the camp commandant responded to orders issued from Berlin stating that allied prisoners of war were not to be allowed to fall into the clutches of the advancing Russian army. At 11 p.m. the German guards marched the men out of Stalag Luft III, with long lines of prisoners of war walking in a westerly direction under armed guard. The exodus was a harrowing experience; freezing conditions and deep snow covered the entire area. The walking was relentless and took place over two complete days, with meagre rations of foods available. The prisoners were loaded onto a cattle truck for a further three days until they reached their destination at Marlag Nord.[56] On 18 March 1945, Barcroft escaped from Marlag Nord, situated not far from Darmstadt. Walking through Darmstadt he experienced a hostile civilian population, and was forced to take to the woods to seek shelter.[57] Four days later, Barcroft walked back to Marlag, where he eventually made contact with the advancing allied forces.

CHAPTER 6

Flt Lt Philip Anscombe DFM AFC, pilot – GQ Club

Philip Charles Anscombe was born in Eastbourne, Sussex, on 24 October 1913. At this period in time, the south coast was at the forefront of early aviation development. A factory responsible for early aircraft production was situated just along the coastline from Eastbourne, at Peacehaven. The local newspapers were frequently producing stories that no doubt inspired the young generation with romantic notions of flying.

It was the aviation developments in the First World War that provided the platform that resulted in Philip's application to join the Royal Air Force. Progressing through the military courses and volunteering to become aircrew at the earliest opportunity, he attended an air observer's course in February 1937. His first flight in an aircraft took place on 1 July 1937, whilst serving in 12 Squadron, who were equipped with the Hawker Hind aircraft.[58] An aircraft capable of carrying up to 500 lb of bombs, Philip occupied the rear-facing cockpit position that was equipped with a Vickers machine gun. He was also the bomb aimer.

The following year Philip was posted to 39 Squadron at Risalpur, India. The squadron was deployed for operations against the tribes on the north-west frontier, countering disturbances in the Badar, Algad, and Maintoi valleys. Bombing sorties were frequently flown after leaflet and other information messages had been dropped on the selected targets.

In May 1938 the squadron returned to its original base at Risalpur, where Philip took part in the king's birthday parade fly-past on 9 June. In January 1939 the squadron returned to Miran Shah, where it intensified the bombing raids against various tribal positions. By early summer in 1939 it became apparent that the situation in Europe was likely to escalate into conflict with Germany, and volunteer pilots were therefore sought. Philip applied immediately, and was accepted for training as a pilot in the rank of corporal.

Philip was posted to the UK for his training, which he completed at 15 Elementary Flight Training School and 10 Flight Training School at Tern Hill. The air experience with 39 Squadron and his own natural ability saw him graded as an 'above average' pilot.

In December 1939, Philip was posted to 90 Squadron, where he started to fly the recently acquired Bristol Blenheim bombers, at the time regarded as the most modern light bomber within the RAF. Each pilot in 90 Squadron was allocated 20 hours in the air a month. Just four months later, Philip was posted to 17 Operational Training Unit RAF Upwood, where he continued to fly Blenheims. To his great disappointment, however, he was selected for an instructor's position. The advancement of suitable students to undertake full-time instructional duties was urgently required. The declaration of war against Germany caused such measures to be imposed, and the selection of instructing staff was of high priority. Philip was awarded the Distinguished Flying Medal as a result of his operational service in Waziristan in 1939, the notification appearing in the *London Gazette* in October 1940. Philip was now wearing the ribbons of the DFM and the India General Service Medal 1936-39 upon his flying tunic.

In May 1941 he was posted to 14 SFTS as a navigation instructor and, in December 1941, to 14 Pilot Advanced Flying Unit at RAF Ossington. In November 1942, Philip joined 20 OTU at RAF Lossiemouth, flying the Vickers Wellington.

It was on 10 January 1943 that Philip came to owe his life to his personal parachute, a GQ-made chute that was designed and operated in exactly the same way as the more frequently used Irvin. Climbing aboard his Wellington T2713, Philip took off shortly before 6 p.m. on a night navigation exercise for his student crew. The crew performed well, but the Wellington suffered from the loss of an engine after oil pressure resulted in overheating. Philip gave the order for his crew to bail out, and unaware that his rear gunner had not done so, Philip himself bailed out into the night sky. The GQ parachute deployed itself correctly, and Philip floated to the ground as his Wellington crashed near Ladybank Fife, Scotland.

Philip had saved his own life with the aid of his GQ parachute and became eligible to join the elite GQ Club. His descent was brought to a crushing end when he impacted upon the ground, causing sustained compressed fractures of the twelfth dorsal and first lumbar vertebrae. The injuries resulted in him being hospitalised at the military hospital at Larbert. Only later did Philip find out that PO Frost, the rear gunner, had remained in the Wellington. When the aircraft crashed, the rear turret was torn away, resulting in Frost's death. By coincidence, Frost and Anscombe both came from Eastbourne. PO Frost was laid to rest in the Ocklynge Road Cemetery in his home town.[59]

It was to be a full year before Philip was able to fly again. The remaining years of service were undertaken in Station Flight, RAF Halton, followed by Communications Flight in HQ 22 Group, for which his services were recognised with the award of the Air Force Cross in 1946.

The GQ Parachute Co. lapel badge was inscribed, 'G.Q. Parachute Saved My Life – F/O. P. C. Anscombe, 10th Jan. 1943', and numbered, 'No. 152'.[60] Retained within the numbered card box of issue, the badge became a treasured possession for Philip Anscombe, who retired back to Eastbourne in 1947. Unlike the Irvin Caterpillar Club, GQ issued no membership cards, but each recipient of the lapel badge did receive a large certificate on which featured a mounted colour plate with a parachute descending through the clouds. Above the illustration was a gold foil-embossed GQ Parachute badge. Each certificate was hand calligraphed in perfect detail; the script read:

> Whereas by virtue of your successful
> accomplishment of a descent from the upper
> airs of this planet by Parachute we have
> thought fit to nominate and appoint you
> [name of recipient]
> To be a member of the G.Q. Club.
> We do by these presents bestow upon you.
> The dignity of membership and hereby
> authorise you to have hold and enjoy the
> privilege of wearing its gold badge of two wings
> No ... without challenge let or hindrance.
> Given under our hand this day ... 19

'GQ' PARACHUTE COMPANY LTD. STADIUM WORKS. WOKING. SURREY

It appears that some minor differences exist in the style and content of engraving upon the GQ lapel badges. However, the individual numbering system upon each badge clearly enables reference to any documentation, including the certificate, to act as provenance to its origin. Sadly, with the passage of time, certificates themselves are now regarded as most rare.

CHAPTER 7

Wg Cdr William Douglas DFC & bar, pilot – Guinea Pig Club

William Anderson Douglas, born in Edinburgh in January 1920, studied at Edinburgh College until volunteering for service with the Royal Air Force Volunteer Reserve in April 1939. William was selected for service as a pilot and attended number 7 Flight Training School in September 1939, with a subsequent posting to 603 (City of Edinburgh) Squadron in early 1940. A swift posting to serve as a staff pilot within two bombing and gunnery schools took place during the following months. This appears to be a rather strange duty imposed upon Douglas. His duties were to fly staff officers between various airfields. He was later posted to 610 (County of Chester) Squadron in September 1940, another Auxiliary Air Force unit equipped with Spitfires, and remained there until February 1941.

William returned to 603 Squadron towards the end of February 1941, when he finally participated in a number of cross-Channel operational sweeps. This was a particularly active period of intrusion sorties over occupied France. On 14 June, following engagements with several BF109 Luftwaffe fighters, William submitted claims of having damaged two enemy aircraft in combat. Seven days later he was able to complete a combat report with a further claim for the destruction of a BF109, south-west of Calais. Proving himself to be of strong character within the squadron, his operational effectiveness was soon recognised. On 23 June, again near Calais, Douglas entered into combat with the Luftwaffe. The ferocious engagement resulted in William sustaining serious wounds inflicted by returning cannon shell splinters. His Spitfire, serial W3110, also suffered significant damage, but William was able to fly it back to England – both the aircraft and himself requiring urgent attention. The Spitfire was repaired and returned to service a lot quicker than her pilot.

After initial medical attention, Douglas was transported to the East Grinstead Hospital in Sussex. During the latter months of 1941, operations commenced upon the wounds inflicted by the large cannon shell splinters. Both his legs and one arm required surgery, which was conducted by Archibald McIndoe. These operations qualified Douglas as a member of the Guinea Pig Club. The pioneering surgery carried out by Archibald McIndoe and his team was not purely restricted to burn injuries, as reconstructive plastic surgery was a significant part of the portfolio of the work they undertook.

In April 1942, Douglas returned to 603 Squadron, where he and the other squadron pilots and aircraft were to be transported to the island of Malta on the United States aircraft carrier Wasp. Operations commenced immediately upon arrival for 603 Squadron to be engaged in the protection of Malta. On 11 May 1942, in a crowded sky over the island, Douglas collided with another Spitfire during the aerial interception of enemy JU88 bombers. PO 'Barny' Barnfather was in the second Spitfire. Sufficient height was available to both pilots, who managed to escape and survived by deploying their parachutes.[61] Both were saved by the RAF air-sea rescue launch that was based on Malta, and were swiftly returned to continue defending the island from the consistent aerial bombardment. Douglas was to quickly raise his score with a JU88 on 25 April, and in May, with another two BF109s destroyed. A brace of JU87s as probable, and another damaged followed directly. Appointed to command the squadron in July, he added a further JU88 and a damaged Italian MC202 to his tally that same month.

The critical situation over Malta reduced, and the decision was made to withdraw 603 Squadron. Douglas was regarded as tour expired and due a rest from operational flying. He returned to the UK, where he became an instructor at 58 Operational Training Unit. It was whilst serving at the OTU that the award of his Distinguished Flying Cross was announced. The original recommendation, written by 603 Squadron's commanding officer states (*London Gazette*, 4 December 1942):

This officer took part in 12 offensive sweeps over Northern France in June 1941, during which he destroyed one M.E. 109 and damaged another. In June he was shot down and wounded, but returned to operations in November 1941 and, on his next sortie, took part in an operation in which the Squadron sank two, and damaged two out of eight flak ships. On 22 April 1942, he led a Squadron of 11 aircraft from an aircraft carrier to Malta. He has flown nearly 47 hours over the island and in that time he has destroyed four, shared in the destruction of another two, probably destroyed one, and has damaged five enemy aircraft. On 10 May 1942, he destroyed one Ju. 87, shared in the destruction of another, and probably destroyed a third. Altogether he has destroyed or shared in the destruction of twelve aircraft. Squadron Leader Douglas has inspired the whole squadron with his keenness and example, and has by his fine leadership, has shown himself to be a first class Squadron Commander.

A refresher training posting to 453 RAAF Squadron provided the opportunity to add another Luftwaffe aircraft to Douglas' tally. Flying once more in a Spitfire, he recorded one JU87 as probably destroyed. This short service posting was followed by a move to the Fighter Leaders School at RAF Charmey Down. Developments in fighter aircraft support to the army had proved effective – close support flying upon specific targets, often very close to the front lines, required training. Pilots underwent instruction upon target recognition and operational deployment. These operations were primarily undertaken by the ground attack squadrons within the RAF Second Tactical Air Force.[62] Eager to fly operationally once more, Douglas was given command of 611 (West Lancashire) Squadron in August 1943. Based at Southend, 611 Squadron's Spitfires carried out a mass of operational sweeps over Holland and France in the lead-up to the Normandy Landings. Douglas claimed a further JU88 south-west of Saintenay on 10 June 1944, and a BF109 over Omaha beach on the 14th. He was awarded a second Distinguished Flying Cross, signified by a bar to his original DFC. The recommendation published in the *London Gazette*, 26 September 1944:

> Since being in command of No. 611 Squadron, Squadron Leader Douglas has successfully completed 105 offensive sorties. These sorties include numerous shipping reconnaissance patrols and shipping strikes along the coast of Holland, involving long sea crossings, fighter sweeps and escort operations with bombers. Latterly they have also included 17 sorties over the Normandy beaches, ten of which were at first and last light, some in very bad weather conditions.
>
> Since D-Day, Squadron Leader Douglas has destroyed one enemy aircraft and probably destroyed another. In the former action, which was at night, Squadron Leader Douglas, finding that his gun-sight was not functioning correctly, closed to point blank range regardless of the return fire to which he was being subjected. On opening fire he caused the enemy aircraft, a Ju88, to explode and his own aircraft to be damaged by the debris which was thrown back.
>
> Throughout this, his second tour of operations, Squadron Leader Douglas has at all times shown the keenest offensive spirit and has been a fine example

to his Squadron. Through his untiring efforts he was able to train his squadron up to a pitch when it was able to operate not only at night, but also in bad weather at night, thus ensuring that it was able successfully to fulfill its mission during the opening phases of the invasion of Europe with the minimum of loss.

Wg Cdr Douglas, an ace-status pilot 'guinea pig' was released from the Royal Air Force in December 1945.

CHAPTER 8

Flt Lt Ralph Carnell, Battle of Britain Hurricane pilot – Guinea Pig Club

At the age of sixteen, Ralph Carnell took advantage of the Royal Air Force Apprenticeship Scheme – for which selection examinations were provided across the country. He was successful, and signed on for twelve years' service in 1929.

The aircraft apprentices, known as 'Halton Brats', completed a weekly time table of 20 hours technical training, 9 hours physical training, drill, and games, and 8 hours on general education. Barrack duties, homework, inspections, and recreational activities (including sports and model aircraft clubs) were compulsory and all part of being a Halton Brat. Each apprentice was assigned to the trades of carpenter, fitter, sheet metal worker, or electrical, and guaranteed a trade qualification on completion of their training. RAF Halton and Cranwell were renamed 1 and 2 School of Technical Training respectively.

It was the examination progress, and marks gained in the final examinations for each apprentice trade, that determined the graduating rank and rate of pay for all cadets passing out from Halton. The apprentices that scored most highly were frequently offered cadetships to RAF Cranwell, where a commission was the likely outcome.

Ralph Carnell had enlisted in January 1929 as an aircraft apprentice; his qualification to become a fitter was achieved in December 1931. In addition, an opportunity to volunteer for pilot training was presented to him, which he accepted with great enthusiasm. Early training was slow but progressive; he was a dedicated student and naturally gifted, which resulted in him gaining his wings and full qualification in early 1937. Ralph was posted to 111 'Treble One' Squadron at Northolt, one of the first squadrons in the world to have been selected to receive the 8-gun monoplane fighter unit, the Hurricane. An exciting development in the history of the Royal Air Force, RAF Northolt became the centre for media attention when the first Hawker Hurricane aircraft arrived at the airfield. Any recently trained pilot would have most certainly wanted to be a member of that particular squadron. Promoted to the rank of flight sergeant, Ralph flew in the squadron's Hurricanes at the outbreak of hostilities. Numerous defensive patrols and reconnaissance sorties were undertaken by Treble One from January 1940. They operated from aerodromes at Croydon, Debden, Hawkinge, Martlesham Heath, Northolt, and Tangmere. Ralph went into true combat over Dunkirk that May.

On the official starting date of the Battle of Britain, 10 July 1940, Ralph was engaged in aerial combat over Folkestone, Kent. He engaged and damaged a German Dornier bomber, but upon his return he was compelled to make a crash-landing at Hawkinge, Kent. His aircraft had sustained damage as a result of accurate return fire during the combat. Quickly back in action, Ralph damaged a ME109 fighter on 25 July and destroyed a JU88 Bomber on the 31st. On 16 August, amidst a fierce air battle, Ralph was shot down over Kent and crashed at Palmers Green Farm, Brenchley, near Paddock Wood. Hurricane P3029 was a write off following the crash, which had taken place shortly after midday. Miraculously, Ralph survived the impact, but the fire that had engulfed the cockpit of his aircraft resulted in him receiving serious burns. Ralph was admitted to the Queen Victoria Hospital, East Grinstead, where he became a patient of Archibald McIndoe, remaining in his care for nearly a year. The early Battle of Britain burn victims paved the way for many later casualties, from within all commands of the air force, to receive treatment from McIndoe.

Two years later Ralph was commissioned as a pilot officer, but despite the successful treatment of his burns, he did not return to Fighter Command. Ralph undertook a flying instructor role until being posted to 684 Squadron, a Mosquito photo-reconnaissance unit in Calcutta, India, in the spring of 1944. A further near-fatal experience took place on his transit journey to India, when the aircraft crash-landed in the jungle. Sustaining minor injuries, Ralph was able to join his new unit slightly later than he had wished for. The Mosquito was a joy for him to fly, and tasked with many photographic reconnaissance sorties, he remained actively employed until the cessation of the war in 1945.

In September 1946, Ralph joined the Aircraft Control Branch as a flight lieutenant. He continued in that role until being placed on the retired list as a squadron leader in August 1963. This Battle of Britain fighter pilot served within the RAF for twenty-eight years, suffered terrible burns at the height of the country's plight, yet received no recognition in the form of any gallantry medal. He died in June 1984.

CHAPTER 9

Flt Lt Cedric Stone DFM,
Spitfire pilot – Caterpillar Club

Cedric Stone was born on 30 December 1913 in Sussex. Having been educated at Collyers Grammar School in Horsham, he left school early in order to train at Plumpton Agricultural College on the outskirts of Lewes, Sussex. Upon completion of his training, he returned to the family-run farm.

Life was hard work, and continued that way for a number of years. Cedric started to study aeronautical engineering, having always harboured an interest in aviation. The only time available was after the long hours working the farm, but dedication brought its reward and an opportunity arose to work within the aviation industry.

Cedric was employed as an aeronautical engineer in the Parnall Aircraft drawings office.[63] His passion was to learn to fly, so he took lessons at the nearby Rearsby grass airfield flying club near Leicester. This was a difficult task, as he was sending money home to help support his aging parents at the Sussex farm. His wages of £4 per week had to stretch far, but with dedication, he managed to study at night for his flying exams whilst juggling his time at Parnall's drawing office during the day.

During 1938, troubles within Europe were brewing. At this time, Cedric decided to join the Royal Air Force Volunteer Reserve, though he was still required to continue his important drawing work at Parnell. He was issued with a RAFVR badge to wear on his jacket, indicating that he had volunteered for service, and was sent the official request to join the RAFVR on 1 September 1939. His allocated service number was 754154. Flying training commenced in June and continued through to August 1939 at Ansty, the air service training school near Coventry. Issued with his pilot's flying logbook, Cedric made the following entries within the first pages, and at the newly promoted rank of sergeant:

27 June 1939   1st Air Experience in the Tiger Moth.

12 July 1939   1st SOLO a 10 minute sortie within a Tiger Moth.

21 August 1939 Flying Assessment and graded as 'Average'

Between March and June 1940, Cedric was posted to 1 Elementary Flying Training School Hatfield (EFTS), where student pilots had the opportunity to clock up several hours of basic aviation instruction on a simple trainer like the Tiger Moth. Pilots who showed promise went on to more advanced training. Others found different specialisms, such as wireless, navigation, or bombing and gunnery. On 8 June 1940, Cedric undertook a flying assessment and was graded as 'average'.

After 53 hours of training on Tiger Moths, Cedric became a qualified pilot. Following the assessment, he returned to 9 Air Experience Flying Training School, Ansty, for a further period of training and assessment, where he was graded as 'above average' on 28 June 1940. Cedric moved to 8 Flight Training School Montrose in Aberdeenshire, a venue which provided the opportunity to fly the Miles Master's Mk 1 aircraft, and enabled experience of single-wing flying to be gained. As the war began to gain momentum, it was clear that the Royal Air Force was going to be tested to its limits. Cedric was eager to join the service, and wanted the training to be completed as soon as possible.

The 15 September 1940 is regarded as the date when the Luftwaffe assault upon Great Britain was at its height. The gallant Spitfire and Hurricane fighter pilots within Fighter Command were about to defend London in a massive air battle, and one event captured the hearts of many that day. It was the desperate and valiant act committed by Flt Lt Ray Holmes of 504 Squadron. This pilot sliced the end from his Hurricane wing during combat with a Luftwaffe Dornier bomber directly over London. The tail severed from the bomber, causing it to plunge downwards, both wings collapsing the fuselage and crashing close to Victoria Railway Station. This was to become the most photographed German crash site during the Battle of Britain, and no doubt also one of the most reported and commented events across the Fighter Command bases.

Cedric's training and progress was rapidly approaching the standard required for operational flying. He was posted to 7 Operational Training Unit, Hawarden, North Wales. Equipped with Spitfires, this unit was preparing fighter pilots for air fighting skills. Within the unit were battle aircraft, towing targets across various ranges to enable the novice Spitfire pilots the opportunity to fire the guns and gain the skills required to engage and hit moving targets.

Cedric flew a total of 4 hours and 35 minutes in the Spitfire between July and October 1940. He was then assessed as ready for an operational posting within Fighter Command. During the first week of October he was posted to 64 Squadron. The Battle of Britain was still taking place and Cedric was about to join one of the participating squadrons, achieving his personal aim to become a Spitfire fighter pilot.

The Battle of Britain took place between 10 July and 31 October 1940. During this period of time, any pilot flying an authorised operational sortie with any of the eligible fighter command squadrons became a 'Battle of Britain pilot'. Records indicate that some 2,928 men were awarded the Battle of Britain bar, thus acknowledging the importance of the defence of the country in the air from July to October 1940.

Fully qualified and eager to fly, Cedric was posted to 64 Squadron. They were a Battle of Britain fighter squadron, who had been in the thick of the fighting in the sky over southern England. Casualties had been high and the squadron had been rested up north, but as he joined them on 7 October 1940 they were soon to be returned to fighting.

Unfortunately for Cedric, he had contracted 'trench mouth' in September 1940, a severe infection that required hospital treatment. It had caused some complications in the completion of his training, but he had managed to continue flying – with some restrictions on rigorous fighter pilot exercises. When he arrived at 64 Squadron he was still suffering from the condition and his face swollen. Cedric was therefore allocated to the position of duty pilot, which included work in the control tower acting as safety pilot. Cedric did several circuits and training sorties, as well as local flying alongside the flight leader, who provided protection. The squadron moved south to RAF Coltishall in November 1940, where Cedric was reinstated to full flying duties by the commanding officer of 64 Squadron, Sqn Ldr McDonnel. Cedric Stone had missed becoming a Battle of Britain pilot by just a couple of days. Though based at Coltishall, 64 Squadron operated from RAF Hornchurch from 10 November 1940 as part of the Hornchurch wing, with Kenly Airfield being frequently visited. Cedric flew several sector reconnaissance sorties from those airfields. It was to be an eventful time for him. He recorded an incident in his logbook on 24 November, where upon landing with eleven other Spitfires, he crashed. Cedric himself quotes:

Kenly airfield had been newly repaired after a bombing raid. On the 24th November I approached to land faster than I should. The result was that the flaps didn't come down due to the speed; with no breaking effect caused by the flaps not working I was forced to use my foot brakes. These in turn were used too violently and the soft ground caused the aircraft to tip on its nose breaking the propeller. I was called into the CO's office for a reprimand.

The commanding officer issued a red ink 'Carelessness' caution within Cedric's flying logbook.

Unfortunately, three days later, Cedric experienced another less than perfect landing. Flying a standing patrol during the evening, his Spitfire was reported to have crash-landed owing to a fractured air system. As the month came to an end, 64 Squadron joined in Fighter Command's planning to thwart the Luftwaffe raids along the ports and other coastal targets being attacked. Daily sweeps were made by numerous fighters, with the Luftwaffe sending significant numbers of aircraft to attack on a daily basis. In addition to the fighter sweeps, other bombing raids were being conducted across major cities and industrial targets. The Battle of Britain, as such, had taken place, but the war was still very much present above the skies of Great Britain. The planned invasion by German forces continued to be regarded as 'postponed' only. The constant Luftwaffe reconnaissance sorties meant observations were taking place that retained the option to carry out a planned operation 'Sealion' in the spring of 1941, should that be Hitler's directive.

Cedric settled into the sector sweeps and reconnaissance sorties alongside his fellow 64 Squadron pilots, with five sorties being flown by him during December. He became accustomed to the procedure of checking the days shift for readiness, checking that the aircraft allocated to him had been correctly fuelled, armed, and radio checked, accepting the aircraft against his signature on the log sheet, and then awaiting a call to scramble or fly the pre-arranged duty.

With a slow start to the year, February saw Cedric engaged in nine operations. During March, the squadron saw an increase in scramble responses; Cedric was on standby response and called into the air on four occasions on the 3rd, and once more the following day. The duration of time in the air ranged from 80 to 90 minutes on each response. The Spitfire serial P7982 became a regular aircraft for Cedric to fly during the month, climbing into the cockpit on twenty sorties, which included fighter protection operations over two shipping convoys. Cedric had reached a total of 76 hours experience within the Spitfire; 33 hours and 25 minutes operational. He was by now regarded as an 'experienced' fighter pilot. Fighter Command returned to the 'big wing' requirement in 1941. Offensive sorties (known as 'circus' sorties) were being undertaken across occupied France. These involved greater numbers of escort fighters, and each wing was made up of three squadrons commanded by the post of wing commander (flying). The Hornchurch Wing was part of the seven wings being commanded at this period in time. It was made up from 64, 54, and 611 Squadrons, all overseen by Wg Cdr Farquhar. Circus 7 was flown in the early afternoon of 13 March 1941, with six 139 Squadron Blenheim aircraft attacking Calais airfield. The bombers were covered by heavy fighter protection, including Cedric with 64 Squadron. Enemy BF109s of JG51 were scrambled to intercept, and 64 Squadron was attacked near the target. Sqn Ldr Aenas MacDonell was shot down, baling out to become a prisoner. Cedric felt the loss of his squadron leader, as not only was he on the same operational flight when he was shot down, he had also flown with him on many occasions. MacDonell's qualities as a leader, pilot, and gentleman were very much respected by Cedric. After escaping by parachute, MacDonell landed in the English Channel. He had been shot down by Maj. Werner Mölders, *kommodore* of JG51. An E-boat rescued MacDonell from the sea, and he became a prisoner of war until 1945. He was mentioned in dispatches for his meritorious service whilst in captivity, having served as the adjutant in Stalag Luft I at Barth.

Cedric went on to fly a large number of sorties recorded as 'Barrow Deep patrols'.[64] During April and May 1941 Cedric and his fellow 64 Squadron pilots frequently maintained a presence within this patrol sector.

In addition to the Barrow Deep patrols, offensive sweeps were carried out. These were sections of twelve Spitfires flying across the English Channel to the French coast. This was an exciting development for Cedric, as he was now flying a wide range of operational sorties. Convoy protection was still being performed, as well as the standing patrols over Maidstone and surrounding areas.

On 7 May Cedric was scheduled for another convoy protection, for which A Flight provided six aircraft. It was going to be a busy day for him as he was also roistered to fly in a sweep over Manston to Calais, and Dunkirk later that morning. Returning to the events of the convoy patrol, they are best recorded in the words of Cedric himself:

My Spitfire Squadron marking SH F, P7840 was detailed to patrol a convoy of ships rounding the coast at Dover and steaming North past Deal. In fact we were some 30 miles north flying as 12 aircraft. The squadron had not noticed, or decided not to alter course for the two aircraft I saw in the distance. I called up 'am investigating 2 aircraft at 3 o'clock'. I felt they could be hostile

Flt Lt Cedric Stone's Spitfire 'L', in which he shot down two Luftwaffe ME 109s in August 1941.

although recognition had not been definite. As I neared the pair, one fired his guns. That confirmed to me that they were preparing an attack. I switched on the range equipment and the fire button. I put the propeller into fine pitch. By then the pair were over the coast line and on my sight. I made a steep turn right towards them as their leader came into my sight. I pressed the firing button. The 'de wilde' ammunition flash showed the path of my bullets as they hit his spinner, then the engine, then the cockpit. Having turned on his back and headed for the sea, his number 2 became my next target. I was excited but the centrifugal force of the turn had kept me firmly in my seat. I leapt around excitedly looking for my next kill. He had gone into the low cloud base and I soon followed flying through the murk of the cloud half on instruments. I then suddenly became aware that we were over the shipping convoy and one of the balloons of the convoy was in fact on fire near my wing. I was lucky not to be caught by its cable. Obviously the 2nd ME109 had set it on fire so I was very near to him. I had to take violent avoidance to escape contact with the balloon. I eventually broke off the engagement after deciding that my target had left the area. I headed for base, the bad weather made me land at Manston. The aircraft was refuelled and rearmed. I phoned my squadron to tell them where I was. They congratulated me and said the convoy had confirmed my kill. They said the 2 German aircraft were lining up to make another bombing run at the time that I destroyed one.

Cedric was able to file his first combat report to confirm his success in shooting down the Messerschmitt ME109 aircraft, probably from II JG52 or II JG53.

The 64 Squadron operational record book for the above incident was written with some humour. It quotes:

> A Flight was patrolling a big convoy off the North Foreland by 0800 and by 0830 they were in combat. Stone (Was it very close? Well it looked enormous) bagged a Me109 which flew across him at point blank range, and 'Cub' P/O Taylor had a beam squirt at another which was potting the convoys' balloons. B Flight relieved A Flight and also found trouble. 'Tiddles' P/O Tidman found a Me 109 fresh from balloon potting flying across and below. 'Tiddles' recovered from the shock sufficiently quickly to dive at him and squirt as he climbed into the cloud. No claim could be made.

The following day, 64 Squadron left Hornchurch for a week at Martlesham Heath, before moving to Turnhouse on 16 May. They were not to remain there for long, moving to Drem in East Lothian, Scotland, four days later. Despite being rested from the busy south-east group operations, 64 Squadron were still required for some scrambles and standing patrols, though minor by comparison with the busy stations they had left. One opportunity presented itself for Cedric to add to his combat score. On 10 June, he was vectored to intercept a reported intruder or bogey between Dunbar and St Abbs Head, close to Edinburgh. The chase failed to locate the intruder, but on the next day he was again scrambled – however this time it was a friendly Blenheim that he located.

It was reported that RAF station Drem had a pleasant and well-used sergeants' mess. The facilities were excellent as evidenced by Cedric's mess bill, dated 1 July 1941. Meals, teas, and general messing required a payment of 14s 10d. It also provided the most fitting location for a leaving celebration when Cedric departed 64 Squadron, having been posted to 72 Squadron. He joined 72 Squadron as they were returning to the south to become operational from Biggin Hill and the satellite aerodrome of Gravesend, Kent. The squadron became involved in flying a non-stop succession of fighter sweeps, rhubarbs, and bomber escort missions. Converting on to the

Mk VB Spitfire in July 1941, Cedric was once again to enter the fighting front with greater opportunity to engage with the German Luftwaffe pilots. He was now flying within the Biggin Hill wing, under the command of Sqn Ldr Desmond Sheen RNZAF, commanding officer of 72 Squadron. Sqn Ldr Sheen was an ace-decorated Battle of Britain pilot.

It was not long before Cedric was flying alongside Sqn Ldr Sheen on circus operations over France, providing fighter cover for the Royal Air Force light bombers attacking marshalling yards and communication targets. In addition, there was a return to protecting the Thames estuary Barrow Deep patrols and wing sweeps, which involved significant numbers of Spitfires on offensive patrols.

On 7 August, Cedric flew to St Omer via Gravelines, where the target was the Longuenesse aerodrome. Soon after crossing the French coast, the eleven Spitfires involved in the operation were attacked by fairly heavy flak, but though enemy aircraft were sighted in the St Omer area, they did not engage with the Spitfires. Two days later, Cedric took part in a twelve-aircraft sweep led by the commanding officer. Taking off at 5.25 p.m., they swept across the English Channel, crossing the French coast at Hardelot. No enemy aircraft were seen. The sweep progressed to Calais and returned to base shortly after 7 p.m. On the same day, Sqn Ldr Douglas Bader of 610 Squadron flew as part of a 100-Spitfire attack on Gosnay power station, an ammunition factory at Marquise, near Boulogne Harbour. A huge dog fight ensued with five Spitfires being shot down. One of these was Sqn Ldr Douglas Bader, who had to bail out of his damaged aircraft. The successful and safe landing of Douglas was thanks to his Irvin parachute, however he was without one of his artificial legs, which had become trapped in his aircraft. This incident qualified him to become a member of the Caterpillar Club. The following day, it was Cedric's turn to attack the Gosnay power station. He took off at 12.45 p.m. on a similar sweep, when they too engaged with the enemy over Calais and St Omer. The engagement saw two ME109 aircraft claimed as damaged. The offensive continued, and fighter escort to bombing operations attacking the Gosnay Power Station kept Cedric very busy in the air.

On 16 August, he started the day on an early sweep to France, leaving the airfield at 7.25 a.m. and returning at 9.05 a.m. Some enemy aircraft were seen, but no engagement took place; the sun was fairly low in the sky and conditions were difficult for the pilots. At 12.15 p.m. he again took off on an escort to bombers attacking Marquise, and once more enemy aircraft did not engage despite being seen. They returned at 1.35 p.m. Cedric took off in his Spitfire on yet another circus bomber escort. This was the third operation led by Sqn Ldr Sheen that day, all aircraft taking off at 5.40 p.m. and forming up over Hastings on the south coast. The following account was written by Cedric:

16/8/41 Flying at about 27,000ft in line abreast deep in France, one of the squadron alerted us by saying over the intercom 'Enemy attacking 7 O'clock' The leader immediately wheeled round to the left and although I closed my throttle instantly, I could still be the victim of a collision. I could go no slower, but my C.O. still came nearer to me by virtue of his turn. I could go no quicker or tighter without running into the pilot on my left. I slowed to stalling speed and spun down. I lost some 5000 feet before fully recovering and regaining speed and allowing my instruments to settle. By that time the squadron was out of sight and away. I now depended upon my compass settling down and showing me where north and south was. It was then that I saw a speck on the horizon. Then there were 2 specks. They then became 4 ME109s. As they came closer it was obvious that I was their target. I got prepared, sight switched on, safety catch off, fine pitch and I was ready for firing. I needed to calm myself and had to sit quietly to align my sights. By this time the 2 pairs had reached me. One took up position on one side and the other on the other side. By this time I was doing a barrel roll, turns and other manoeuvres to make myself as difficult a target as possible. Then one crossed my sights. I pressed the button to fire. He was hit and I believe went down. I had no time to observe before the next one came in for attack. A short squirt with my fire button put him off and he started smoking. I saw no more of him because the 3rd was on his way to destroy me. A burst hit him and the 4th decided to reconsider his attack. I had no more ammunition. The thought was I may have to ram him and we'll go down together. He put his nose down and went for home. What course do I fly for the UK? I put my nose down and aimed north. I collected myself together, sorted my instruments and realigned my compass. I had been perspiring and could see nothing through my goggles. I pressed them to my forehead which allowed me to reset my instruments. I was too far into France to see the coast line. I felt that I was in very hostile country and unarmed. I needed to get out as fast as my Spitfire could take me. Nose down, course pitched. I was soon insight of the coast with some cloud cover. I crossed the channel as soon as I could; the white cliffs of Dover were most welcome on route for Biggin Hill. I landed at Biggin Hill almost without petrol and no ammo. I was in one piece and without a single enemy shot on my aircraft. I was very shaken, shivering and frightened. I had a nightmare or two subsequently.

Flt Lt Stone wearing a Mae West
life jacket on the wing of his
Spitfire 'Moshesh', named after a
Basutoland chieftain.

Sgt Stone was later credited with one ME109 destroyed and a further
ME109 damaged. Having gained the nickname 'Killer Stone' within the
squadron, Cedric had become a regular pilot in the Spitfire serial W3431,
squadron code RN, identification letter L. The following day, Sqn Ldr Sheen
led an offensive patrol against German shipping between Cape Gris Nez and
Calais. The target was quickly located, along with the patrolling ME109s.
During the engagement Sqn Ldr Sheen damaged one ME109 during the
melee. Flying at 12,000 feet, Cedric spotted a ME109 approaching from
his port side. In anticipation of the ME109's flight path, he opened fire at a
range of 80-100 yards. Suddenly the ME109 filled his sight ring. The enemy
aircraft whipped over on his back and was seen diving vertically towards
the sea. One of the other Spitfire pilots confirmed that the ME109 had hit
the sea. On consecutive days, Cedric submitted further combat reports, with
another aircraft endorsed as destroyed.

Cedric's morale could not have been higher at this time. This is evident
from his logbook entry on 28 August 1941, when he flew his Spitfire on a
solo 35-minute sortie named 'Aerobatics Handcross'. This was a personal
celebration of his combat claims of three aircraft destroyed and one damaged.

The aerobatics were carried out over his family's farm in Handcross, Sussex. It would have been an easy task for his parents to recognise the Spitfire's identification lettering, and they were no doubt proud to see Cedric demonstrating his flying expertise and skill in the air.

Sqn Ldr Sheen added his signature to Cedric Stone's flying logbook at the close of the month. This was a standard procedure to calculate the hours flown by each pilot. Another important signature was to be penned into the back page of the logbook as well. It related to an incident on 26 August. Cedric provided the following explanation:

> I needed to test flight my spitfire before being accepted for the next operational patrol. As I took off the cross wind veered me towards the six foot fence. The excitement of my recent success provoked me a little. I lifted the undercarriage before I was completely airborne. The spitfire sank about two feet just enough for the propeller to plough up the ground. I pulled back the stick as I did so the tail wheel caught the fence causing me to not gain enough height. The trees ahead were level as I ploughed through them, the wingtips were torn off. This was the worst crash of my life.

The signature in the back of Cedric's logbook provided the following detail:

> 26 August 1941
> 'The pilot retracted the undercarriage too soon after take-off, Error of Judgement.'
> Entry Authority IIG/29/79/4/TRG.
> Group Captain Commanding RAF Station Biggin Hill. (Temporary) S F Vincent DFC AFC

Despite this being an entry Cedric would not have wished to be recorded in his logbook, it is a rare example of Gp Capt. Vincent's signature. He was only at Biggin Hill for a month before being swiftly promoted to air commodore of Fighter Command. He was the only pilot to have shot down enemy aircraft in both world wars.

September 1941 was a period of less operational flying for Cedric, with circus sorties to St Omer, Le Touquet, Cape Griz Nez, and Rouen. At the close of the month Cedric had recorded a total of 265 operational hours in Spitfires. The grand total of hours reached was now 517. Sqn Ldr Sheen signed Cedric's logbook for the last time at the end of September, as he was about to leave the squadron and be replaced by Cedric Masterman, another significant name in aviation history that would be added to Cedric Stone's flying logbook within the coming weeks.

One of Sqn Ldr Sheen's last duties with his beloved 72 Squadron was to type the recommendation for the award of the Distinguished Flying Medal to Sgt Cedric Stone. The recommendation was signed and submitted on 24 September 1941, and the final departure of Sqn Ldr Sheen took place after his last sorties in early October. Cedric flew with him as he led the Biggin Hill Wing on an offensive sweep to France, and a diversionary sweep where he claimed another ME109 during combat over Abbeville. Cedric himself flew circus operations to Ostend Power Station, Neiuport, and the docks at Boulogne.

Cedric Masterman, commanding officer of 72 Squadron, called Sgt Stone to his office: 'I have the pleasure of announcing the award to you of the Distinguished Flying Medal.' A letter signed by the commanding officer of Biggin Hill, Gp Capt. Broadhurst, was handed to him.

The letter was dated 4 October 1941 (ref. BH/2655/2/PI):

His Majesty the King on the recommendation of the Air Officer Commanding-in-Chief has been graciously pleased to award to you the Distinguished Flying Medal.

Wg Cdr Masterman said, 'I am asked to convey the Air Officer Commanding's congratulations with which my own are coupled.' He went on to inform Cedric that he had also been gazetted as a commissioned officer – becoming PO Stone – and that he needed to obtain his officer's uniform. On 15 October Cedric gathered the following clothing, which was entered on the internal return and receipt voucher: two jackets, two pairs of boots, one cap, one pair of trousers, one tie, three collars, one pair of gloves, one pair of socks, and one pair of gaiters. Submitted as a result of taking a commission, he was now responsible for the purchase of his own uniform and equipment. Other equipment and clothing was retained, with an agreement to return once the private purchase of equipment and uniform had taken place. This was a normal process for anyone entering the chain of promotion and gaining a commission. Cedric wrote to his parents to seek an advance of £10 in order to acquire some immediate uniform, doing so in the knowledge that the gratuity payment of £20 in respect of the award of his DFM (Kings Regulations & A.C.I., paragraph 310) was pending. In fact, this payment was not drafted into his bank until February 1942.

On 20 October, 72 Squadron moved to Gravesend, and Cedric returned to flying several operations in Spitfire W3431 – RNL clearly being a favourite aircraft of his. His position within the squadron was now senior; he was highly experienced and a commissioned officer wearing the ribbon of the DFM. This experience was rewarded with elevation by the commanding officer to 'yellow leader' on several practice sorties. Cedric was posted to a navigation course at RAF Grange during December, and as the year closed he was assessed as an 'above average' fighter pilot and 'exceptional' pilot navigator. Cedric returned to RAF Gravesend to re-join 72 Squadron in January 1942, where he led the squadron on two convoy patrols along the Thames estuary on the 17th. It was, however, one of the last times he would fly with the squadron. On 23 January Cedric returned the last of his NCO issue equipment to the stores, entering his signature on the internal return and receipt voucher.

Cedric took time to reflect upon his personal position at the close of January. By his own admission, he was suffering from the stress and trauma of having flown the Spitfire in combat for the last fourteen months. Not many pilots had achieved what he had, with three confirmed ME109 aircraft – and one other probable – destroyed. Cedric requested to be posted overseas as an operational fighter pilot; he knew that such a posting would provide a period of rest during the transportation by ship.

On 3 February 1942, Cedric was posted away from 72 squadron and regarded as tour expired. He attended the personnel distribution centre at Wilmslow, where he was provided with a rail warrant to travel to Glasgow in readiness to embark on the steamship *Neohellis*[65] on 13 February. After eleven weeks of passage, the convoy reached the Red Sea, subsequently arriving at the port of Tufiq on 16 April 1942. The passage, although uneventful, had been enjoyable for Cedric, and having rested, his thoughts turned to the new opportunity of flying in North Africa.

He was posted into 73 Squadron on 28 April. At that time he knew little of the structure or role of work he was about to commence. After crossing mile upon mile of sand, Cedric completed his journey, arriving at 73 Squadron's base, where he was met by Sqn Ldr Derek Ward, the commanding officer. Cedric was to be his B Flight commander within the squadron, one of the most forward in the desert at that time. The front line was close, and the tented accommodation was frequently being attacked by German raiders. The squadron were flying Hurricane Mk II aircraft, and were about to be thrown into the intense desert battles with the allies, as they were pushed back towards Egypt by the building German offensive. The air war over the desert was very different to that which Cedric had already experienced. It was explained that all combats were likely to take place over barren areas, away from habitation or ground forces. Any claims regarding the destruction of enemy aircraft had to be substantiated, requiring them to be witnessed as being on fire, crashing into the desert or with the pilot seen to have bailed out.

Cedric commenced flying the Hurricane Mk II as 73 Squadron flew from Sidi Hanaish. Over several days he gained experience on the aircraft and the unusual flying and navigation conditions across the desert. This introduction also saw Cedric admitted into the 10 SA field ambulance, where he was treated for gastro enteritis. It was not only the flying that needed adjustment. Water was seriously rationed and always tasted less than fresh; the diet was very different, too, and the incessant desert flies were difficult to contend with.

Cedric flew a full sector reconnaissance of El Adem and Gambut on 22 May, where he sighted three ME109s who made no effort to engage. On the 26th, 73 Squadron moved to El Adem. The next day, German ME109s strafed the landing ground at El Adem with one aircraftsman, DeBono,[66] being fatally wounded. The Germans had advanced and engaged in a tank battle only 15-20 miles south-west of their location. The squadron was ordered back to Gambut; Cedric wrote in his flying logbook, 'Jerry encircled El Adem.' The Hurricanes took off at 3.15 p.m., en route to west Gambut. One pilot, Sgt Sands,[67] was later reported as missing during that flight. Cedric landed without incident at 3.45 p.m. The desert war was producing a moving picture of lands held and lost on a daily basis, and movements between landing grounds were becoming a frequent event for 73 Squadron. Cedric might have relaxed on the transit to Egypt, but he was far from experiencing a relaxed or stable overseas flying posting. Cedric had arrived with 73 Squadron at the time of Rommel's advance, who were intent on reaching Alexandria. The German attack was against the front line, extending from Gazala to Bir Hakim, their aim to destroy the British troops with superior tanks and artillery. British and free French troops suffered great losses. Cedric recorded his thoughts of these times:

> It was a cruel lifestyle, constantly raided and dangerous. We hunted and were ourselves hunted. Issued with tents for night-time sleep, we found the tents became the target for enemy morning raiders. Individuals soon bivouacked in holes in the desert providing a degree of protection. We were constantly on patrols deep into the desert offering a gesture of help to the front line, the far end of which was held by the French. Casualties were daily and sometimes heavy.

Cedric led B Flight under the command of Sqn Ldr Ward DFC and bar.[68] The operations flown in early June from Gambut were patrols and reconnaissance sorties that covered the Bardia, Gambut, Hachiems, El Aden, and Amund areas, all of which had German aircraft engaged in offensive actions. Stukas were seen on occasions, but withdrew immediately if threatened. ME109s frequently stalked the areas looking for easy targets. The 12 June was an intense day of engagements, with several scrambles taking place. During the late evening a large force of Stukas, JU88s, and ME109 fighters were intercepted, with five Stukas and one JU88 being shot down.

On 13 June, Cedric was scrambled in an attempt to engage two ME109s, who eventually turned and departed. Eight other ME109s were similarly chased by other members of the squadron. The following day, 73 squadron was stalked by further German fighters during a sweep of El Adem. Cedric was experiencing a game of cat and mouse, never sure if a trap had been set.

On 16 June the commanding officer was on a scramble with twelve Hurricanes instructed for El Duda, when they were jumped by ME109s – this resulted in Flt Lt Robin, a newly arrived pilot, being shot down. Cedric's personal account fully explains the events that were about to take place:

We'd been on a long patrol, several alerts but each fizzled out. We returned short of petrol. The CO and his No. 2 landed almost together. I was flying a circuit about 1000 ft. above him as he passed under me to touch down. Suddenly I saw a fire ball. I looked down horrified. He was in the middle of it and his No. 2 flew straight into it. I saw an enemy leaving the area of the fire. I immediately turned towards it. It seemed ages before the Hurricane gathered speed. I'm sure my Spitfire would have been more manoeuvrable or quicker or was it the different atmosphere I was flying. The enemy aircraft was some way ahead out of range. I was full throttle through the gate. The enemy was climbing and so was I. I was some 15000 ft. and totally concentrating on catching the unseen enemy. Suddenly I felt the most frightful bang. My poor old Hurricane lost heart, immediately thinking her engine had seized. Suddenly in a spin with no control, I was unable to stop the spin. I realised I had been hit. My tail plane didn't work. I was descending out of control at 400 ft. per minute. I knew I needed to get out. I detached my helmet, tubes and connections. I undid my seat straps and belt and opened both the door flaps. I took a plunge. Halfway out of the door I was thrown back into my seat. The same thing happened again. In a couple of minutes I'm dead! I tried the other side and seemed to clear the aircraft but suffered an enormous bang on my head. I struggled to find the rip cord, pulled it and released the parachute. A terrific jerk and I could see the parachute canopy open. During the few minutes to fall to the ground on my parachute, I suddenly heard gun fire. The ME109 was trying to shoot down my parachute. I grabbed the parachute cords and pulled them. I don't expect that did much good but the German passed by and I was still in one piece. I caught a glimpse of my No. 2 who was trying to defend me. The German had completed a circuit and was preparing a second attack on my parachute and myself. I again tried to make it difficult for him to hit me. I then thought I could see my No.2s crashed aircraft and his parachute coming down in the same area. My head and neck were causing serious problems. I was having to hold my head up with the help of my other hand. As soon as my feet touched the ground, I released the parachute, held my head and ran like mad for about 100 yards. I was in no man's land but wanted to make some distance from my white parachute, I knew I was a target for him. It was some time before anything moved. Then somebody approached me. I recognised a tracked gun carrier. Two hefty bearded dark skinned Seiks spoke to me in English. I sent them over to my No. 2. They came back with him and lay him on the floor with his parachute wrapped around a badly wounded leg and thigh. All 80 yards of silk in the parachute and still red blood showed through. I was placed on the floor at his side. I soon realised something serious was wrong with my neck. Any slight movement was sheer agony. The casualty clearing station was 5 miles away. My No. 2 was dealt with immediately, but nobody knew what was wrong with me. I was dispatched back to my squadron arriving in time to be given a place on the floor of the C.O.s caravan. The Germans had broken through our lines and were mauling our columns and men. I was put on a 500 mile journey to Cairo and a medical centre near Ismailia. Mile after mile of rough road driving through the night I reached the hospital medical centre.

Cedric had become a member of the Caterpillar Club, but who was it that shot down his gallant commanding officer, PO Woolley, his number two, Sgt Goodwin, and himself? The German ace Hans-Joachim Marseille[69] had been responsible, one of the most remarkable pilots to have flown during the Second World War. PO Stone was the 100th allied aircraft that he had shot down. Marseille went on to record 158 victories before he lost his life having to bail out from an aircraft suffering mechanical breakdown in the air over North Africa. A strange coincidence was that Cedric suffered some broken bones in his neck after striking the tail of his Hurricane when descending by parachute, whereas Marseille struck the tail of his ME109, causing fatal injuries.

How many pilots experienced the horror of becoming a target whilst descending on a parachute? It had been a precedent that the aircraft's

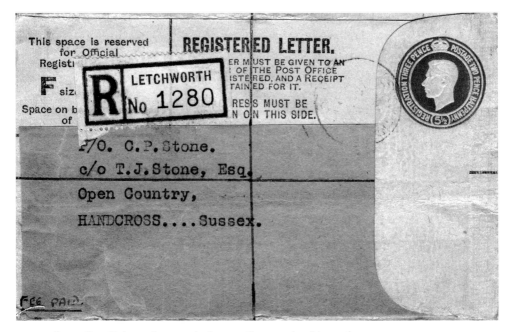

Caterpillar Club envelope used when sending membership cards.

CATERPILLAR CLUB

P/O. C. P. STONE

is a member of the Caterpillar Club, having saved his life by parachute

Signed

Hon. Secretary European Division

Flt Lt Stone's Caterpillar membership card.

destruction was the primary reason for pilots to engage in aerial combat. As war progressed, the understanding that the same pilot could return time and again to the skies changed all that. If the pilot was killed, the respective enemy was truly denied that fighting capability; Marseille clearly believed in that policy. Cedric's Hurricane was the first objective – Cedric himself was then considered equally so. It is probable that the engagement with the Hurricane flown by Sgt Woolley saved Cedric's life.

Cedric was examined at 27 General Hospital, a huge tented hospital close to Ismalia, where the broken bones in his neck were discovered. Several weeks of treatment were required before he was able to support his head normally. Haifa, Palestine, was his next destination, where further recuperation took place, with frequent return visits to the 27 General Hospital. Cedric was advised that he would be unable to fly for a minimum of one month, and even after then it was not to be operational. This resulted in him being posted to the Aircraft Delivery Unit, Cairo. The immediate duties required of him were that of assistant adjutant. In August 1942, he was able to commence non-operational flying – the best he could hope for in light of the injuries he had sustained.

A letter dated 30 August 1942 arrived from the adjutant of 72 Squadron, England. Cedric had written explaining his eventful experiences and enquiring about his old friends. The reply advised him that Wg Cdr 'M' was on 'the G.C. Island'. Observing the censorship rules the reference was obviously Wg Cdr Masterman, Cedric's old commanding officer. The reply also congratulated Cedric upon his membership to the Caterpillar Club.

On 26 October 1942, an airgram arrived from Irvin Air Chutes of Great Britain, Letchworth. Addressed to Cedric at the Aircraft Delivery Unit, it confirmed his enrolment into the Caterpillar Club:

Dear P/O Stone.

Many thanks for your letter of October 5th, and I am indeed glad to hear that you saved your life with one of our chutes.

I have much pleasure in welcoming you as a member of the Caterpillar Club, but regret that at present we are unable to obtain caterpillar pins. We have therefore decided to give membership cards with the promise of a pin as soon as they are again available.

I will send your membership card out to you as soon as possible, and when we do obtain more caterpillars I will certainly send yours to your home address as requested. Wishing you the best of luck

Yours sincerely

Leslie Irvin Honourable Secretary.

Flt Lt Stone's Caterpillar Club letter.

Cedric had passed a refresher course with 1 Aircraft Delivery Unit, and was now authorised for flying the various aircraft arriving at the ADU from UK factories. These aircraft units were landed at the west African ports, assembled, and flown by ADU pilots to an aircraft pool facility in Cairo. From this location the aircraft were moved directly to the front line squadrons, as and when needed. The transit across Africa was lengthy and dangerous to fly, covering at least 5,000 miles. This work engaged Cedric right through 1943.

In February of that year, Leslie Irvin applied his signature to the Caterpillar Club membership card. The card and engraved pin, with a personal letter signed by Irvin, was posted by registered delivery to Cedric's home in Sussex.

Promoted to the rank of flight lieutenant, Cedric was posted to 249 (Transport) Wing RAF Central Mediterranean Forces (Naples, Italy) 216 Group. A later move to 249 Wing brought duties flying the southern Italy and Cassino areas. During mid-1944 Cedric flew Hurricane LB680 to several front line locations. This included the recently captured airfield at Jesi Drome; Cedric had been requested to locate and trace many missing aircraft spread across the rapidly moving front line airfields in Italy. This he did with great success. In addition, he had flown a mercy mission onto the beachhead at Anzio, where emergency blood supplies were needed, as well as surveying Corsica and Sardinia for the ferry division. The overseas posing was drawing to its close and Cedric was classed as tour expired, boarding a Liberator at Naples on 8 September 1944, en route to England. Upon arrival, Cedric was posted to 1 Ferry Squadron Pershore, Worcestershire. He was still classified as 'non-combat' status due to the injuries sustained in 1942. This unit was responsible for many aircraft movements from the UK to overseas units. Cedric soon found himself returning to North Africa. On one journey he took a Beaufighter via Pershore, Rabat, Marbel Arch, west Cairo, El Adem (where he had been shot down in 1942), Castlebenito, and Blida. He then returned, via Gibraltar and Whitchurch, to Pershore in a Dakota.

In December 1944, Cedric was posted to the Metropolitan Communication Squadron, Hendon. RAF Hendon in London was ideal for Cedric, as he was close to family and friends. The squadron was a high-profile one, with responsibilities for the movement of important documentation and cabinet ministers. At the end of the month the grand total recorded within his flying logbook had reached 1,349 hours and 45 minutes.

On 1 January 1945, Flt Lt Cedric Stone's name was published in the *London Gazette* as having been 'mentioned in despatches' for his work in Italy. He was able to wear the 'oak leaf' adjacent to the DFM ribbon on his tunic, a fitting reward for the work undertaken with 216 Group. In addition to the MID oak leaf, Cedric wore the tiny Caterpillar Club badge just beneath the DFM medal ribbon.

The war in Europe was drawing to a close. Cedric's flying during April 1945 included several local trips for boys in the air training corp. On 24 April, Cedric took up an old favourite, the Spitfire, for a 30 minute air test. On the very same day a letter was sent to him from St James's Palace inviting him and his family to attend the investiture of his Distinguished Flying Medal. He was required to be at the palace no later than 10.15 a.m. on 8 May 1945. Within the letter was his ticket of admittance, number 4,713.

Flt Lt Stone's medal group, including the DFM with Caterpillar pins.

On 8 May, Cedric attended Buckingham Palace to receive his DFM from the king, with his parents sitting in the second row of the magnificent state room. The investiture was for some 200 recipients of gallantry medals, awarded for services during the war. Victory over Europe had only just been announced, and London was awash with celebrations – it would have been a proud man who walked up the slope towards the king after his name was called. Cedric saluted, shook hands, and was addressed by the king, 'Why have you been so long in coming to receive this?' Cedric replied that he had been in service overseas and had been unable to attend earlier. His Majesty thanked Cedric for his service and wished him luck. He saluted once more turned and walked away, with the DFM medal pinned to his chest. The Caterpillar Club pin was worn on his tunic, not an official award but displayed with equal pride.

The next day, Cedric returned to operational duty, flying a stretcher case between Hendon, Lynehan, and Wroughton. Gp Capt. Veale, Adml Evans, and Lord Leven were carried across the country. July was a busy month with several flights, including visits to Tempsford, the SOE special duties airfield, Brussels, Frankfurt, and many other airfields. The grand total recorded within Cedric's flying logbook had reached 1,585 hours and 50 minutes.

Flt Lt Stone was released from active service on 4 September 1945. In November 1949, Cedric was notified that his service within the RAF Volunteer Reserve had been calculated and that he was to be awarded the Air Efficiency Medal.[70] The letter forwarded a section of medal ribbon that is still attached today and held within Cedric's flying logbook. The award was subsequently issued in May 1951, engraved to 'F/L C. P. Stone'.

CHAPTER 10

Sqn Ldr Terence Carr DFC AFC, pilot – Goldfish Club rescuer; PO Dunn, Sgt Savill, Sgt Gibbons, Sgt Allen & Sgt Riley

Terence Howard Carr was serving as a regular officer in the Royal Air Force prior to the outbreak of the Second World War, and had experienced operational flying in southern Kurdistan. He went on to serve in 230 Squadron, flying the Short Singapore III flying boats,[71] before moving into 206 Squadron during January 1940 – who operated the Anson and then the Hudson aircraft. Employed primarily on reconnaissance duties, the squadron was tasked to carry out several offensive operations, such as attacks on enemy ports, vessels of opportunity, and dangerous flak ships. In May 1940, Terence was posted to take command of 220 Squadron, frequently leading Hudsons on patrols over the Dunkirk beaches during the epic retreat of the British Expeditionary Forces (BEF) from France in June of that year. For this and other offensive operations, he was awarded the Distinguished Flying Cross. The following details were taken from the official recommendation (*London Gazette*, 9 July 1940):

> Squadron Leader Terence Howard Carr. This officer has commanded No. 220 Squadron during a week of intensive operations, personally leading on all bombing attacks on enemy targets, on Rotterdam and elsewhere, and in other operational flights against the enemy. He has led his squadron in four long flights by day and night and it is largely due to his high courage and example that his squadron has achieved successful results.

As part of Coastal Command, 220 Squadron received many requests to conduct searches for missing aircraft. On 24 September 1940, a Whitley aircraft from 77 Squadron, identification number P5046, was returning from an operation over Berlin. The aircraft suffered severe damage from flak while flying over the city, however the captain, PO Dunn, took the decision to try and limp the aircraft home despite the damage. In addition to Dunn, there were four other crew members: Sgt Gibbons, Sgt Savill DFM, Sgt Allen, and Sgt Riley. Radio contact was still possible, but despite this, communication was lost when the aircraft ditched into the sea approximately 80 miles off the east coast of England. Terence Carr played a significant role in the locating and eventual rescue of the sole survivor, Sgt Riley, from the crew of P5046. What follows is the official account of the events that took place, as recorded in the *London Gazette* on 17 March 1941. The following details were taken from the official recommendation for the award of an AFC to Terence:

> Wing Commander T. H. Carr, 220 Squadron, No. 18 Group. This officer was pilot of an aircraft, which took part in a search for the crew of a bomber, reported down in the sea on 24th September 1940. A rubber dinghy was located, but bad weather conditions made it very difficult to keep this in sight, and a high-speed launch, proceeding to the rescue, was forced to turn back by heavy seas. Wing Commander Carr maintained contact with the dinghy for five and a half hours, only giving up when darkness set in. The search was continued in vain on the next two days, but on the 27th September, during his second search that day, Wing Commander Carr found the dinghy and remained over it for four hours, until surface craft reached and rescued the sole survivor. This officer displayed skill and cool judgment in his search, and great determination in maintaining contact for nine and a half hours, under conditions of great strain.

Two of the airmen who tragically lost their lives from within the dingy, PO Dunn and Sgt Savill, had been involved in a sea rescue from a ditching three months earlier. Sgt Savill, the wireless operator, who was only on his second operational sortie, had been a crew member aboard Whitley P5046, which was involved in a dramatic ditching and subsequent fight for survival on the 19 June 1940. Savill and Dunn received immediate awards of the DFM, with the other three crew members receiving DFCs. The citation for the awards appeared in the *London Gazette* on 12 July 1940, as follows:

> These officers and airmen were the crew of an aircraft, piloted by Pilot Officer Dunn, and detailed to carry out a bombing attack on the Ruhr one night in June, 1940. After being subjected to heavy anti-aircraft fire for some fifteen minutes, during which their aircraft was repeatedly hit, they were attacked by a Messerschmitt 109. The first attack disabled the inter-communication gear

and also wounded the air observer, Sergeant Savill, and the wireless operator, Sergeant Dawson. The rear gunner, Pilot Officer Watt, was unable to warn the captain of the enemy fighter's second attack but, by quick reaction and skill in aiming, he delivered a good burst of fire at short range which destroyed the enemy. During this second attack, however, one engine was disabled. Despite these difficulties the target was successfully bombed before a course was set for home. For three and a half hours the aircraft, flying on one engine, steadily lost height until the North Sea was crossed at only 400 feet. During this time the navigation was ably carried out by Sergeant Savill, despite the pain from his wound, while Sergeant Dawson, operating the wireless apparatus, secured a number of essential homing bearings, thus materially assisting in assuring the safety of the crew. Pilot Officer Montagu, who was the second pilot, made necessary preparations for abandoning the aircraft and his personal example of coolness and efficiency was of the greatest assistance to his captain. Pilot Officer Dunn displayed resolution, courage and determination in piloting his badly damaged aircraft, but was forced to land in the sea close to the south coast. This crew showed the greatest determination, courage and gallantry throughout the operation.

The survival of all the crew from the sea off Hastings led to them becoming members of the Goldfish Club.

Following the successful rescue, Sgt Savill DFM, returned to operational flying one month later and completed a further twelve sorties, including two to Italy. On the night of 23 September, the target was the aircraft factory at Spandau, on the outskirts of Berlin. During a successful bombing run over the target, their Whitley bomber had encountered heavy flak and a piece of shrapnel punctured one of the fuel tanks. By good fortune no fire took hold. On the return flight, despite the pilot's best efforts to conserve fuel, the aircraft steadily lost height and, as he headed out across the North Sea, it soon became clear that it would not be possible to reach the home coast. Accordingly, an SOS message was sent out and preparations were once again made for a ditching, this time in heavy seas. The pilot made a good landing under the circumstances and all the crew made it safely into the dinghy. One of the crew, Sgt Riley noted that his watch had stopped on impact at 5.50 a.m. Their flight time had been almost 8 hours, and they were still about 100 miles from the English coast. The rescue services had responded to their distress signal and a Hudson was sent out to locate their dinghy, but without success. However, another was sent mid-morning and managed to locate the tiny craft in rough seas. The aircraft stayed over their dinghy for another 2.5 hours, until relieved by another that maintained position for a similar period. A rescue launch that had already set out was forced to return after taking on a lot of water in the heavy seas.

Conditions were even worse for the poor airmen in the waterlogged dinghy who were soaked through and very cold. That afternoon, a Hudson dropped a container of rations within 10 yards of the men, but despite their efforts in the very rough seas, they were unable to reach it before it disappeared from sight. Early the next day, a group of Hudsons set off to resume the rescue operation with the assistance of two royal navy destroyers, but it was not until mid-morning that an aircraft located the dinghy. The position was fixed, but owing to fuel shortage the aircraft had to return home before they could guide the destroyers to the location. Meanwhile, one of the airmen had been lost. Cold and tired, he had fallen into the sea, and whilst his comrades were able to pull him back into the dinghy the first time, he fell overboard a second and was lost forever.

Eventually, another Hudson was able to locate their position and circled over them for several hours until the early afternoon. Yet attempts to get supplies to the men had again failed and, with fuel low, the aircraft was forced to return home. At dawn the following day, five aircraft took up the search, combing a huge area of almost 5,000 square miles. The destroyers were located, but enemy aircraft in their vicinity had to be repeatedly driven off, and the rescue launch was again forced to return home. The aircraft reached their endurance limits and once again were forced to return to base. Night fell and the weather deteriorated, resulting in the loss of another crew member, swept out of sight.

The search was resumed the following day in the continuing bad weather, but it took until the early afternoon to locate the airmen once again. At that time only one of the three airmen in the dinghy was moving, but at last he was able to reach the supply-drop undertaken with accuracy by the rescue aircraft. The Hudson maintained station over the dingy for several hours and witnessed another of the men falling overboard into the sea. At last, a launch from one of the destroyers reached the dinghy to find Sgt Riley alive and Sgt Allen dead. The dinghy had been drifting for 84 hours in appalling conditions, and had been swept a distance of almost 90 miles. Sgt Savill DFM, and his captain PO Dunn DFC, had tragically been two of the three crewmen lost overboard and swept away.[72]

The sole survivor, Sgt Riley, was able to apply for his personal membership of the Goldfish Club.

CHAPTER 11

Flt Lt George Dove CGM DFM, air gunner – Guinea Pig Club

At the age of eighteen, George Frederick Dove was employed by the Post Office, cycling around Scarborough delivering telegrams. George sought some excitement, however, and enlisted in the Royal Air Force in 1938. Following his formal training, George's operational career commenced as a wireless operator in May 1940 with 10 Squadron, who were equipped with the Whitley bombers at RAF Dishforth. George completed a significant number of early wartime operations as a wireless operator with various captains, but later retrained to become an air gunner. The tour of duty led towards a most unusual recommendation for the award of the Distinguished Flying Medal, with twenty-five individual entries relative to his service. Such lengthy extracts are not encountered often. The author has selected a few examples from within the text of the document as published on 18 April 1941. The original recommendation states:

> Prior to being posted from this unit this Wireless Operator / Air Gunner had completed a total of 31 operational missions totaling 230 flying hours. Of these missions, 26 were successfully completed and eight were carried out in the capacity of 1st Wireless Operator. Details of the successful missions are given hereunder.

> 20.5.1940. Captain of aircraft – Sgt MacCoubrey DFM.[73] The object of this mission was to destroy road bridges over the River Oise to interfere with enemy movements. The bridge at Hannapes was bombed from 4,500 feet by this crew but no results were observed. AA fire was encountered and searchlights active.

> 3.6.1940. Captain of aircraft – F/O Nelson DFC. A successful attack was carried out on the oil plant at Homberg. Direct hits were obtained and huge

white sheets of flames were seen. This fire could still be seen when the aircraft was 60 miles away on the return flight. Heavy AA fire was experienced but no damage or casualties were sustained.

20.7.1940. Captain of aircraft – F/O Henry DFC. A successful attack was made on the aircraft factory at Wenzendorf. All bombs were dropped in two sticks but low cloud and the glare of searchlights prevented the observation of results. AA fire was fairly accurate and searchlights were active in large numbers.

16.8.1940. Captain of aircraft – F/O Henry DFC. The Zeiss works at Jena was the objective of a successful attack on this date. Bombs were seen to straddle the target and fires were seen as the aircraft left the area.

23.9.1940. Captain of aircraft – P./O. Bridson. Invasion barges and shipping at Boulogne were successfully attacked on this occasion. Bursts were seen in the No. 3 basin and fires broke out. Heavy and accurate flak from A.A. guns was experienced and the aircraft was hit several times but no casualties were sustained. Searchlights were operating in fair numbers.

29.10.1940. Captain of aircraft – P./O. Peers. A successful attack was made on the docks and shipping at Wilhelmshaven. All bombs were dropped in one stick from 10,000 feet and bursts were seen in the target area. Intense opposition from A.A. guns and searchlights was encountered but no damage or casualties were sustained. On returning to base, the aircraft circled the aerodrome, received permission to land but flew on and finally crashed at Slaggyford. The aircraft was completely wrecked but the crew escaped with superficial injuries.

This N.C.O., though a slow starter, eventually achieved a high degree of efficiency as a 1st Wireless Operator. He possesses a quiet personality and has proved himself sound and completely reliable. His conduct on all operations has been in accordance with the highest traditions of the Service.

George Dove had accomplished thirty-one operations; his tour of duty was complete. His final operation resulted in the Whitley P4957 being completely written off when it struck the ground on its return from Wilhelmshaven.[74] Such accidents frequently saw entire crews killed, yet the pilot and his four sergeants all escaped unscathed apart from minor injuries. Regarded as tour

A Whitley crew member boarding the aircraft carrying his parachute pack.

expired and rested to recover from his injuries, George Dove became an instructor at RAF Warmwell in November 1940.

Instructing posts were valuable in passing on skills to newly qualified aircrews, but without exception, the commencement of the second tour of duty was keenly sought by the majority of instructors. George Dove was posted to 101 Squadron, a Lancaster unit operating out of Stradishall, in early 1943. As an experienced air gunner, wearing the medal ribbon of the DFM, he was swiftly embraced into a crew captained by Ivan Hazard. They completed four operational sorties, but it was on returning from his fifth sortie, on the night of 14 February, that his aircraft was seriously damaged by an Italian night fighter.

Cooper's *In Action with the Enemy* (William Kimber, 1986) takes up the story:

> The target that night was Milan, in northern Italy. Sergeant Ivan Henry
> Hazard was a pilot with 101 Squadron and this night would be the occasion

A Whitley tail gunners position.

for a unique record in the annals of awards for gallantry. Hazard and his crew took off from Holme-on-Spalding at 6.50 p.m. After successfully bombing the target from 11,000 feet at 10.41 p.m., they were attacked by a fighter – a CR. 42 biplane – six minutes later. The Fiat got in a burst of fire from about 100 yards, but as it turned away was seen to be hit by return fire from the Rear Gunner, Sergeant Airey, and the Mid-Upper Gunner, Flight Sergeant George Dove, D.F.M. The Fiat went down in flames and was claimed as destroyed. In all, the gunners fired over 300 rounds between them.

The Lancaster, however, had been severely damaged. Machine gun bullets had exploded incendiaries still in the bomb bay which had failed to release and there were numerous bullet holes in the starboard centre petrol tank. The intercom had been damaged and fire had broken out in the rear part of the fuselage; then the burning incendiaries had exploded, leaving a large hole in the fuselage floor. Sergeant Leslie Airey had been hit in the legs during the attack and received facial burns. Flight Sergeant Dove recalled:

'The fighter's first burst hit the petrol tank and wounded Airey, the Rear Gunner. Another set the incendiaries alight. Airey replied and set the enemy plane on fire. Then I gave a burst and saw it fall away blazing. While I was firing, flames and smoke rolled into my turret. My window was burned and ammunition began to explode. I scrambled down and picked Airey out of his turret, but owing to the fire and a hole blown in the bottom of the aircraft, I couldn't carry him forward.'

In the meantime, Pilot Officer Moffatt, the Bomb Aimer, had mistaken the pilot's orders to prepare to bail out, and went out by parachute. Pilot Officer F. W. Gates, the Wireless Operator, Sergeant J. F. Bain, the Engineer, and Sergeant W. E. Williams, the Navigator, all set about extinguishing the flames, while Sergeant Airey, lying on the floor at the rear of the aircraft, continued to try and beat out the flames about him. Then the port engine caught fire so the pilot put the aircraft into a dive to blow it out, leveling out at 800 feet. With the Rear Gunner being wounded, abandoning the Lancaster was out, so Hazard would have to try and make a forced landing somewhere. By now the starboard outer engine was failing. All the escape hatches had been jettisoned in preparation for instant escape, the intercom was now totally dead and the oxygen had gone. But then Gates, Bain and Williams, succeeded in putting out the fuselage fire, and as Hazard had blown out the engine fire, he decided to try and get the aircraft and themselves home.

Hazard managed to haul the crippled bomber up to 15,500 feet to cross the alps, but then had to feather the starboard outer engine which now failed and he was compelled to make a detour and steer through the peaks rather than fly over them. The Navigator, Sergeant William Ernest Williams, taking the course the pilot had been steering, worked on his dead reckoning, until he obtained an astro-fix. All his navigation was above 10/10ths cloud and his work was instrumental in Hazard getting them back to England. Williams did not receive any wireless aid until he reached the English Channel and for a period of over five hours he navigated solely by D.R. and astro readings. So as not to violate Swiss territory, he deliberately overshot his estimated time at the turning point in France by five minutes.

After leaving his position to help with the fires, Sergeant James Fortune Bain, the Engineer, returned to find his starboard tank holed and leaking. He turned on the balance cocks and manipulated the petrol system throughout the return flight with the greatest skill, and on landing only some fifteen gallons of petrol were still in the port inner tank.

Pilot Officer Frederick William Gates, the W./Op., having done his share in putting out the fires, had then, with the light of a torch, rendered first aid and applied a tourniquet to Sergeant Airey's leg and given him morphine. Later he re-established intercom contact with the forward part of the aircraft by shortening the wiring, despite having to negotiate the gaping hole in the fuselage floor on several occasions. On reaching the French coast Gates returned to his set and sent out S.O.S. signals and in making contact, was able to direct Sergeant Hazard towards the fighter field at Tangmere, in Sussex, where they landed safely in spite of having no hydraulics and only 10 degree of flaps.

It was only after landing that George Dove mentioned that he had been burned on the face and hands when the flames had risen to his upper turret.

Sgts Bain, Airey, and Williams were all recommended on 16 February for awards of the CGM (Conspicuous Gallantry Medal); PO Gates the DSO (Distinguished Service Order); Hazard the pilot and his gunner George Dove were recommended for the Victoria Cross.

The air officer commanding 1 Group, Bomber Command, approved the recommendation for the VC, The commander-in-chief's recommendation failed to support the VC's, however, which was downgraded on 11 March to immediate awards of the CGM.

Five CGMs and the DSO to the wireless operator Gates, were published in the *London Gazette* on 23 March 1943. The original recommendation – for the Victoria Cross – states:

On the night of 14 February 1943, the Lancaster aircraft in which Flight Sergeant Dove was the Mid-Upper Gunner, took part in an operational sortie to Milan. Shortly after bombing had been carried out this aircraft was attacked at 200 yards range by an enemy night fighter which opened fire and ignited 4 x 30lb. incendiaries still in the bomb bay of the Lancaster.

The Rear-Gunner, although wounded in the leg, had replied and succeeded in setting the engine of the enemy fighter on fire. The Lancaster was already on fire amidships and the flames had rapidly risen up to the mid-upper turret where Flight Sergeant Dove remained at his post although burnt about the face and hands. In spite of this he handled his gun with cool determination and got in a good burst as the enemy aircraft turned away in a climbing turn to starboard, as a result of which it dived in flames and was destroyed.

Hearing over the inter-com that the Rear-Gunner was wounded, Flight Sergeant Dove got down from his turret into the flames which were exploding ammunition in the ducts, and made his way to the rear turret. Despite his own injuries, and the flaming inferno behind him, and the fact that his inter-com and oxygen was unplugged, he succeeded in extricating the Rear-Gunner.

Flight Sergeant Dove did not leave his comrade to attend to his own injuries until the fire was subdued and he was relieved by another member of the crew. Nothing was known of Flight Sergeant Dove's injuries of which he made no mention until after landing at base. By his determination, courageous action and fearless disregard for danger this N.C.O. displayed gallantry of the highest order.

The remarks of the station commander:

By his cool, calm and determined valor. Flight Sergeant Dove has added yet another act of heroism to the epic of the Royal Air Force.

In spite of flames, which were roaring through the mid-upper turret, he displayed a complete disregard of his own safety in a perilous situation and continued to man his guns with such grim determination, and to handle them with such accuracy, that the enemy fighter burst into flames and undoubtedly was destroyed. Thereafter, he descended from his turret into the flames which must, by now, have seemed to him inextinguishable, to attend to the Rear-Gunner.

Despite the fact that to attach his parachute and bail out through the aft door of the fuselage was a simple matter and a ready escape from the raging fire, he deliberately abandoned this chance of saving his own life and proceeded past the door to extricate the Rear-Gunner from his turret. This he did successfully regardless of his own suffering from second degree burns about his face and hands. His object achieved, he rendered valiant assistance to the remainder of the crew in subduing the flames.

Thence onwards, Flight Sergeant Dove displayed fortitude of the highest order by making no mention of his injuries to his Captain or crew, so that their attention should not be distracted from their duties, but remained quietly unattended on the rest bed until a safe landing had been completed.

I regard Flight Sergeant Dove's indomitable courage, skill and fortitude as exceptional, and one worthy of the award of the Victoria Cross.

Sgt Hazard returned to the squadron and was assigned Lancaster bomber serial number ED446. This aircraft had undertaken just five operations since its construction, all with 101 Squadron. On 20 March 1943, Sgt Hazard took ED446 up on an air test, the normal procedure to test maintenance work or other applications in preparation for an operational sortie. The pilot made a very low pass over Hornsea beach – this was not an unusual occurrence experienced, as pilots frequently undertook such actions that were nicknamed 'beating up' – but the end of his run, the tail wheel struck a concrete pill box on the beach. This occurred as he pulled back on his control column and the tail section dipped as the aircraft rose into the air. The impact caused the Lancaster to break up in the air; the forward section crashed into the cliffs and blew up, whilst the tail section fell on the beach below. The crew of ten, including Hazard, Bain, and Williams, all died instantly. George Dove was not amongst the casualties, as he was still being treated for his burn injuries at the East Grinstead Hospital. George had joined the exclusive Guinea Pig Club, having received extensive treatment to his facial injuries. Keen to continue his tour of operations – and like many of the Guinea Pig members – George pressed to be deemed medically fit in order to return to his squadron.

George Dove did return to 101 Squadron as a newly commissioned pilot officer, but he failed to obtain permission to fly. He was grounded for medical reasons and posted to non-operational duties as a gunnery instructor.

It is estimated that no more than thirty aircrew were to be recommended for the Victoria Cross during the Second World War. George Dove was also one of only eleven men to be awarded the combination of the Conspicuous Gallantry Medal and Distinguished Flying Medal during that period of aviation history.

Post-war, George served for ten years as a flight lieutenant and commanding officer of the Scarborough Squadron in the Air Training Corps. The badge of the Guinea Pig Club would obviously have created enthusiastic discussion and acknowledgement from the cadets, some of whom followed in the footsteps of George Dove's historic RAF service.

CHAPTER 12

Sqn Ldr Jack Purcell BEM, air gunner – Goldfish Club

Jack Purcell was born in Clapham, London, in May 1920. Upon reaching the age of twenty, Jack volunteered for aircrew duty within the RAF, enlisting in July 1940 during the Battle of Britain, when the threat of invasion was a plausible possibility. Jack completed his initial training, and having qualified as an air gunner, he was posted to 218 'Gold Coast' Squadron within Bomber Command in August 1941. At this time, the squadron was flying the Vickers Wellington aircraft at RAF Marham, Norfolk, with the identification letters 'HA' painted upon the canvas fuselage. Jack joined his crew and completed the standard acceptance sorties undertaken at the start of an initial posting.

Jack's first operation was to attack Ostend on 2 September 1941. The captain of Wellington X9810 was an extremely experienced pilot, Sqn Ldr Gibbes,[75] who had previously been awarded the Distinguished Flying Cross in 1940. At 8.22 p.m., the aircraft left the runway at Marham for what was expected to be a short operation. With Sqn Ldr Gibbes leading a crew made up entirely of inexperienced sergeants, including Jack on his first flight as the front gunner, Wellington X9810's luck ran out when the aircraft was struck by flak during the flight and crashed into the sea off the Belgian coast. The squadron's operational record book takes up the story:

Nothing was heard from this aircraft after it left base. The entire crew was posted as missing. Later it appeared that the aircraft had come down in flames over the sea; nose first, as a result of being hit off Ostend. The pilot's cockpit was about ten feet under water, the only part of the aircraft not on fire. Squadron Leader Gibbes, D.F.C., struggled to get out of the pilot's escape hatch but it was jammed. After various things seeming to fly past him and very weak as a result of trying to hold his breath in between the intervals of taking in water, he found he was too weak to open the astro hatch when he located it. Eventually, after what seemed like an age, he found a break in the fuselage, where the Sergeant Front Gunner (Jack Purcell) was just getting through. They struggled out and the Sergeant tried to blow up the Squadron Leader's flotation jacket with his mouth, but he could not manage it. The Squadron Leader cannot remember getting into the dinghy, his only memories being an endless moment in which he had his head under water for what seemed like an eternity. For three days and nights the crew drifted. On the first morning they heard a bell buoy, but the tide swept them past it. They rationed their supplies. On the third day they could see buildings and could hear trains but they were still being washed in and out by tides. Eventually, they were washed ashore near Margate. For four of the crew, including the Front Gunner, this was their first operational flight. It was Squadron Leader Gibbs' 36th raid.

Jack had sustained burn injuries in the crash-landing, and requiring hospital treatment, had a delayed return to operations – his recovery lasted nearly two months. The survival in the dinghy enabled Jack and his fellow crew members to become members of the Goldfish Club.

When Jack returned to operational flying, his first raid on 4 November 1941 was once again to Ostend. The difference this time was that he returned safely to Marham and no doubt breathed a sigh of relief as he went into his first operational post raid de-briefing session.

On 26 November 1941, Jack was the front gunner in Wellington Z1103. The crew was entirely manned by sergeants and the target for the operation was Emden; it was the longest raid so far in Jacks short list of completed operations. At 5.15 p.m., the pilot, Sgt Helfer, lifted the Wellington off the runway. The navigator completed his task well, reaching the target area and bombing through a significant cloud base. On the return journey, flak caught them as they crossed the enemy coastline. At the time, it was not thought to have caused any damage to the aircraft, however Jack was soon to experience another near-fatal experience and his second ditching. The squadron's operational record book holds the story:

Bombed Emden, 10th/10th cloud, N.A.P. sent. Flak from Islands when returning. A fuel check was taken by the Navigator, the gauges showing 130 gallons in tanks. D./R. position from coast - 100 miles. In 15 minutes the loss of 50 gallons showed on the fuel check, now only 80 gallons in tanks. As the coast was not reached by E.T.A., the captain decided to come down to 3,500 feet. The aircraft flew at this height for some while and not seeing coastline the captain asked for a priority fix at 10.21 hours. This showed him to be 100 miles from the coast. The nacelle tanks had been punctured some 20 minutes before the priority fix was received. The W./T. receiver was now U./S and no bearings could be received, but the transmitter could be used and so an S.O.S. was sent at 22.30 hours, as it appeared doubtful whether it would be possible to reach the coast. The coast was reached at 22.55 hours and searchlights pointing west along the coast were seen and a green Very light was fired from the ground. We turned west and flew along in the direction of the searchlight. The engines started spluttering and the captain decided to land on the water as near the coast as possible. The reason the captain decided not to land on the beach was because of the possibility of it being mined - and it was! Prior to landing on the sea the containers were jettisoned and the flotation bags pulled. The dinghy inflated automatically. The aircraft sank within five minutes. All of the crew successfully got into the dinghy and cut it adrift with the knife provided. Immediately one marine distress signal was let off. The crew drifted for about two hours. The crew then saw a light flashing on the water which they answered S.O.S. with the flash of a torch. An R.A.F. Launch approached from the sea direction, piloted by the Coxswain of the Wells lifeboat. The crew, apart from being cold and slightly bruised, were uninjured, thanks to the captain's decision to land on the sea and not on the beach.

Once more Jack's life, along with that of his crew, was saved as a result of the dingy. His second survival through the use of a dinghy enabled him to submit a further Goldfish Club application. An additional badge in the form of a second 'Blue Wave' was able to be stitched below the original embroidered badge. This was rarely seen but very proudly worn by the few that survived more than one ditching. An operation against Brest followed swiftly on 16 December 1941, with two further operations in the New Year.

The recognition of Jack Purcell's actions resulted in an announcement published in the *London Gazette* on 6 January 1942, confirming the award of the British Empire Medal. The original recommendation states:

Sergeant Purcell was the front-gunner of an aircraft which, whilst carrying out an attack on Ostend, received a direct hit from heavy anti-aircraft fire. Although an attempt was made to bring the aircraft back to England, it eventually crashed in the sea some ten miles off Orfordness. On impact the captain was thrown down into the bomb compartment but, after being submerged in 15 feet of water, he eventually escaped, in semi-drowned condition, through the broken off tail of the aircraft. Sergeant Purcell, who was suffering from burns about the face and hands, had helped the captain to climb out of the wreckage and then supported and encouraged him for about half an hour until it was possible to reach the dinghy. In spite of the captain's continual suggestions that Sergeant Purcell should leave him and get to the dinghy himself, the Sergeant refused to do so. There is little doubt that the captain's life was saved as a result of the determination and bravery shown by Sergeant Purcell. He subsequently displayed courage, cheerfulness and powers of endurance during the three days which the crew spent floating in the dinghy.

Jack remained with 218 Squadron, which converted onto the newly received Stirling bombers. He joined a new crew captained by Flt Lt Livingston, and they undertook a sortie together to Billancourt on 3 March 1942. Wg Cdr P. D. Holder DFC was aboard for the ride.[76] The next mission to Essen on 8 March saw the crew once again carrying guests. Sqn Ldr A. W. Oldroyd AFC, and David Thornton-Smith, the war artist.

Wg Cdr Holder joined the crew for a further flight on Jack's next sortie against Cologne on 13 March. The remainder of the month saw operations against Essen on the 25th and 26th, followed by Lubeck on the 28th. April proved to be an even busier month, with operations to Cologne, Essen, Hamburg, Poissy, Pilzen,[77] and Gennevilliers. The final operation that month was to drop sea mines off Kiel, and this provided the unexpected opportunity for Jack to fire off his guns against a ship within Kiel Bay.

On 19 May 1942, Jack received his British Empire Medal from the king at Buckingham Palace. Although in full military dress attire, there would have been no sign of his Goldfish Club badges – these were sewn onto his battledress flying jacket. Returning to his squadron, Jack flew another mining operation, and return visits to Gennevilliers and Pilzen,[78] culminating on 30 May with the first 'Thousand Bomber Raid' against Cologne. Jack received a commission to pilot officer in June; operations to Bremen three times, followed by Emden, and completed his tour of operations on 16 July.

Jack Purcell BEM was posted to the operational training unit at Moreton-in-Marsh as a tour-expired instructor. He was back in the trusty Vickers Wellington, but the quiet life eluded him with raids on Düsseldorf and Bremen in September 1942. Jack remained employed as an instructor late into the summer of 1944. He was awarded a 'mention in dispatches'[79] (*London Gazette*, 8 June 1944), and promoted to flight lieutenant in December 1945. Jack was finally placed on the retired list as a squadron leader in May 1969.

CHAPTER 13

Sgt Woolston, pilot – Goldfish Club; Sgt McKay, Sgt Chandler & Sgt Wood

On the night of 30 June 1941, a Hampden bomber with a crew of four sergeants set off from RAF Scampton shortly after 11 p.m. They were intending to attack Dusseldorf, but never reached the target.

The Hampden had crossed the North Sea and was some 10 miles beyond the Dutch coast, when the port engine began to fail. The serious drop in power was sufficient for the pilot, Sgt Woolston, to recognise that the remaining engine would be placed under additional pressure. He decided to turn for home, but a few minutes later, blue flames and sparks lit up the sky as the port engine stopped altogether. The aircraft was now well out to sea, yet hope still existed that they would reach England. That hope was based upon the pilot's ability, as a month earlier he had brought another Hampden back on one engine after sustaining flak damage over the Frisian Islands. This time, the starboard engine started to overheat and power was beginning to be lost. The aircraft went into a spin, falling several thousands of feet before Sgt Woolston could recover the situation. Unfortunately the aircraft was forced into another spin, and with no more than a few hundred feet above the sea, and still fighting at the controls, Sgt Woolston ordered the crew to brace themselves for a ditching. The wireless operator sent out his SOS, but it was not received as the engine failure resulted in insufficient power for its transmission.

Travelling at roughly 80 mph, the Hampden approached the water with full flaps, but unable to lose any further speed, it crashed onto the water at 2.30 a.m., the tail striking the water first. As soon as the aircraft hit the water the dinghy was automatically released, but it inflated in the sea upside down. The Hampden started to sink as the crew climbed onto the wing. Sgt Woolston leapt into the sea in an effort to right the dinghy. Unfortunately as he did so it flipped over in the sea, and he found himself under the dinghy.

Hampden Bombers.

The rest of the crew swam to the dinghy and managed to assist everyone into it. Sgt Woolston, having swallowed a quantity of sea water, suffered the consequences immediately and was sick several times. The Hampden had floated for no more than a couple of minutes, which meant there was insufficient time to recover the emergency pack or the carrier pigeons from within its fuselage. Dawn broke, providing first light to assess the emergency supplies within the dinghy, thirty-six Horlicks tablets, small bottle of rum, a few ounces of chocolate, some boiled sweets, and a rubber bottle containing 1.5 pints of drinking water. The crew were hopeful that rescue would come quickly, however this that was not to be the case:

First Day: Sgt Woolston and one other crewmember were consistently sick as a result of sea water consumption. The remaining crewmembers were reasonably fit and well, the day was warm and enabled some clothing to dry. Each man received half a tin lid of water and three Horlicks tablets. The night was cold, cramp affected everyone, and the wireless operator's Sidcot suit was ripped apart to provide some warmth.

Second Day: Fairly heavy sea, cloudy sky. The sea was washing over the sides of the dingy, requiring the crew to bail out all the time using the small canvas bag in which the chocolate and tablets had been kept. The two sick men recovered from the condition they were experiencing. Spirits were high until they saw a mine, which explained why no shipping had been sighted. The water ration was half a tin lid in the morning and again in the evening, and three Horlicks tablets.

Third Day: The sea was still entering the dingy and required continuous bailing. There was no sickness. Boiled sweets were sucked to try and supplement the water and tablets. No sightings of shipping or aircraft. A fishing line was made by unraveling a piece of cord from the dinghy; tying the pieces together it was about 40 feet long. Spinners were made from a piece of tin. Plenty of fish were seen but none took the spinners.

Fourth Day: Three Blenheim aircraft sighted in the morning, only 200 yards distant and just 150 feet high. The crew attempted to wave and flash with the two signal mirrors; they thought they had been sighted, but after an anxious wait they did not reappear. The water ration was halved to conserve as best possible the precious contents remaining.

Fifth Day: The sea at last became calmer, so the crew used the water-logged, inoperable distress flares as paddles and attempted to progress westwards. The navigator's watch was still working, enabling shift times of half hours to be rotated during the day. Each man was issued with half a cube of chocolate three times a day.

Sixth Day: At midday three launches were sighted within 2 miles of their position, but they turned away and disappeared over the horizon. A motor boat engine was heard but nothing seen, also the noise from what they presumed had been the engines of a submarine. Weakness set in and paddling was reduced to an ineffective level, the pumping of the bellows to keep inflating the dinghy was now a difficult task to maintain. Some greenfly and wasps were seen, making them think that landfall must be close.

Seventh Day: The water ration gave out, Sgt Woolston's tongue became hard and thick, and the surface began to lose its skin.[80] Salt water was used to swill the crews' mouths.

Eighth Day: All four men were very weak, and their tongues were swelling and cracking. In the evening a Hampden and two Hurricanes appeared from the west and turned north, almost over the dinghy. The signal mirrors were used but not sighted.

Ninth Day: With little hope left and desperately weak, the crew was resigned to think the worst.

At RAF Hemswell, Sgt Donald Whiting of 144 Squadron took off in his Hampden aircraft, with a course set across the North Sea at 2,000 feet. This was to unknowingly bring him within sight of the dinghy. At 8.20 a.m. Sgt Whiting's Hampden came out of the sun no more than a quarter of a mile from the dinghy's position. They used the mirrors and gathered what strength they had in waving. The mirror signals were spotted, the Hampden did a half turn and banked towards the dinghy issuing on its Aldis lamp the signal 'Help Coming'. Sgt Whiting dropped a dinghy with great accuracy, landing only a few yards from the survivors. Knowing that water would be in the dinghy the crew mustered what strength they had and managed to reach the supplies, tying the two life rafts together. Sgt Whiting circled the survivors for 4 hours, only leaving when two Blenheim's with a fighter escort arrived. Soon afterwards, the sight of an RAF high-speed launch greeted them at 12.30 p.m. It was now 9 July 1941. Once on board the rescue launch each man drunk a quart of water and managed to eat a little chocolate. They were taken to Great Yarmouth and then to hospital, where full recoveries were made.

On 25 August 1941, the pilot responsible for their rescue, Sgt Whiting, took off for a bombing raid on Mannheim. The bomber crossed the channel before darkness, making an easy target for the German night fighters. His Hampden aircraft was hit by flak on the outward journey, and during the return fire took hold whilst over Brussels. Sgt Whiting ordered the crew to bail out. The navigator, PO Hayward, survived, despite his parachute having insufficient time to open properly. He sustained minor injuries and became a prisoner of war. Two further crew members deployed their parachutes, but they opened too late, causing fatal injuries. The Hampden hit the ground near the Ninove-Halle road, close to Puttenburg Castle, Pepingen (near the Belgian village of Brages). Sgt Whiting and his two crew now rest in the town cemetery in Brussels.

CHAPTER 14

Sqn Ldr George Davies DSO MID, pilot – Caterpillar Club

Sqn Ldr George Geoffrey Davies was born at Wavetree, Lancashire, on 5 March 1920. He was educated at the Liverpool Institute before emigrating to Australia with his parents. George continued his education at Geelong Grammar school in Victoria, following which he found employment as a clerk at Borthwick & Sons, a meat firm.

As soon as he was legally permitted, George set out to fulfill his ambition to fly. His employment allowed him to finance lessons in a Tiger Moth aircraft, and he subsequently gained his flying license in 1937. A year later George's mother became very ill, and with the probability of war ever present, he decided to apply for service in the Royal Australian Navy, but still harboured the desire to fly. There was no need for pilots in the navy at that time, however. With the Royal Air Force actively encouraging applications, George wrote to England to apply for a short-service commission of seven years. He received a favorable reply and left Australia, arriving in England in June 1939. Posted to Sywell, Northants, George commenced his training in the Royal Air Force on 13 September 1939. War had been declared against Germany just ten days previously.

George experienced a lull in the progression of training, which resulted in a decision to place him and several other colonial recruits into the reserve. Once in the reserve they would be called for as and when needed. This was a most unsatisfactory situation, which was made known by the men it concerned. Having gained a commission, George just wanted to get on with his flying training. After strong representation, the decision was reversed, and those affected were able to continue with pilot training.

George was posted to the Initial Training Wing at Cambridge, but billeted at St Johns College before moving to Hatfield, and from there to Cranwell. The excitement of flying Hawker Harts at Cranwell provided the possibility of his selection for Fighter Command. During the course, to the trainee pilot's disappointment, the Harts were exchanged for twin-engine Oxfords. This gave a clear indication that the route of training was to be within bombers. On leaving Cranwell, George attended 27 War Course at 10 Operational Training Unit, RAF Abingdon. In company with George was a fellow pilot officer, William Fullerton,[81] who later became a double Caterpillar Club member.

Posted to 102 (Ceylon) Squadron in January 1941, George's operational career commenced with a sortie to Rotterdam on 10 February, flying as the second pilot in a Whitley bomber. Unfortunately the Whitley suffered a port engine failure on the return journey, which resulted in a forced landing at Buckenham in Norwich. George had experienced a bumpy start to his operational career, which continued as they had a crash-landing at Sedgefield after his very next sortie to Cologne, and a 'through the hedge' landing following a raid on Lorient in late March.

April 1941 commenced with sorties to the German targets of Kiel and Emden, and in May, a brace of outings to Hamburg and Bremen, in addition to a strike on the Scharnhorst and Gneisenau at Brest. On the night of 11 May, George took control as first pilot. His Whitley Z 6576 was 'shot up very badly', but he managed to return to base. Brest became the selected target for his crew on 10 June. With luck having appeared to elude him for quite some time, the operations to Aachen, Brest, Dortmund, Essen, and Osnabruck proved successful. Once more however, his Whitley was shot up by a night fighter on a raid to Schwerte. Bremen was the next operation, taking place during the night of 14 July in his Whitley K 6820 with crew members PO E. Anderson, PO N. Bennett, Sgt W. Swain, and Sgt N. Stockdale. It was to be a most significant operation for George, resulting in the award of the Distinguished Service Order. The immediate award recommendation states (*London Gazette*, 8 August 1941):

> This Officer was Captain of Whitley aircraft Z 6572 detailed to carry out a bombing sortie against Bremen on the night of 14-15 July 1941. At about 0215 hours, when over the target area, the aircraft was held in a concentration of searchlights and was heavily fired on by flak. The flak ceased suddenly while the aircraft was making its run on to the target, and although this indicated the immediate presence of enemy fighters, the Captain continued on his bombing run and warned the Rear-Gunner to keep a very sharp look out for enemy aircraft.
>
> Very shortly afterwards, the Captain saw tracer and cannon shell passing very closely on both sides of the fuselage of his aircraft and felt considerable

movement on the control column, indicating that the control surfaces had been hit. At the same time the Rear-Gunner called out to him that he had been hit by bullets from the enemy aircraft. The Gunner was in fact killed in this first attack, and the rear turret rendered useless.

The aircraft then went out of control, the nose going up until it stalled and went into a left hand spin at a height of 10,500 feet. The Captain wound the tail adjusting gear well forward to try to gain control by using the elevator trimming tabs, as the elevator control wires to the control column had been shot away. He found, however, that the stop on the tail adjusting wheel prevented it from being moved forward for more than half a turn, and with great presence of mind the Captain instructed the Navigator to get the axe and hack away the stop. The Navigator did this and by winding the wheel fully forward and by skillful use of rudder and engines, the Captain succeeded in righting the aircraft after having lost 7,000 feet. However, it was only by skillful use of engines and elevator tabs that the Captain was able to maintain the aircraft in level flight, and soon after coming out of the spin the aircraft was again attacked by enemy fighters and later by light flak.

During the whole of this most hazardous experience the Captain showed the utmost determination and coolness and was alone responsible for extricating the aircraft and the remainder of the crew from almost certain destruction. He continued to fly the badly damaged aircraft, still exercising exceptional control, until he reached Driffield, to which airfield he had been diverted owing to fog at Topcliffe. Knowing that his elevator controls were shot away and only a few weeks before having seen an aircraft stall and crash at Topcliffe while trying to land in the same position, this Officer still stuck to his post and gave no thought whatever of abandoning the aircraft. With great skill and care he succeeded in landing at Driffield with no further damage to aircraft or crew than that sustained over enemy territory.

I cannot speak too highly of this most marvelous effort on the part of an Officer who has already done exceptionally good work during a number of previous sorties. His coolness, courage and devotion to duty saved the lives of the remainder of his crew, and brought back to this country a valuable aircraft. I strongly recommend him for the immediate award of the Distinguished Service Order.

In the words of Air-Vice Mar. Coningham, who approved the award of his immediate DSO, it was 'one of the best shows of the War by a Captain of an Aircraft in his Group'. In the words of his group captain, George displayed 'almost miraculous airmanship in bringing his aircraft and crew safely

Davies' Whitley Z6820 damaged over Bremen, 14 July 1941.

back to this country', probably no understatement when one considers the damage inflicted on his Whitley, which counted over forty holes (including the petrol and oil tanks), two tyres shot through, and the elevators clean shot away.

George wrote the following entry into his pilot's flying logbook:

> Operations Bremen MLR 719[82] Camera.[83] Hell of a time over target. Clamped in searchlights. Fighter attacked and killed air gunner Stockdale R.I.P.[84] Elevator shot away. A.S.I. useless BXF Driffield. Port & rear wheels punctured. Good write up Awarded D.S.O.

Several newspapers carried accounts of the DSO awarded to George Davies, with one providing further detail of the night fighter attack upon his aircraft:

> Suddenly all the Anti-Aircraft fire stopped and he [George] knew that fighters must be about. He had scarcely had time to warn the rear gunner when he

saw tracer bullets coming at him from the front, while cannon shells seemed to be coming from below and up from the rear. The navigator sat unperturbed at his bomb sight with bullets and shells crashing past him and released the bombs on to the target. The captain heard the rear gunner call out 'I'm hit' He answered 'Stick it' Then again he heard the rear gunner say 'They've got me' and that was the last he heard of him.

Seemingly unperturbed by this hair-raising episode, George went on to complete his next mission, to Cologne, just five days later. Again coned by searchlights, he escaped without any damage to his aircraft or the crew. Then, on his very next mission to Frankfurt, on the night of 5 August, his Whitley was once more shot up 'over Aachen and Antwerp on return'. A further mission was flown in August, to Bremen, followed by others in September to Berlin, Huls, Kassel, Mannheim, and Stettin. George flew the final sortie of his first tour against Kiel on 7 November. Having completed nearly two full tours of operations, acting Flt Lt George Davies DSO was rested from operational flying. He was mentioned in despatches in January 1942, and posted on an instructor's flying course at the Central Flying School at Upavon. He subsequently qualified as an instructor, and was posted to 22 Operational Training Unit, Wellesbourne, Mountford. This proved to have been an administration error, as he should have been sent to 19 OTU at Kinloss.

Despite a late arrival, the experienced pilot, wearing the ribbon of the DSO, was quickly embraced as a valued addition to the unit. Unfortunately, on 24 March 1942, whilst flying the training Whitley N1437 from Kinloss, the aircraft suffered engine failures upon take-off. The correct procedure for such an emergency was undertaken, and George tried to land straight ahead, but struck a clump of trees instead. The pupil in the left-hand seat[85] was killed by one of the aircrafts spars that passed through his body. George himself was trapped by the knees. The aircraft caught fire and George was badly burnt, suffering second- and third-degree burns. The burn injuries were so extensive that his chances of survival were rated as slim. George was taken to Aberdeen Infirmary, where it was decided that he required specialist medical services at the burns unit at East Grinstead. The RAF liaison officer at the hospital provided guidance, but his condition was assessed as too fragile for the journey. He went to the new unit at Stracathro, near Brechin, Scotland, instead. Stracathro was an emergency medical service hospital accepting casualties who had suffered injuries as a result of the blitz raids by the Luftwaffe. Built in the grounds of Ballochmyle House,

Sqd Ldr Davies instructing his pupils wearing full flying equipment at 19 Operational Training Unit.

the mansion was used as residential accommodation for the hospital staff. The hospital itself consisted of thirty-two main wards, each containing approximately forty beds. Harold Gillies, the renowned plastic surgeon and cousin to McIndoe, attended EMS hospitals across the country. Gillies supervised the treatment of George's burn injuries whist tutoring Jack Tough, who performed George's skin grafts. Tough went on to become surgeon-in-charge of the plastic surgery unit at Stracathro EMS in 1943. The combination of expertise and medical treatment resulted in a gradual recovery for George. A nurse, Jo Lowis, was constantly by his side, and like several Guinea Pigs at East Grinstead, a marriage between a patient and nurse resulted in 1943. The absence of receiving operations undertaken by Archie McIndoe himself excluded George Davies from membership of the Guinea Pig Club.

After his initial recovery, George was posted back to RAF Kinloss, but was unable to fly as a result of a severed tendon behind one of his knees. In January 1943, through sheer determination, he managed to attain the standard required to return to flying, but with a stipulation that he was only

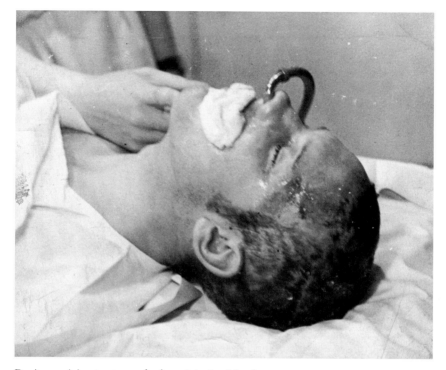

Davies receiving treatment for burn injuries, March 1942.

able to fly single-engine aircraft. On 10 April 1943 George returned to his pilot's logbook, where he wrote a short entry to record the incident from the 24 March 1942: 'Crashed E/Failure on take-off, Scott Killed, self and Harris burned, Stracathro Hospital. Grand total of 665 hours 5 minutes.' He applied his signature and turned the page.

Glad to be able to fly once more, George was posted as staff officer to Sir Hugh Walmsley.[86] In September 1943, George was promoted to the rank of squadron leader and appointed as deputy chief flying instructor at 23 Operational Training Unit Pershore. He was desperate to return to operational flying and decided to contact Hamish Mahaddie,[87] a personality known to him from his early operational duty.

Hamish was in a position to 'pull a few strings' as the saying goes, having been responsible for the early selection of the right men to form the path finder group. A posting for George swiftly followed, initially to the 44 conversion unit at Waddington, where he flew the Lancaster for the first time and subsequently joined 8 Group Path Finder Force, who were undertaking initial and customary path finder force[88] training at RAF Warboys. He joined

Sqd Ldr Davies on 13 July 1944, the day before he was shot down.

156 Squadron, PFF operating with Lancasters, in March 1944. Numerous sorties followed, commencing with trips to Lille and Aachen that April. In the former operation, his Lancaster was in collision with another aircraft over the target, which resulted in a return to base on just two engines. The operational records quote: 'A Lancaster came weaving in from starboard and hit our aircraft with its port wing, our inner and outer were hit, port outer feathered just as bombs gone.' It is an interesting point that Sqn Ldr Davies' crew consisted of six commissioned officers, indicating the experience that was sought at that time for path finder squadrons.

The months of May and June witnessed a busy schedule, with many operations carried out to attack a mixture of French and German targets – Coubronn, Hasselt, Mardick, Marquise (daylight), Middel Straete, Montdidier, and St Pol (daylight). Many of these targets were associated in the overall planning for D-Day. The operation to Hasselt took place on 11 May, where flares were dropped by the master bomber but no instructions were given to the supporting aircraft. George's Lancaster ND534 was attacked from below, sustaining unknown damage. Still carrying the entire bomb load, George landed the aircraft back at base. One of the aircraft's tyres had been punctured by the night fighter attack, which caught fire and caused terrible handling issues on the runway which then becoming blocked. The crash tender and fire service contained the situation, averting a seriously dangerous situation for all involved.

In July 1944, operations to Paris and Tours took place, but disaster struck on 14 July in an attack on the V1 rocket site at Revigny-sur-Mer. Having taken off in Lancaster PA948, George was acting as the deputy master bomber, a duty that entailed protracted time spent over the target instructing the bomber force. The target area was reached but the weather conditions were poor. At 1.53 a.m. George engaged in radio communication with the master bomber, who cancelled the operation. That was the last anyone heard from Lancaster PA948, which was set ablaze by an enemy night fighter.

In an interview with Oliver Clutton-Brock, author of *Massacre Over the Marne* (Patrick Stephens, 1994),[89] George recalled the final moments aboard his blazing aircraft:

Due to thick ground haze the attack was abandoned by the master bomber, I had been down low and was climbing up again on the way home. At approximately 02.30 hrs the aircraft was attacked by a night fighter from below and the port quarter astern. No warning was received from the gunners, I immediately corkscrewed to port. I had been hit by cannon shell or bullets in my left thigh and wrist. The rear gunner cried out, 'we're on fire, skip'. I suspected that one of the Tis[90] had been hit as the fire had a pronounced red glare. I immediately opened the bomb doors and gave the Bomb Aimer his instructions for jettisoning TIs and bombs. Felt them go and tested on toggle, but the aircraft was still blazing away. The smoke by this time was absolutely solid, suffocating. Couldn't see or breathe, turned oxygen right up and clamped mask to face, but was still unable to breathe. I therefore opened the port side window and stuck my head out. I heard the Engineer gasping and told him to do the same at his side. Judging by the draught he did so. I continued corkscrewing by touch as I was still unable to see the instruments.

I closed the bomb doors as soon as the load had gone in order to cut the draught. However, the fire was still going strong, and the smoke was filling the cockpit. The aircraft controls then went u/s completely. The flames were coming through the floor and I was on fire personally (helmet, hair, face, silk gloves, hands, scarf).

I then ordered the crew 'Jump! Jump!' and a few seconds later 'Bail out, blokes, and let me know as you go.' I heard the Rear-Gunner say 'I'm going Skip!'. I felt the draught from the front as if the escape hatch had been opened. Still holding my head out of the port window (at intervals), I saw (I think) two parachutes open. I heard no more from any other crew member, although my intercom was still working.

I therefore called up the crew but received no answers. I decided it was time to get out, the controls being u/s, and I could see the ground which was pretty close. The aircraft was, as far as I could judge, in a shallow diving turn to port (the throttles having been left open as, due to lack of control, they were the only means of attempting to keep the nose up).

I unplugged after taking a couple of deep breaths out of the window and made for the forward escape hatch, feeling for the Engineer on the way. I could not find him and presumed he had got out. By this time flames were roaring in the cockpit between me and the hatch. I sat back for a final effort and leaned out of the side window for another breather. Next I found myself out of the aircraft, presumably blown through the window. Rather dazed by smoke, heat and burns (eyes, hands, arms and hair) and bruised, I remember feeling a blow on my left side and leg. Then I remembered to pull the rip-cord and the parachute opened immediately. I hit the ground about 60 seconds later, crashing 50 or 60 feet through trees. The aircraft appeared to hit the ground a few seconds earlier (or may have been TIs burning).

I was unconscious for a period. Discovered I was in a wood of some sort – thick undergrowth and tall trees close together. My face was burned, left eye very bad (thought I was blind). My right eye was half closed with burned eye-lids; left leg suspected broken shin bone; flesh wound in the left thigh; had lost one tooth and had small flesh wound in left wrist. Hair was burnt off to within one and a half inches or so of scalp. Nose and mouth burned. Back badly bruised and altogether shaken and knocked about.

It was then half-light and I calculated it to be about 0330 or 0400 hours. Set watch. It went but stopped later. Hid my chute and Mae West, opened my emergency rations and escape kit and stowed it about my person. Had a swig of brandy. I then transferred all my sock and stocking to my left leg and stuffed the bottom with kapok from my Mae West, and cut up part of the chute canopy for bandages.

I found it not impossible to bear my weight on my left leg so I lopped off a stout branch for a crutch. I had another small swig of brandy and started off to try and find a way out of the wood.

Heading South in the direction of St. Dizier, it took me about 30 minutes to find any sort of track through the trees, and a further two to two and a half hours to get to the edge of the wood (after retracing my steps three or four times).

By this time I could hardly see and I had to hold the compass about two inches away from my eye and blink rapidly in order to see at all. At the edge of the wood I could see a road running N.E.-S.W. At approximately 0600 hours I headed South on the road (not being able to make rough going over fields). There was a dyke about three to four feet on the left side of the road. I walked along the left side as continental traffic drives on the right-hand side. So I imagined locals would walk on the left in order to face oncoming traffic. I headed South by West, intending to keep to the road until I sighted some civilisation.

I stopped at the bottom of a hill for a rest. A Hun lorry was coasting down the hill, which I didn't hear. It contained one officer and five men who with pistols invited me to enter, which I did after being relieved of my knife and stick. Apparently it was a guard ration lorry. They then turned the lorry round and took me to St. Dizier.[91]

I sat for four hours in an office and then was moved to the Town Hall. There I was questioned and searched. I gave regulation answers. I was given a receipt for articles taken from me during the search.

A short time later, George was whisked away from the town hall by the marquis, in an audacious escape organised during an American bombing raid, and placed in a safe house somewhere near the Belgian border. The intention was for him to be moved 'down the line' of an escape organisation. His freedom was short-lived. The Gestapo raided the hideout and arrested George and at least five or six other RAF aircrew. It is possible the group had been betrayed.

George was taken to the Luftwaffe interrogation holding camp Dulag Luft,[92] and allocated prisoner number 4,900. His registration card recorded distinctive marks of scars to his right hand and forehead. He was later moved to Stulag Luft I at Barth Vogelsang. Here he was surprised to discover that he had also collected a broken jaw while being thrown clear of his blazing Lancaster.

On 23 July 1944, the Air Ministry Casualty Branch wrote to Mrs Davies at her operational base, Stradishall, advising her of George's status as 'missing in action'. Wg Cdr Bingham-Hall, commanding officer of 156 Squadron, had previously intimated to her that little or no chance existed for his safe return. This statement was based upon the report that a PFF aircraft had been seen to explode in the air whilst over the target.

On 23 August the Air Ministry wrote to Mrs Davies once more (it must be presumed this letter was based upon information provided by the French resistance responsible for his escape from the town hall in St Dizier):

Dulag-Luft. **Kriegsgefangenenkartei.**

Gefangenen-Erkennungsmarke Nr. 4900 4 b.	Dulag-Luft Eingeliefert am: 24.7.44 H.

NAME: D A V I E S

Vornamen: George Geoffrey

Dienstgrad: S/Ldr   Funktion: P-

Matrikel-No.: 87 415

Geburtstag: 5.3.20

Geburtsort: Liverpool

Religion: C of E

Zivilberuf: Student   (*Buchhaltung*)

Staatsangehörigkeit: Brite

Vorname des Vaters: George

Familienname der Mutter: Harper

Verheiratet mit: ja

Anzahl der Kinder: -

Heimatanschrift: *Frau :*
Mrs.J.M.Davies
3 Grange Ave.
Hunts Cross
Liverpool, Lancs.

Abschuß am: 15.7.44   bei: St.Dizier   Flugzeugtyp: Lancaster

Gefangennahme am: wie oben   bei:

Nähere Personalbeschreibung

Figur: mittel

Größe: 1.76

Schädelform: lang

Haare: hellbraun

Gewicht: 65 kg

Gesichtsform: lang

Gesichtsfarbe: blass

Augen: blau

Nase: kräftig

Bart: Schnurrbart

Gebiß: gesund

Besondere Kennzeichen:
Narbe auf der recht.Hand
kleine Brandnarben am linken Schlüsselbein.

Rechter Zeigefinger

Von zuvorkommenden Wesen.

Fingerabdruck

Sqd Ldr Davies' POW registration form with fingerprint and mug shot.

Madam,

I am directed to advise you that information has been received that your husband, Acting Squadron Leader George Geoffrey Davies DSO RAF, landed in occupied territory and is alive and well.

In the interests of your husband and his benefactors you are asked to keep this good news to yourself and not ask for further information or attempt to communicate with him in any way. It should be appreciated that if your husband is caught it not only means that he will become a prisoner of war but that those harbouring him will no doubt serve the death penalty. In these circumstances it is felt sure that you will cooperate.

Any more definite news will be passed to you immediately it is received.

On 12 September an additional letter advised that the International Red Cross had informed the Air Ministry that George was now confirmed as having been captured and reclassified as a prisoner of war. This information was at last true confirmation that George was safe and well. It was followed by a most rare event in October, when the Air Ministry wrote once more, reporting that a letter written by George had been read over the German wireless on the 15th of that month. The text of the broadcast was typed out in the letter as follows:

Dearest [Dot?] At last I am at a permanent address. You may write to me here [once every week?] Also send as many [indistinct] as possible this address. I am allowed to have as much incoming mail as I like. [Indistinct sentence] [May I send out?] Only three letters and four postcards per month [Few words indistinct] I have written a post card to you already. Please contact the Red Cross about sending me parcels of cigarettes and chocolate. Please let my Adjutant know that I have with me (1) gold wrist watch, (2) silver flask, (3) silver cigarette case. Please contact Frank and see what he thinks about the car. Contact Lloyds about savings certificates for Mother. Ask Adjutant about caterpillar for bailing out. My tankard was in the mess bar. Will write next letter to Mother and postcard to you darling. All my Love.

This transcript of the radio transmission is a rare example of application to the Irvin Caterpillar Club being actioned by a station adjutant. George was immensely lucky to have escaped with his life, the direct result of the parachute, which only operated safely within the barest of time margins. Lesley Irvin applied his signature to the membership card that recorded Sqn Ldr G. G. Davies DSO as a member and recipient of the gold pin.

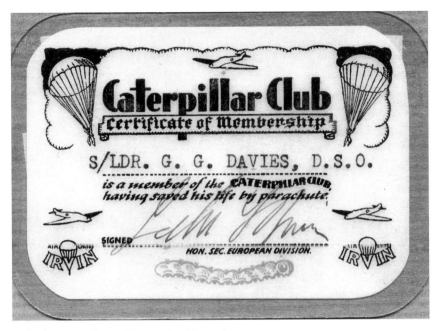

Sqd Ldr Davies' Caterpillar membership card.

In 1945, George was liberated from the prisoner of war camp, eventually reunited with his wife, and later sought to establish the fate of his crew from the night of 15 July 1944. From his crew of seven, only one in addition to himself had survived. Flt Lt K. Stevens had managed to escape by parachute and avoid capture until 4 August, when he became a prisoner of war. FO Plantana DFC, FO Lockwood DFC, Flt Lt Robinson DFC, FO Holbrook DFC, FO Coker, and FO Debrock all lost their lives. Sadly the body of FO Debrock, who originated from Belgium, was not found until March 1945, and was later repatriated to his home country. The remaining crew all lie together in the cemetery at Ancerville.

In 1949, tiring of civilian life, George rejoined the RAF in the commissioned rank of flight lieutenant. He held a number of training appointments and later served with 38 Squadron in Malta and at HQ Coastal Command. George retired as a squadron leader in 1963, but continued working as a systems manager with special responsibilities for Nimrod and Tornado equipment. George Davies died in September 1991.

CHAPTER 15

Sgt Philip Felton, navigator – Goldfish Club; Sqn Ldr Harrison-Broadley

Sgt Philip Felton was a navigator, flying as a crew member within Bristol Blenheims in some of the most harrowing low-level operations undertaken against enemy shipping in the early years of the Second World War. His pilot was John Harrison-Broadley, a commissioned officer, respected by his crew for his abilities in the air and his powers of leadership.[93]

John Harrison-Broadly's widow received a letter from Philip written after her husband's death in November 1983. The letter explains the events that had unfolded over forty years before, when they had to ditch their aircraft, becoming prisoners of war, in 1941:

> As his Observer, my main duties were navigation, bomb aiming and I had twin browning machine guns in the floor of my little nose compartment which I fired to the downward rear by means of a mirror. The other member of our crew in the Blenheim, Stuart Thompson,[94] was the wireless operator/rear gunner. Stuart escaped from our prison camp in Sulmona in Italy, when the Italians surrendered in September 1943. He was killed in a flying accident soon after the war.[95]
>
> Stuart and Harrison-Broadly had already completed a tour of operations (30 missions) before I joined them. I was fresh from initial training, having just lost my pilot and WOP/AG in a flying accident at our operational training unit. I was asked to join HB and Stuart as their observer, and went with them to 21 Squadron at Watton. We were equipped with Blenheim's, a twin-engined medium bomber with a bomb load of 1000 lbs, usually four times 250 lb. bombs and our top speed was about 200 mph.
>
> Soon after I joined them, on the 21 May 1941, we went on my first operational mission, which was a daylight raid on an oil refinery and power station at Gosnay, Bethune, in occupied France. We were part of a large

Sgt Philip Felton.

formation of Blenheim's', escorted by 200 fighters. We were led by Wing Commander Webster and our flight was led by Squadron Leader Cooper. Harrison-Broadley was then a flying officer. Stuart and I were sergeants.

We successfully bombed the targets and returned safely after a three-hour flight. I soon realised what a superb pilot HB was. Three days later, on the 24 May 1941, we set off on my second daylight mission. With eight other Blenheim's led by Squadron Leader Cooper, we were to bomb the German aerodrome on Borkum – one of the Frisian Islands off the coast of Denmark. Before we reached the target, we encountered a small enemy convoy, which we attacked, aborting our mission to Borkum as our intended surprise would have been discovered. We returned safely after a flight of four hours.

A day or two later, we flew up to Lossiemouth, in Scotland, from where we were to attack the German airfield at Stavanger in Norway. However, before we had been sent on this mission, we were ordered to return to Watton where we picked up a new Blenheim which had been especially adapted for use in the North African desert. We were to fly to Egypt with 82 Squadron and take part in operations in North Africa. On the 13 June 1941, we flew from Portreath in Cornwall to Gibraltar, a distance of 1000 miles, which was our maximum range.

We stayed in Gibraltar for a few days, waiting for a zero or following wind for our next leg of the journey to Malta. This was again, our maximum range. We had a fifty-gallon drum of petrol in the bomb bay, which I was to pump into the petrol tanks, when needed. We arrived at Malta on the 17 June 1941, after a flight of eight hours with only a few gallons of petrol remaining! Malta was under siege at this time and was heavily bombed each day. The North African campaign was going badly for our forces and it was vitally necessary to stop the supplies for the German armies under General Rommel, which were ferried in convoy from Italy to North Africa.

The senior RAF officer on Malta, Air Marshall Hugh Pugh-Lloyd co-opted us to attack these convoys. On the 18 June 1941, in daylight, we attacked a ship off the coast of Tunisia near to the port of Sfax and we returned safely to Malta.

On 22 June 1941, our reconnaissance aircraft sighted a heavily defended convoy near Lampedusa, which is an Italian island halfway between Sicily and North Africa. With five other Blenheim's of 82 Squadron, led by HB, then a flight lieutenant, acting squadron leader, and with flight lieutenant Watkins leading the other vic of three, we found and attacked the convoy, which was defended with intense anti-aircraft fire from the escorting destroyers. We flew low towards our target ship, dropping our bombs as we flew up between the masts; at this moment we were hit in the port engine and a wing tip hit the ships mast; we staggered up a few hundred feet – HB fighting to control the aircraft. We started to descend rapidly; I opened the escape hatch above HB's head. Shortly after, we crashed into the sea. I was shot forward into the nose and hit my head on the bombsight and severed my temporal artery. Stuart had thrown out our rubber dinghy and we all swam to it and climbed in. We cut the line tethering us to the aircraft, which was beginning to sink. Some five hours later, we were picked up by an Italian destroyer and taken prisoner.

Whilst we were in the dinghy, it was around midday, I bled copiously from the wound in my head until, in the hot sunshine, the blood congealed. We could see the Island of Lampedusa about five miles off, but without paddles, we could make no progress towards it with our hands. I was soon too weak to do more than slump on the floor of the dinghy in a pool of my blood. Some five hours later, when an Italian destroyer came to pick us up, HB and Stuart climbed aboard, but immediately I stood up, I passed out, but vaguely remember the Italians hauling me aboard the destroyer. They cut my clothing off and clipped the wound together with something like a bulldog clip. They put me in a bunk and plied me with sweetened brandy, which I thoroughly enjoyed. Later that day, they landed me on another Italian Island off the African coast, called Pantelleria, where I was put into a hospital where a doctor sewed up my wound.

Pantelleria is a waterless, volcanic cone; the hospital was airless and hot. There was no water for washing, only bottled water to drink and that was strictly rationed. I had no food, only occasional tidbits given to me by a nun who visited me daily bringing me either a raw egg or a peach or an apricot. Not surprisingly my wound festered and the doctor re-opened it, purged it and sewed it up again. (One year later, a large piece of Perspex came out of the wound!).

A week or so later, I was flown to Palermo in Sicily where I was locked up in the Bersagliere Barracks. As I toiled, wearily, up some stone stairs, my room was three flights up; I passed a huge hamper full of green figs. I was invited to help myself; they were absolutely delicious.

After another week or so, I was flown to Rome where I was interrogated by a board of senior officers of the various Italian armed services. But of course, I had been taught that all I was allowed to say in answer to their questions was to give my name, rank and number. As I persisted with this formula, the interrogation was soon over and I was given a blank sheet of paper and told that I could write home. This of course was ruse on the part of the Italian authorities, hoping that I would disclose some valuable information to them. My letter, therefore, which my parents never received, contained nothing of any value to the enemy.

From Rome, I was put on a train, guarded by two Cariboniere and travelled to Sulmona in the Apennine Province of Abruzzi. From Sulmona, I was taken by truck to the prison camp – PG 78 at Font d'Amore in the foothills of the Apennines about ten miles from Sulmona. A sheer grey and white cliff some 2000 feet high towered over the camp, which comprised of long brick huts, terraced up the slope to the foot of the cliff. From the camp we could see the tiny village of Font d'Amore and the valley beyond.

In the camp I met up with Stuart again and we were together for the next two years. HB was also in this camp but in a separate compound reserved for officers. Stone walls surrounded each compound with broken glass on the top. However, we climbed into the officer's compound and met HB. He was in a shiny new Italian Air Force Officers uniform with the rank of squadron leader. We visited him two or three times in the following weeks, but then our visits were discovered and forbidden with threats of being shot. So we never saw HB again.

John Harrison-Broadley was recommended and later awarded the Distinguished Flying Cross, evidencing the heroic action taken over the convoy on 22 June. At the time of the award he was listed as 'missing in action'. The aircraft containing Flt Lt Watkins, as mentioned in the account by Philip, suffered similar intense anti-aircraft fire from the convoy. Watkins was seriously injured, leaving his foot hanging by shreds of muscle and raw flesh, with additional injuries to his buttocks and leg that reduced his ability to control the Blenheim. He did succeed in gaining sufficient control, however, for the air gunner Sgt Chandler to shoot down an attacking fighter. As a result of his injuries the observer sergeant, Sargent, took control of Blenheim Z9545 and flew the aircraft back towards Malta – notwithstanding having never flown an aircraft. Watkins gained consciousness as they reached Malta, and through immense strength and bravery, he returned to the pilot's seat and landed the aircraft safely. This act of bravery was recognised by Wg Cdr Atkinson and Air-Vice Mar. Stevenson, both recommending the award of the Victoria Cross to Watkins, and the immediate Distinguished Flying Medal to Sargent. Despite these recommendations, Watkins did not receive the Victoria Cross. The recommendation was downgraded to the award of the immediate Distinguished Service Order.

Returning to Philip's letter:

The weather was very hot in the summer and the huts were airless and crawling with bed bugs, centipedes and scorpions. The toilet facilities comprised of a hole in the ground winter and summer. We tried to sleep on the ground outside of the huts, but this was forbidden, again, on pain of being shot. The daily ration was a 200g of maize bread, a pannekin of rice, a pannekin of macaroni. (A fifty cigarette tin was used as the measure) and a piece of hard cheese rind once a week. No meat or vegetables. The winters were very cold with lots of snow. (It has become over the years, a ski resort!). There was no heating in the huts, so we were always cold.

In the winter of 1942, the camp was snowed in and no supplies could get to us and so for a whole fortnight, the only food we had, was one boiled onion per day. Nobody suffered from obesity! One of our scourges was tapeworms, which of course stole most of our meager food. We had a weekly newssheet, written by some dedicated people, and there was often 'a birth notice of a tapeworm', giving its length instead of its weight! Luckily, Red Cross food parcels occasionally supplemented our meager rations – these were about twice the size of a shoebox containing tea, powdered milk, sugar and usually some tins of McChonachie's meat stew.

In September 1943, Italy surrendered and the guards left the camp. The senior British officer ordered each NCO to take charge of thirty other ranks and climb into the mountains, there to await the arrival of our forces. But, we were a long way north of the allies landing at Salerno and our forces evidently, did not get to our area until nine months had passed. We had no food or water and after a week or so, the Germans came up the mountain and rounded us up.[96] A week or so later they crammed us into cattle trucks, fifty men to a truck; we were taken by train to Germany. It took several days, with no food or water, in freezing conditions as we travelled through the Brenner Pass in November. We did stop off at Innsbruck where we made a beeline for the toilets, but after a few minutes the guards butted us off the toilets with their rifle butts and herded us back into the cattle trucks. Many men had dysentery and the conditions inside of the trucks were indescribable.

Upon our arrival in Germany, we were taken to a concentration camp at a place called Zeitheim. The conditions there were appalling. Long unheated huts, with a long wooden shelf extending the whole length of the hut to be used as 'beds'. An out-door pump heavily lagged with straw was the only washing facility. The Germans apologised to us, saying, that the camp was only meant for Russians, Jews and pigs. After a few weeks we were moved to Stalag IV B at Muhlberg on Elbe, halfway between Leipzig and Dresden. Again long huts, containing about 200 men with three-tiered bunks in blocks of twenty-seven. There was a wood stove for cooking only. Daily food rations consisted of 200 grams of black bread, two pounds of potatoes, (many rotten) vegetable skilly – no meat and a weekly piece of the most foul smelling cheese that I have ever experienced.

Thank goodness for the first year we had fairly regular Red Cross parcels but none for the last six months when we really starved. When the Germans guards retreated before the advancing Russians, we roamed the countryside outside of the camp, which was mostly forest and farmland. We were looking for food. We met lots of Russian peasant soldiers who were also looking for food. They would put their hand in their pocket and give us some of whatever they had found. Perhaps dog biscuits, cattle cake, oats or wheat. I went with a group of prisoners to a farm where we saw a huge sow in a pen. We decided to kill it, but no one even had a knife. So we went out onto a nearby road and flagged down a Russian lorry. By sign language, we told the officer in charge that we wanted him to come with us and shoot the pig. Very reluctantly he accompanied us back to the farm and despite the protests of the poor farmer, he shot the pig. Immediately, a crowd of slave farm labourers appeared, built a straw fire and burnt the bristles off the sow, gutted and quartered it in no time. As the prime movers, we were given a hind leg, which we bore away in high glee. How to cook it presented the next problem, we found a fairly clean dustbin, filled it with water, built a fire and boiled the leg of pork. When it was cooked, we gorged on the meat until we were full to bursting. Very soon after, however, we were all violently sick. Sometime later, we found a sack of oats and a large bag of sugar and we feasted on porridge for a few days with no ill effects.

Soon we were rounded up by the Russians and taken back to the prison camp to await collection by our forces. After about a fortnight, we were formed into columns and marched off to a town called Reisa – it took us all day. We were there for a few days before an American Transport Company manned by Black Americans came in a convoy of Lorries to pick us up. As we left the camp in the Lorries, on our way to the American Zone the Russians had assembled a band to bid us farewell, but all they got for their pains were jeers and catcalls from the frustrated ex-prisoners. In the American Zone we were given some 'K' rations; these were their emergency iron rations which consisted of a large cardboard box, containing lots of luxury food, drinks and cigarettes. There were biscuits, butter, tins of meat, milk, cheese, marmalade, and jams – a wonderful selection of food to a starving person. From my normal weight of 12 stone, I had descended to 8 stone! A day or so later, we were flown in Dakota's to Brussels in Belgium. My four years as a prisoner-of-war was over and what a joy is was to see the White Cliffs of Dover and my family.

Long after the events of 22 June 1941, Philip Felton penned a letter to P. B. Cow & Co., who confirmed that his survival and that of his crew from Blenheim Z6422 enabled membership of the Goldfish Club.

CHAPTER 16

Flt Lt Gordon Bennett, pilot – Late Arrivals Club

Gordon Turner Bennett was one of many young men who volunteered for aircrew service within the Royal Air Force during 1939. He commenced an intensive program of pilot training in October 1940 that progressed well and resulted in Gordon successfully gaining his wings. Gordon was selected for twin-engine aircraft and posted to 13 Operational Training Unit at RAF Bicester. Having flown Blenheim bombers and clocked up sufficient flying hours in his logbook to achieve full qualification as a pilot, Gordon was posted in late June 1941 to RAF Great Massingham, Norfolk, with 107 Squadron. Equipped with Blenheim aircraft, Gordon swiftly commenced upon his first operational sortie on 8 July, a low-level anti-shipping sweep of the Danish coast. Two days later, he participated in a 'zero feet'[97] attack on the harbour at Cherbourg. Following these challenging operations, Bennett was posted to the Middle East, where he joined another Blenheim unit, 45 Squadron, operating over North Africa and part of the Middle East Command's light bomber force. Six Blenheim squadrons, including 45 Squadron, were supported by two free French squadrons in September 1941. The free French squadrons were identifiable due to the RAF roundels being painted over with the Croix de Lorraine.

Operational sorties were slow to begin with for Gordon, with just two flown from Habbaniya in Iraq during late August. Moving to Fuka, Egypt, 45 Squadron commenced a tour of operations in the western desert. Gordon flew two successful operations with them in early October, attacking the railway marshaling yards at Bardia. In November, the squadron diverted their attention to commence attacks on road communication targets, with three such daylight operations mounted in the vicinity of Sidi Omar.

It was on 22 November that four Blenheim aircraft of 45 Squadron failed to return from a raid upon El Adem. They had become casualties of enemy

A Free French Blenheim.

fighter attacks, and one of the aircraft was forced to land in the desert. Two crew members were captured and became prisoners of war. The remaining crew member, Sgt Turton of the RNZAF, managed to evade capture and endured a fortnight-long trek across the desert before he reached the allied lines, returning to a rapturous reception from his squadron. Such events like this were longed for by squadron personnel, as the desert frequently failed to allow survival to many downed aircrews.

In December 1941, after moving to Gambut, 45 Squadron were charged with attacking the extensive armour and motorised transport units of the axis army,[98] a difficult target to destroy. These operations required exposure to defensive light anti-aircraft fire and the defensive fighter protection that was almost always present.

On the 4 December, 45 Squadron experienced a traumatic incident, brought about by the enthusiasm of the combined squadrons operating at the base. The free French Lorraine Blenheims and 45 Squadron were awaiting the final green flares to signal the start of an important raid. The ground was such that neither set of aircraft had vision. All responded to the flares and commenced take-off at exactly the same time. Several aircraft struck each other; this avoidable accident took several airmen's lives. Gordon

Free French No. 1 Squadron.

was thankfully unhurt, and on 10 December, he successfully took off in his Blenheim V5948 to attack an enemy convoy. His aircraft was attacked suddenly by several ME109s, resulting in his port outer engine catching fire. With an anticipated forced landing likely, Gordon tried to gain as much ground as possible towards the allied lines. He managed to force-land the Blenheim on the desert sand without inflicting any injuries to himself or the crew. Having taken account of their location, they estimated that they had several days walk ahead of them to get back to the safety of their own lines. The only way to survive was to load up as many emergency supplies as they could carry and start the long trek to safety. With the careful monitoring of their onward journey through the use of a compass and the rationing of water, the crew survived and returned to their squadron after three days.

The story of Gordon's escape was published in the local newspaper and, together with his fellow crew members, they applied for and became members of the exclusive Late Arrivals Club. Publication of successful escapes provided a great boost to general moral, and highlighted the ever-present possibility of survival.

After medication leave, and fully recovered, Gordon resumed his operational activity within 45 Squadron, flying three operations to attack enemy gun emplacements in the region of Bardia. On 20 December, 45 and

Flt Lt Gordon Bennett on a Free French Blenheim.

84 Squadrons provided eight Blenheims, supported by four free French Blenheims, to attack a retreating German and Italian armoured column. Flying conditions were poor but instructions came that the column must be broken up at all costs. Nineteen fighters escorted the bomber force, which was abruptly attacked by Luftwaffe ME109 fighters. Immediately, one 45 Squadron aircraft was shot down, with four allied fighter escorts and a further 45 Squadron Blenheim also becoming casualties. It was a massive aerial combat, with aircraft trying to escape in all directions. Two free French bombers were lost as a result of the continuing aerial battles. One of those aircraft was flown by the French commanding officer, Lt Colonel Pijeaud. His air gunner Sgt Dekros was killed in his turret and the Blenheim caught fire. Pijeaud remained in control as best he could, instructing his navigator Lt Gaston Guigonis to jump. The flames caused terrible burns to Pijeaud's hands and face, but he did manage to bail out of his aircraft. Pijeaud pulled the ripcord and the parachute operated correctly, enabling him to land onto the sand. The burn injuries caused great pain to Pijeaud, his eyes were burnt so badly that he had no vision as the swelling and inflamed tissue erupted across his face. Two days later he was captured by an Italian patrol unit and taken to Derna hospital. Unknown to Pijeaud, his navigator, Guigonis, negotiated five days walking across the desert and reached an allied patrol.

He was in poor shape but had survived. When he arrived at the Squadron base in Gambut, he was informed that they had held a memorial service for his soul the day previously. Pijeaud himself remained in the hospital at Derna. Meanwhile, the British front line offensive was pushing forward, causing the Italian strength at Derna to commence withdrawing.

Lambermont's book, *Lorraine Squadron* (1956), explains further:

> He spent some days in a military hospital, then some British officers who managed to escape took the blinded flier with them. They spent four hideous days on foot in the desert, with no food and no water. Then they were picked up by an Australian patrol. Pijeaud still breathing, held on to the vanishing threads of life until the 10 January 1942. Then he died on board a hospital ship at Alexandria. His last whispered words were: I don't regret a thing.

Gordon Bennett had been fortunate; he survived the escape across the desert and completed his operational tour of duty with the Desert Air Force. It had been a period of intense operational flying. Gordon was posted into an instructor position at 72 OTU in Kenya in early 1942.[99] He applied for, and gained, a commission whilst undertaking his instructing duties. In February 1945, Gordon transferred to 212 Group's communication flight at Benina. His operational service in the RAF was completed and he left the service as a flight lieutenant at RAF Middleton St George in June 1946.

CHAPTER 17

Sqn Ldr Leonard Pipkin DFC & bar, pilot – Caterpillar Club & evader; Sqn Ldr Saxelby, 'Great Escape' participant

Leonard Charles Pipkin was born on 22 March 1912. He grew up and was educated in Lambeth, London, gaining employment as an accountant in civilian life. In 1937 he married and settled down to domestic life, however, following the Munich crisis, he volunteered for the RAFVR with the ambition to fly as aircrew.

Leonard's anticipation of conflict proved to be well founded, and his training was in place when war was declared. Wearing the rank of leading aircraftsman under training, Leonard was mobilised on 2 September 1939, and attended 9 Air Observers Navigation School, RAF Squires Gate, Lancashire.[100]

The training progressed well for Leonard, and he was promoted to sergeant in March 1940. His training and qualifications proved him to be a capable navigator observer. Leonard was successful in his application to be appointed as a commissioned officer for the duration of hostilities in March 1941.

Leonard attended No. 20 Bombing Leaders Course. On 5 May 1941 he produced a lecture on the training of Polish crews within the RAF, which interestingly touched upon the formation of dedicated operational training units for Polish personnel. The lecture proposed that qualified Polish crews should eventually man their own operational squadrons.[101]

Leonard's own posting arrived; he was to join 103 Squadron flying from RAF Elsham Wolds. This Bomber Command squadron was a multinational squadron with trained aircrew from the Commonwealth being posted in as replacement personnel. The majority of these were Canadians, Australians, and New Zealanders. There were other parts of the Commonwealth represented together with additional personnel from occupied Europe who had escaped during the early stages of the war. Belgium had at least

Sgt Pipkin standing left with an RAF Military Policeman guarding a VIP flight, DH95 Flamingo, one of only two such aircraft used for the King's Flight.

four representatives on the squadron at one time or another. Together with British aircrew, the mixture of nationalities generally proved a great success – working together within their own crews and forming close-knit teams. The multinational blend continued with 103 Squadron throughout the rest of the war. It was quite fitting that Leonard's lecture on the 'leaders' course had been apt as to the make-up of personnel on this his first operational posting.

The Royal Air Force service was an adventurous one for Leonard. After his operational training posting at Bitteswell, he took part in twenty bombing raids over occupied Europe. In addition, he escaped from his aircraft by parachute, fought hand-to-hand with an enemy soldier in Germany, and successfully evaded. Leonard's story is one of personal bravery and associated bravery from many who risked all to help him.

Leonard's operation sorties commenced on 25 March 1942 with an attack on Essen. The crew flew in Wellington R1452 and returned safely back to base. The tour of duty had started well for Leonard, but he was not yet allocated to a particular crew. His next operation was to bomb the Poissy motor works in Paris on 2 April. Once again, this was an operation that saw the entire crew return safely despite the aircrafts intercom failure en route

Sgt Pipkin on the left wearing an early Sidcot Flying Suit.

to the target. Any loss of communication between the crew would have been regarded as dangerous, particularly for the rear gunner, who protected one of the most vulnerable areas of attack by enemy night fighters. He required immediate communication with his pilot to shout out emergency directions to avoid impending attacks. An attack on Hamburg on 17 April provided Leonard with the opportunity to demonstrate his navigation ability. He located a pin-point position of recognition that led to his crew making an excellent bombing run on the target.

Flt Lt Saxelby,[102] a pilot on 103 Squadron, was seeking a keen navigator observer for his own crew. Leonard was recruited and flew the vast majority of his following operations within Saxelby's crew. Saxelby had previously flow with Leonard when they were at 18 Operational Training Unit. Their first operation together was to Rostock on 23 April. Once more, the navigation was excellent, with Leonard securing the recognition point of the river and bombing from a height of 12,300 feet. This accuracy was exactly what Saxelby wanted. Two days later they returned to Rostock, followed by yet another operation on the same target on the consecutive night. The month of April concluded on the 29th with a return to Paris, where the Gnome Rhone aero-engine factory was bombed.

The most eventful raid yet took place on 6 May 1942. The target was
Stuttgart. Leonard had no particular difficulty in the navigation, but when
over Karlsruhe, it was thought the Wellington DV697 had been struck by
flak. The dinghy that was stowed in the compartment to the rear of the
starboard engine nacelle had apparently caught fire. Saxelby, thinking it was
as a result of a fire in the engine, cut the power and feathered the propeller.
The fire went out, and after a successful bombing run over the target, he
managed to return to base safely. When the Wellington was examined the
true situation was revealed. The fire had been caused by a falling incendiary
bomb dropped from another bomber flying above their position. They had
been lucky; this type of accident caused fatal consequences over targets
throughout the war. Uneventful operations over Warnemunde on the 8th,
and Mannheim on the 19 April, followed.

The first 1,000 Bomber Raid on Cologne took place on 30 May 1942.
Barker gives a full account of the Pipkin and Saxelby ordeal during that
operation in his book, *The Thousand Plan*:

First man over the target from Elsham Wolds was Clive Saxelby ... after
bombing the target and returning for home, 'They had crossed the Dutch/
German border and were approaching Eindhoven when the fighter picked
them up. The first they knew of the attack was a succession of sharp cracks
and a tearing, rending noise in the fuselage, followed by a strangled scream on
the inter-com. The cockpit had escaped, but the middle section of the fuselage
had been badly hit and was on fire. The fire quickly contaminated the oxygen
system, half suffocating the crew. Saxelby wrenched off his mask but he still
couldn't breathe. He pushed back the cabin window and put his head into
the slipstream, breathing deeply, and as he did so he stared straight into the
silhouette of a Me 110, slanted into a 90-degree bank turning in again towards
him. 'Christ! He's coming back in again!' Saxelby put the nose forward and
spiraled but the fighter followed him down getting in another accurate burst.
The fire in the midsection had caught hold and the fabric was peeling and
burning. Half of the tail plane was denuded of fabric, and the trimmers had
been shot away. The hydraulics were hit and the undercarriage and bomb-
doors were drooping, greatly adding to the load on the control column as
the Wellington spiraled. But the worst danger was the fire and Pipkin, the
navigator, was nearest to the flames. He had no gloves on, but he attacked them
immediately with his bare hands. McClean, the Wireless Operator, clipped on
his parachute and went forward to open the hatch under the cockpit, expecting
an order to bail out. He saw Saxelby struggling with the controls. 'Are you

coming, Sax?' 'Not yet - I think I can hold it' McClean went back to help Pipkin, and between them they extinguished the fire, ripping off the affected fabric and pushing it out through the holes. The Wellington began to look bare and skeletal amidships, but it still flew. Pipkin went forward and shouted in Saxelby's ear. 'Everything's fine, we're doing well, I know exactly where we are. For God's sake keep her flying.' But Saxelby was finding the weight of the controls too much for him. The plane was still locked in the spiral and the ground was coming up fast. It's no good - I can't hold her. 'Pipkin disappeared, then came back with a rope which he tied round the control column. Saxelby noticed that the skin on Pipkin's hands was shriveled and burnt. Pipkin lashed the stick back and the Wellington leveled out....St. Pierre, the French-Canadian in the rear turret, had been wounded in the leg. (He had sustained shrapnel wounds to his legs and face) His inter-com was cut off, and he crawled forward to see what was happening. He thought he might have missed a bail-out order. Under the astro-dome, leaning against the side of the fuselage, was Roberts, the 2nd Pilot, apparently taking it easy. St. Pierre gave him a prod to attract his attention, and like the body in the cupboard Roberts slid in slow-motion to the floor. This eager young pilot who had come along for the experience had been rewarded by the experience of death.

Wellington DV704 crash-landed at RAF Honnington. The true horror of death had been experienced by the crew. Leonard required medical treatment to the burns on his hands and was admitted to West Suffolk Hospital on 31 May, where he remained for six weeks. Saxelby was promoted to squadron leader and attended a conversion course onto the Halifax bomber. Leonard's burn injuries healed and he was promoted to flying officer. Once Saxelby returned to the squadron, the team re-commenced operations. Exceptional confidence existed between the pilot and navigator; each respected the skill and professional abilities that had been demonstrated over the previous operations. The Halifax was seen to be an aircraft with greater capacity than the old Wellington that it had replaced.

The first operation within a Halifax bomber was to Dusseldorf on 31 July 1942, with Osnabruck on 17 August, and Kassel on the 27th. Both proved to be very successful, with Leonard securing accurate navigation points, leading to good results over the respective targets. Halifax W1219 became Leonard's regular aircraft; in fact, this airframe was to be the only Halifax used by the crew. It was clear that Saxelby was very happy with that particular aircraft, and being in the position of the flight commander, he no doubt made that fact well known.

103 Squadron in 1942, with a newly delivered Halifax.

The next eventful operation for Leonard took place on 28 August, with the target identified as Nurnberg. Leonard located the aiming point on the first run across the target area, but failed to feel the effects of the bomb load departing the aircraft. It was found that the bomb bay doors had not opened. Saxelby orbited the area, keeping clear of the bombing run for 13 minutes, whilst the bomb bay doors were pumped down by hand. This was a heavy task for the crew members who were able to help. A further run was made across the target at a height of 8,200 feet, and again one single 1,000 lb bomb failed to release on this run. Leonard put his arm through the clear vision panel in the bay to release the last remaining bomb by hand. It then took three crew members 20 minutes to pump the doors shut by hand. Just as Saxelby confirmed that the doors were closed, the gauge blew off the top of the accumulator – partially blinding the wireless operator and covering Leonard in hydraulic fluid. The flight engineer was able to stem the leak by clamping the pipe closed.

On 31 August 1942, the air officer commanding 1 Group RAF endorsed a DFC recommendation, submitted by the commanding officer of 103 Squadron. FO Leonard Pipkin had been recommended as a result of his actions over Cologne and his achievements to date in his tour of duty. The notification of the award in the *London Gazette* followed accordingly.

Halifax W1219 was taken to Saabrucken on 2 September, and then to Bremen on the 4th. Both operations were regarded as successful, however three nights later, this was not to be the case. In the knowledge that he had been bestowed the non-immediate award of the Distinguished Flying Cross, Leonard climbed aboard Halifax W1219. Saxelby was, as normal, in the captain's seat, and the aircraft took off from the runway at 1.06 a.m. An operation to bomb Duisburg commenced, with the time over the target scheduled for 3 a.m. Leonard set about his technical calculations and bearings to get the aircraft over the target for that time. As the Halifax aircraft approached the target, two Luftwaffe night fighters attacked. The rear gunner[103] was killed instantly during the first sustained attack. The elevators were shot away causing a stall that induced a spin. An immediate order was issued by Saxelby to abandon the aircraft, just as Leonard was about to release the bomb load. He managed to negotiate through the escape hatch and fall away from the aircraft. Pulling the ripcord of his parachute, anxious split-seconds of emotion must have passed as the trusty Irvin silk exploded into the canopy that was to save his life over the skies of Duisburg. Those instantaneous thoughts would have been replaced by other survival issues as he was suddenly held within a searchlight beam. The searchlight crew retained Leonard within the light, an easy target with the white silk parachute illuminated brightly. The intensity of the light blinded Leonard as he swung into the full beam strength. As he descended, his right boot left his foot, tumbling into the darkness below him.

Falling into an unknown area over Duisburg, Leonard reached the ground and the searchlight left him in the darkness. He had landed in a field on the western outskirts of the city. The first action he took was to tear up the silk parachute and the Mae West life vest. Hiding them in a ditch as best possible, he remembered that in his pocket was a copy of the 'full method of attack' for the night operation over Duisburg, so he destroyed the evidence of the operation as thoroughly as he could. In the knowledge that he would not get far with only one boot, Leonard started to square-search the field to try and locate his missing flying boot. The search lasted just under an hour, but patience and methodical application resulted in success. It was of some good fortune that the large field was stubble. Had the summer crop not have been harvested the boot would never have been located.

Leonard's survival by parachute was the start of an extraordinary story of evasion from deep within Germany. Leonard had saved his life by his parachute, as had the remaining members of his crew, who all became prisoners of war. Leonard was to become not only a member of the Caterpillar Club, but a member of the exclusive group of airmen who escaped capture and evaded through Germany. Leonard became a valuable reference to the Air Ministry. He was to later lecture aircrews on evasion techniques. From his own lecture notes we are able to read his story:

If you are shot down over Germany you can only live on what you have with you and what you can pick up from the fields, you will get no in Germany. Get away from the aircraft during darkness after having hidden your parachute and also find a place to hide for the day. The Germans search the whole area from the Coast to the target between six o'clock and midday.

I started my escape as the all clear was sounded; I mixed with the people as they came from the shelters. Walked a short distance but was confronted with the barb wire defenses of the Ruhr. These are 7 feet high and 6 yards wide, the only thing you can do with these is to get through them as all gaps are held by sentries. About 5.30am cyclist passed me, the Germans start work early. Soon after this I saw some Nazi soldiers coming along the road, I hid in a small coppice which was below the made up road. The soldiers passed above my head only 2 yards away. Crowds of other soldiers came along, I lay flat on my back and covered my face with twigs and leaves and kept my hands behind my back. I later discovered that this road led towards a Nazi camp. At 6am sentries started patrolling the road with a commander giving instructions, they combed the area with about 2 yards separating each of them, prodding the undergrowth as they went. One soldier kept shouting in English "Come here" I knew they were searching for me and my crew. They then went to the woods. During the day I had to lie perfectly still for 16 hours under some thick bushes with sentries patrolling continually a large village to the right of me, a soldiers camp behind me and dense undergrowth ahead.

When the sentries finished it was about 8pm, I began to crawl through the undergrowth over the ditch to the road above. Half way up and about 5 yards away I saw a dozen soldiers so went back again where I lay still for a further hour. I returned and got up to the road at around 9.30pm after a short while I came across another soldier on his own, before I had time to hide again he was level with me. He said something which I did not understand. I acted as if I was deaf and dumb. He then said 'Papiers' and held me in a strong grip starting to march me off to the camp. When he let go of my arm for a second I tried to escape but he was prepared and got me down and knelt on my stomach and kicked me. I managed to get him over to the ditch and silence his shouts by holding his head under the mud and slime. The struggle lasted 5 or 10 minutes in the ditch, the man was not armed. I lost my identity discs in the fight, they had been in my pocket. I left the dead man in the ditch running alongside a hedge only to see another soldier. I hid in the ditch and let him pass. I was feeling weak after the fight and was compelled to sit down taking some of the endurance tablets. These pulled me together and I was able to get my strength back within half an hour. Both the endurance and chlorine tablets proved extremely valuable.

At intervals during the night people wandered around with torches. I thought it was an organised search but later found out it was farmers setting guards to protect the crops in accordance to the laws. The Ruhr roads are patrolled by Nazi troopers on cycles. During the day I slept in a ditch covered over with branches near a railway embankment and a wood. The only people that may have worried me were the peasant farm workers. I tried to listen to see if I was close to a railway station, at about 6.30pm I climbed up the embankment and saw two soldiers patrolling the tracks. I later found out that this was done at all approaches to stations and slow sections of track.

Walking for three days in water saturated flying boots had caused feet blistering, which was extremely difficult. I obtained moisture from handfuls of wet grass and cabbage leaves; this was enough to quench my thirst. At 1am I located a main road and decided to walk on it to rest my feet, but within just five minutes I had been seen by two Nazi troopers. I found an opening in the hedge and shot across the fields, the troopers took off after me. I saw five haystacks discovering a hole in one in which to hide. I pushed my way frantically inside and lay still, the troopers searched but failed to find me. I remained hidden for two hours. This whole episode proves to show how dangerous it is to be on a road at night. Owing to the curfew one is always going to be questioned or possibly shot on sight.

I returned to walking the fields, when I came across a filthy ditch I was so thirsty I dipped my rubber bag into the water and filled it. After putting in the chlorine tablets I drank it and felt no ill effects at all. I was still in Germany so it would have been most dangerous to ask for water anywhere. The next night I was rather under the weather, I was again walking the fields following the hedges, I had been walking for four nights and every night I was forced to avoid troopers. I had crossed the river Niers at its narrowing at Viersen and continued walking until I reached a farm. I used my escape map once more and calculated that I must have been inside Belgium. I saw a farmer who approached me, he took me towards the farm. I made him take me to the back of the building where I saw a woman and two children. The latter looked at my flying boots, I was taken inside where the door was shut and curtains drawn. A little later a man arrived who spoke some English, he gave me some trousers and the farmer gave me a coat.

The farmer was Jean Berden,[104] a resistance member in Reuver. Petrus Meusen and the chaplain H. L. Dirix, also from Reuver, all assisted with the arrangements to facilitate the movement of Leonard towards the frontier. Leonard Pipkin was one of the very first group of evaders to have escaped through Holland and subsequently reach the UK. Berden, who passed away in the 1970s, recorded that he was very proud of his part undertaken in the resistance. Returning to Leonard's account of his evasion:

> I was given hot water to bathe my feet and their best food which was bread and musty meat. The farmer told me he had just been fined 5000 frs because one of his cows had not given the milk expected. A farmer might have plenty of stock but was not allowed to use it himself. The woman told me I was only just across the frontier and that the area was very dangerous. The farmer laid out maps and told me of the German manoeuvers and exercises. He was going to try and get me a bicycle and show me the way to Holland with an address. I was taken across the River in a boat.

Jean Berden and Petrus Meusen guided Leonard to Beesel, a location just south of Reuver. The river itself was the Maas, which he crossed on 11 September 1942. Two men were waiting to act as a guide:

> We walked to a house and took a cycle. I timed myself and reckoned that I was doing 8 miles an hour at some distance behind the guides. I checked my landmarks and found the farm that had been indicated to me by the farmer. I was hidden upstairs. In the morning Germans arrived for breakfast. I was then given milk and bread and moved on to another farm. I was still wearing flying boots but had been given a civilian jacket to wear. Again I was hidden in the loft; the Germans ate here at lunchtime every day. I rested and waited to be seen by a helper who arranged to get me across the Holland Belgium frontier.
>
> It was too dangerous to cross by the fields and woods so arrangements were made to cycle across as fast as possible when given the signal to join the crowds of workers crossing the frontier returning from work. We were shouted at but did not stop. Cycles in occupied territories have a number plate according to

the sectors in which they may be ridden, and the radius of these sector are about 50 miles. Outside that sector the rider is most likely to be questioned. I was taken to an address in Belgium and then moved from place to place. I ended up on a farm outside Brussels where I stayed for 5 or 6 six days digging potatoes, had good food and regained my strength.

Leonard had been escorted by Abert Coenen, a Belgium, and crossed the frontier at Neeritter, near Roermond. Coenen handed Leonard over to Gertrude Moors at Dilsen. Gertrude was an operative within the Comet Escape Line. Gertrude collected Leonard at a mill near Maestricht and escorted him to Tongres, the home of two sisters, Jenny and Mathilde Ritschdorff. The Comet Line questioned Leonard at length to establish his true identity. The questioning was carried out by a Dr Lindemann:

I was taken by train via Tongres to Liege to the home of two middle aged sisters where I remained for about 9 days. I was then taken to Brussels staying at various addresses when I left for Paris. The train was crowded with Nazi troopers and U Boat men, these soldiers appear to hate each other and fights were taking place. I reached Paris and eventually reached Spain and Gibraltar.

The Comet Escape Line was well organised during 1942, and operated with efficiency. Each evader was known as a 'parcel' and allocated a number. Flt Lt Leonard Pipkin was number sixty-three. Unbeknown to him at that time, Sgt William Randle (later Gp Capt. Randle CBE AFC DFM) was 'parcel' sixty. Randle adds to the story:

I was taken on the train, we had to change trains at Lille and wait there for a connection. While we were standing on the platform from Brussels with our guide, we could hardly restrain ourselves when we saw another group, quite obviously evaders with their guide on an adjacent platform. One of this group was Pipkin. I would put the date at about the end of September. After a longish stay in Paris we went to Biaritz and then St Jean de Luz. We had about a week getting ready to cross the Pyrenees. We were disguised as Basques, denims, rope sandals and berets. It was there one day that I saw the same group from Lille railway station. There was Pipkin clad in denims, wearing rope sandals and a Basque beret. I believe that Pipkin's team crossed the Pyrenees before mine, using the same guides. We crossed on about the 20 October, led by Florentino the Basque and 'Dede' Andree de Jongh. I got to Gibraltar where I was able to talk to Pipkin for the first time.

On 4 October, Leonard's wife Violet received the following telegram at the family home in London. Though she did not know it, Leonard was at this time securing his safety by entering British territory in Gibraltar. The telegram read:

IMMEDIATE FROM AIR MINISTRY KINGSWAY P 2392 4/10/42 DEEPLY REGRET TO ADVISE YOU THAT ACCORDING TO INFORMATION RECEIVED THROUGH THE INTERNATIONAL RED CROSS COMMITTEE YOUR HUSBAND ACTING FLIGHT LIEUTENANT LEONARD CHARLES PIPKIN IS BELIEVED TO HAVE LOST HIS LIFE AS THE RESULT OF AIR OPERATIONS ON THE 7th SEPTEMBER 1942 STOP THE AIR COUNCIL EXPRESS THEIR PROFOUND SYMPATHY STOP LETTER CONFIRMING THIS TELEGRAM FOLLOWS STOP UNDER SECRETARY OF STATE.

On 8 October Violet Pipkin received a letter from the Air Ministry in London:

Madam,

I am commanded by the Air Council to inform you that they have with great regret to confirm their telegram of the 4 October 1942 in which you were notified that in view of information now received from the International Red Cross Society your husband, Acting Flight Lieutenant Leonard Charles Pipkin RAF is believed to have lost his life as the result of the air operations on 7 September 1942.

The Societies telegram quoting official German information states that five of the occupants of the aircraft in which your husband was flying were captured on that day and that one of them has reported that your husband and the two other occupants were killed.

Although there is unhappily little reason to doubt the accuracy of this report it will be necessary to record the casualty as 'Missing believed killed' until confirmation by further evidence, or until in the absence of such evidence, it becomes necessary, owing to lapse of time, to presume for official purposes that death has occurred. Action to that effect would not however be taken until at least six months from the date when your husband was reported missing.

The Air Council desire me, in conveying this information to express their profound sympathy with you in your grave anxiety.

I am, Madam, your obedient servant.

As Violet Pipkin read this letter, Leonard was negotiating the final link with the Comet Escape Line – a journey over the Pyrenees Mountains. Returning to his lecture notes, he makes reference to this:

> About this journey I am not going to say anything other than you need to be very fit to make the 9 hour journey over the Pyrenees. There are swamps and rivers to be waded through, and the trip must be completed in one night. In Spain be very careful of the guards they are very conscientious. Be cautious in approaching the British Consulate as the guards outside will demand your identity card. Do not have false identification papers in Spain, it will lead to much trouble whereas if you have none you will be sent to prison but will be rescued by the Consulate.
>
> Remember when walking through occupied territory wear an old civilian suit but keep yourself reasonably decent looking, shave. Belgian identity cards can be used in France a photograph of you is vital for this.
>
> Make sure that all your crew know how to use a hand held compass and while flying over enemy held territory the navigator should give the crew an idea where they are every quarter of an hour so they will not be lost on bailing out. Parachute drill should be practiced in full kit. Unless our crew had been drilled there would not have been a ghost of a chance of more than two or three people getting out. We only had 7 or 8,000 feet to get everybody out with the aircraft vertical.

People like Jean Berden and Gertrude Moors were quite extraordinary. Gertrude was a member of several resistance groups, and played a significant part in the escape of Leonard Pipkin and twenty-four further allied airmen were assisted directly by her. As a result of German infiltration of the Comet Line, she was captured by the secret Fieldpolizei on 18 June 1943. Severely tortured in the Prison of St Gillis, Brussels, and in the Begynestraat, Antwerp, Gertrude was condemned to death on 2 July 1944. She never betrayed her country, or her fellow partisans. Gertrude died in Ravensbruck in March 1945. She was posthumously decorated by Belgium, and by both British and United States governments.

Leonard Pipkin eventually arrived back in Great Britain on a transport flight from Gibraltar on 24 October 1942. The Air Ministry valued highly the de-briefing reports compiled by successful evaders upon their return to the country, and after medical attention, the report completion was seen as being of the utmost priority. On 26 October Leonard was interviewed, and the account of his forty-eight days of evasion was submitted and distributed

Sgt Pipkin after his escape and evasion.

Memorial card to Sgt Pipkin's Comete line operative, Gertrude Moors, murdered in Ravensbruck March 1945.

to many secret departments under reference MI9/S/P.G.(-)934. That same reference was submitted upon a recommendation for honours and awards:

Recognition for which recommended. Military Cross
Flight Lieutenant 62260 Leonard Charles PIPKIN D.F.C. Navigator 103 Squadron No1 Group.

Particulars for Meritorious Service.
See most secret letter No. M.I.9/S/P.G.(-)934.

Strongly recommended for the Award of the Military Cross for Gallantry on the ground.

The military cross award to members of the Royal Air Force was a rare occurrence. The MC was primarily awarded to captains, commissioned officers of lower rank, and warrant officers in the army. In 1931, the award of this medal was extended to gallant conduct on the ground by officers of the Royal Air Force. Clearly, the long evasion in Germany, and the enforced hand-to-hand conflict with the soldier in the ditch, fulfilled the apparent qualifications for the award of the Military Cross to Leonard. In 1942, ten Military Cross medals were awarded to members of the RAF, mainly for services while a prisoner of war, evasion, and escape, and to members of the RAF regiment for actions on the ground. During the Second World War, a total of eighty-four medals were awarded. Leonard was not to be one of those few. The recommendation was changed by the air vice-marshall, A. O. C., 1 Group, on 27 November 1942, his pen striking out the words 'Military Cross' and replacing them with 'Bar to DFC'. Covering letter BC/S23191/ P of 3/12/42 on S.86798 was also recorded. The events surrounding the gallantry medals awarded to Leonard Pipkin all occurred with swiftness. The original Distinguished Flying Cross recommendation from August was published on 10 November 1942. On 18 December *The Times* newspaper published the award of the bar to the DFC:

The King has approved the following award in recognition of gallantry displayed in flying operations against the enemy.

Bar to Distinguished Flying Cross.

F/Lt L.C. PIPKIN D.F.C. R.A.F.V.R. 103 Sq.

Sgt Pipkin's DFC and Bar Medals complete with Caterpillar Club pin.

'In September this officer was the navigator of an aircraft detailed to attack a target in the Rhur. In most hazardous circumstances he displayed courage and devotion to duty in keeping with the highest traditions of the R.A.F.'

Leonard continued to serve within Bomber Command touring many airfields in order to lecture upon escape and evasion through Europe. It would have been made clear to him that no further operational flying would be possible over Europe, a procedure designed to protect those people and contacts he had gained during his successful evasion. Leonard returned to 103 Squadron, where he visited the parachute packing section at Elsham Wolds in order to thank the staff. The Caterpillar Club application forms requested, if possible, to know which parachute had been responsible for the saving of a life. Careful records were maintained on all parachutes by these departments on every operational airfield. Without doubt, Leonard applied to Irvin Chutes around this period. Another area of work undertaken by Leonard was promoting awareness for 'Wings for victory' – Sheffield had a target of £4,000,000 to raise for 100 Lancaster Bombers between 29 May and 5 June 1943. Having been promoted, Sqn Ldr Leonard Pipkin DFC and bar appeared in full uniform on page five of the *Daily Star* newspaper, officially opening the event.

In July 1943, Leonard returned to an operational station. He was posted to RAF Wymeswold in Leicestershire as senior navigation officer. Leonard was in charge of all navigation training undertaken at Wymeswold, a position of senior responsibility. He carried out these duties for over a year, before a tragic event was recorded within the station records book during August 1944: '31.8.44 S/Ldr L.C. PIPKIN. Station Navigation Officer died.' *The Echo* published the following report on the inquest of Leonard, dated 8 September 1944:

Tragic End to Rabbit Shoot

Squadron Leader L Pipkin died in Loughborough Hospital on Wednesday night following shocking injuries received when, it was surmised he opened the door of a motor car after he had been shooting rabbits in a field at Burton on the Wolds. The gun went off and he was shot through the abdomen. A fellow officer and friend Squadron Leader Borrell heard the shot some distance away and ran to his aide. The Coroner Mr Deane said it was indeed a tragedy, for that this young man had faced all perils of his calling with such efficiency and bravery and had earned two decorations for so doing. To meet his death in that way was so simple and so terribly sad. The Coroner proceeded that he was perfectly satisfied it was a pure accident.

Violet Pipkin laid her husband to rest in Hendon Cemetery London. Well over a dozen floral tributes were laid by his graveside from the airfield. The beret worn by Leonard during his escape across occupied Europe, with its Paris label, became a treasured keepsake.

CHAPTER 18

FO Patrick Flynn DFC, pilot – Caterpillar & Goldfish Clubs

Patrick J. R. Flynn was born in 1921 London. He volunteered for service in the Royal Air Force Volunteer Reserve with aspirations to become a pilot. Successful in the subsequent selection of potentials, he awaited his training with great expectation. The uncertain British weather and ever-present threat of the German Luftwaffe meant that the skies over the UK were no place for eager young men to learn to fly. To overcome these problems, the British Government sought to establish aircrew training schemes in a number of locations both within, and outside, the Commonwealth. The United States of America was one of the locations identified where British and Commonwealth airmen undertook flying training in the (then) neutral USA. A number of schemes were established, amongst them the Arnold Scheme,[105] which Patrick Flynn attended in 1941.

Patrick returned to the England to continue with his training in air gunnery. He was commissioned as a flying officer in February 1942 and posted to 124 (Baroda) Squadron, who were equipped with Spitfires and operated from RAF Gravesend. It was not long before Patrick was seconded to 57 OTU, returning to 124 Squadron in September that same year, and flying from the now infamous RAF station at Tangmere[106] in the new pressurised high-altitude Spitfires. These Spitfires were able to operate up to 28000 feet, facilitating the ability to escort the USAAF Flying Fortresses on daylight bombing raids.

An interesting posting took place for Patrick in January 1943. The abbreviation MSFU appeared on his official documents. The Merchant Shipping Fighter Unit had been set up at the old Liverpool civil airport at Speke under the command of Wg Cdr E. S. Moulton-Barrett.[107] The MSFU were equipped with Hurricanes, specially adapted to be catapulted from selected merchant ships in an attempt to combat the success the German

FO Flynn's Catapult Hurricane displaying the letters 'I' (aircraft V6756) and NJ (Merchant Ship Fighter Unit).

Condor[108] bombers were having, when attacking allied convoys. Once the adapted Hurricanes, or 'Hurricats' as they became known, had been launched, there was no return to the ship. Once the fuel had run dry the pilots had to bail out, with no guarantee of being rescued. Merchant and escort ships faced great dangers of being attacked if they removed themselves from the protection of the convoy. Ironically, Patrick was posted onto this specialist unit at a time when they were about to be withdrawn. The U-boat and Luftwaffe Condor threat against the convoys began to reduce as a result of the combined proactive allied operation's against them. The RAF felt it was uneconomical for such an expensive resource to be maintained, and therefore on 8 June 1943, HQ Fighter Command issued the following order, which was relayed from the admiralty to HQ 9 Group RAF:

> My Lords would like to express their great appreciation of the services rendered by the RAF in providing this valuable service for our convoys, and it is with great regret that we are now forced to recommend that this association of the RAF and Merchant Navy should now be brought to an end.

Luftwaffe Condors were in fact still very active and proving effective. On 16 June, the 740 ton *Sudin* was attacked off Iceland, and on 8 July the small 87-ton trawler *Mistletoe* had been bombed and sunk. Condors had also been engaged by both the royal navy and free Norwegian surface ships.

Patrick commenced life at sea with Convoy SL133,[109] aboard the steamship *Empire Tide*. The convoy was homeward bound from Sierra Leone, departing from Gibraltar on 23 July 1943. The convoy comprised of forty ships, and was accompanied by the last two MSFU-equipped ships in service, as the unit had been officially disbanded on the 15th. Leading the extreme port column of the convoy was the *Empire Tide*. The *Empire Darwin* led the starboard column. The first three days proved uneventful, even though during daylight hours Patrick was ready for a launch at short notice, in some instances sitting in the cockpit of his aircraft, which was perched on the catapult rack high above the ship's bows. Salt water spray was a constant problem, with the aircraft frequently becoming damp. Gun barrels would start rusting and corroding inside the mechanism – covers were made to prevent salt spray from penetrating wherever possible.

It was not known to the allies, but the German intelligence network had gathered sufficient information to advise the Luftwaffe of the disbandment of the MSFU. Convoy SL133 was presumed to have no close air support at that time. On 26 July, the convoy was 250 miles off Cape St Vincent when a Luftwaffe Condor made a reconnaissance at a position where no effective air support would have been available from Britain or Gibraltar. A decision was made not to dispatch the 'Hurricats', even though the launching drill was a well-proven system of events. The MSFU would hoist the recognition flag that advised all shipping masters. The pilot started the engine, whilst the catapult officer checked that the locking bolts and pins had been removed from the trolley that held the rocket installation. Flags were then waved between the catapult officer and the ship's master. The pilot, upon seeing both flags, went to full engine power, locked the throttle, and pressed himself into his seat in anticipation of the massive thrust that was about to launch his aircraft into the air. A launch could be achieved within 3 minutes.

Two days later, in the early evening of 28 July, Convoy SL133 made further contact with a Luftwaffe Condor. Fortuitously, however, a United States Air Force B-24 Liberator was sighted simultaneously. The convoy was passing roughly 800 miles due west of the Condor airfield base at Bordeaux. As such, it was considered best to hold the protecting 'Hurricats' in reserve. A request was made for the Liberator to engage the enemy aircraft. The subsequent aerial battle was intense. Both aircraft suffered damage from their respective air gunners. The Condor suffered sufficiently to send it crashing to the waves. The Liberator appeared to have suffered less damage during the engagement, but that aircraft also crashed into the sea shortly afterwards.

The Condor had obviously reported the location of the convoy and its engagement with the Liberator as two further Luftwaffe Condors appeared and approached the convoy. Barker refers to the events in his book, *The Hurricats*:

… Pilot Officer J. Stewart was launched from the Empire Darwin, and despite his guns jamming after 800 rounds he managed to shoot down one of the Condors before having to bail out, Meanwhile yet another Condor was silhouetted on the horizon dead ahead, height 1500 feet, distance about 12 miles. The duty pilot on Empire Tide was a Londoner named P. J. R. Flynn, inevitably dubbed 'Paddy' Flynn, and he was as extrovert and exuberant as Stewart was reserved and phlegmatic. Like Stewart he had never been in combat. Stamping around with impatience at having missed the chance of a launching, he had been imploring his crew to get the firing mechanism serviceable. This they eventually succeeded in doing, and at 2036 the decision was taken to launch. 84 seconds later the Hurricane was airborne.'

Flynn climbed to 200 feet, and was able to engage with the Condor in a matter of minutes, 'Coming up astern of the Condor on the port quarter, Flynn opened fire with a two-second burst at 300 yards. There was a short burst from the port lateral machine-gun of the Condor and as Flynn closed directly astern he saw that the gunners in the front and rear turrets were firing at him point blank …

Breaking off he executed a climbing turn into the sun, then began a series of beam and quarter attacks from the port side up sun. As with the other two Condors, the pilot took no violent evasive action but relied on his gunners. On his second run Flynn concentrated his fire on the cockpit and knew he was on target, but he had to fly through blistering return fire and his Hurricane was repeatedly hit, mostly in the wings.

Even the impetuous Flynn realised that he would first have to silence the Condor's guns. Breaking off again, he began his third run by spraying the fuselage between the rear turret and the lateral gun position on the port side before closing to 100 yards and finishing up with a short burst of fire directed at the front turret. Again he saw his tracer stabbing its mark.

Having as he hoped silenced the gunners, he went now for the outer and inner port engines, but the answering fire was as withering as ever. The Perspex of the cockpit hood behind his head suddenly splintered, and a gaping hole appeared in the port wing. For compensation he had to be content with increasing spurts of smoke from the Condor's port engines …

As he closed in for a final attack, a bomb from the Condor fell away right in front of him and he nearly flew into it. Soon afterwards he felt the blast from the explosion as it hit the sea. Then, as the Condor pilot jettisoned the rest of his bombs, Flynn fired a final burst that exhausted his ammunition. He left the Condor pouring smoke and rapidly losing altitude …

Every pilot catapulted from one of the adapted merchant ships was likely to become a member of the Caterpillar Club. The risks were high for these specialist pilots, with the Mae West life vest or the one man dingy the only support available to assist survival in the sea. In effect, MSFU pilots were always eligible for an endorsed membership[110] to the Goldfish Club.

In Patrick's case, he was some 40 miles distant from the convoy. Out of radio transmission range, his Hurricane had suffered from a smashed Perspex canopy and holes in his port wing – the result of cannon fire during the aerial engagement with the Condor. He managed to gain sufficient height and commenced a search for his convoy. After what would have been 10 minutes of anxious flying, Patrick sighted the convoy, however the radio was still unable to transmit, so he circled the convoy, waggling his wings. At a height of around 2,000 feet, Flynn abandoned his much-trusted aircraft, which crashed into the sea, lost forever. Flynn's parachute deployed perfectly, and he landed in the sea, operating the compressed air bottle to fully inflate his Mae West. The k-type single-man life raft operated efficiently, and this then enabled him to discard the now unwanted parachute.

With no more than 30 minutes' daylight left, the dark prospect of not being found grew in his mind. Luck was on his side, however, and it was only 10 minutes before HMS *Enchantress* appeared on the horizon. Flynn was recovered from the sea safe and well, his life saved by both parachute and dinghy.

The action in July was recognised by the award of the Distinguished Flying Cross. The official recommendation quotes (London Gazette, 1 October 1943):

Flying Officer Patrick John Richard Flynn (119785) Royal Air Force Volunteer Reserve

This officer had completed his duties in a most commendable manner. In July 1943, his aircraft was launched by catapult and he successfully attacked an enemy aircraft which was menacing a convoy the attacker was destroyed and Flying Officer Flynn returned to the convoy which was suffering further attacks. Although he knew that his petrol supply was limited, he attacked a second enemy aircraft and stayed in the vicinity of the convoy until forced to abandon his aircraft.

During its two years' existence, the MSFU had provided excellent aerial protection to the Merchant Fleet.[111] Its disbandment resulted in Patrick being posted to another Spitfire squadron, 616 (South Yorkshire). Tragically, FO Patrick Flynn DFC was killed in a motor car accident on 14 November 1943. He was later buried in Wandsworth Cemetery, London.

CHAPTER 19

Flt Sgt Raymond Warwick – Late Arrivals Club; PO Hare & PO Chappell

Raymond Warwick was an air gunner serving in 458 Squadron Royal Australian Air Force, flying Wellington aircraft operating in the Middle East. Warwick's entire crew consisted of six men from across the Commonwealth, two from Australia, two from Canada, and two from the UK. Serving alongside Raymond was his fellow Australian, Sgt Alexander Barras. These two men were to become eligible for membership into the Late Arrivals Club by one of the most extreme set of circumstances to be evidenced.

On 16 July, on their first raid to the harbour in Tobruk, enemy flak damage tore the fabric from the Wellington bomber's starboard wing between the engine and the fuselage. The wing spar itself suffered damage, and they were very lucky to escape and return to Abu Sueir landing ground. The Wellington aircraft was built with a geodetic metal construction,[112] brilliantly designed by Barnes Wallis. Warwick's bombing operations on 23, 26, and 28 July were not so eventful, but were successes in that each occasion saw the capacity loads of nine 250 lb bombs dropped accurately onto the chosen target.

On the night of 29 July 1942, Raymond's crew flew in Wellington bomber HF 833 on a further raid to attack the harbour installations at Tobruk. This was a target known to the crew, having visited it on four previous occasions. Taking off at 8.50 p.m., Sgt Chappell, the Canadian navigator, recorded his twenty-sixth operational raid in his flying logbook, entering both PO Hare and Sgt Barras as first and second pilots respectively. In stark contrast to Chappell, Barras was only just commencing his operational tour of duty. They reached the target and commenced the bombing run upon Tobruk at approximately 9,000 feet; as they did so one engine registered rapidly increasing oil temperature and subsequently seized up. Almost immediately the pilot, Canadian Chris Hare, dropped the bomb load and reported to the crew that they were going to have to force-land in the desert. Crash-landing so close to Tobruk was a daunting prospect for every crew member. They were over 400 miles from allied lines, with very little but desert sand across that entire distance.

Raymond Warwick, in a letter to his sister Loriot,[113] later recalled the events that took place:

> It all started off by us being forced to land in the desert a few hundred miles behind jerry lines. Chris made a good job of the crash landing, nobody injured in the slightest. We took off what water and little food we had in the plane and started walking as fast as we could that night. Next day while we were laying up in what shade we could find we mapped out a rough course we thought of taking and somewhere around the distance we had to cover. After a few days everything went hay-wire, we were to change our whole plans as we were almost out of water and the place we had expected to find water we didn't so we had to make what water we had last a couple of days, we rationed ourselves down to a pint of water for three days and quite often we went a day and two days without any water at all, but each time when we felt the game was up something happened as if by miracle, we kicked an empty tin as we thought, and found it had water in it, mostly rusty, we strained it through a cloth and tipped it into our water bottle and so we managed to keep going. We had very little food throughout the whole trip, we lived on emergency rations carried in the aircraft, which is a tablet form, the old belt went up a notch or so each day. We got rather close to the enemy on a few occasions, rather too close for our liking.

Ten days after the crash-landing, the two Canadian crew members, Hare and Chappell had the misfortune to become separated during an attempt to steal water from an Italian truck. Forced to escape a skirmish[114] situation, they departed from the remaining crew, unable to regain contact. During their further attempts to get urgently needed water, the Italian forces chased them away like local thieves. Lucky to have escaped, a further discussion took place that resulted in the two Canadians seeking help from a small Arab village, where the Bedouins gave them directions to the Quattra depression,[115] where they were arrested by an Italian patrol. Transported to an Italian prisoner of war camp in North Africa, both men were then moved to another Italian prisoner of war camp at Sulmona. Hare and Chappell managed to escape at the time of the Italian capitulation in 1943 – in effect the Italian guards abandoned the camp. Both men eluded the efforts of the German forces in capturing the escaped prisoners of war. Assistance

Late Arrivals wearing escape clothing, having reached allied lines. The Canadian pilot, Chappell is in the centre and the navigator, Hare on the right.

from Italian farmers enabled Hare and Chappel to make contact with the allied forces several weeks later. Hare subsequently arrived in the UK on 30 October 1943, closely followed by his fellow Canadian crew member, who later made three simple entries within his flying logbook: 'Captured August 16, 1942. – Escaped September 12, 1943. – Safe October 19, 1943.'

Returning to the other crew members of Wellington HF833, Alexander Barras, Raymond Warwick, Les Jones, and Jim Shirra; Raymond recalled:

Our feet gave us lots of trouble, we had lots of blisters to be attended to. We walked roughly 450 miles and the trip took us 22 days of solid walking. We were all very happy guys when we sighted our own lines and joined our troops, for a while they could not make out what we were as we were all very dirty, not having shaved or washed. Our clothes and ourselves were all the same colour. We could hardly walk, the good food and drink took getting used to again. For a day or so we could not eat a thing that is to hold it down at all. We were put in the hospital for a week and brought us back to ourselves again.

Raymond later said:

Late Arrivals membership badges.

I am in Cairo on leave, the best I have had. I thought I could drink gallons of beer when we were back in the desert walking, we all thought we could, but when we came to it we found differently, we just can't take it, a bottle of beer and I'm done, just can't force any more down, rather a tragedy. When I first arrived I had lost over 2 stones in weight, we are doing fine with eating, heaps of eggs and chicken, fruit salad and ice cream. Our navigator Cliff and Chris I am sorry to say are no longer with us, we lost them in the desert.

When in Cairo, Raymond located a copy of the book, *They Flew Through Sand*. On page 146 a representation of the Late Arrivals Club membership certificate was shown. He wrote his personal details on the page; where his squadron, name, and date of incident were to be placed. In the margin was found the signature of the honourable secretary of the Late Arrivals Club, Sqn Ldr G.W. Haughton. He was the author of the book concerned and also the senior RAF press relations officer in the Middle East. Haughton had himself designed and commissioned the metal winged-boot badges that were awarded to members of the Late Arrivals Club. The amazing 450-mile trek across the desert was recognised with immediate membership to the club for Raymond and his crew.

One of Raymond's crew members, Sgt Alexander Edward Owen Barras, RAAF 458 Squadron, was recommended for the Military Medal[116] for his leadership in negotiating the survival of the four men across the desert. Barras was the first Royal Australian Air Force recipient ever to be given this award. The remaining crew members were 'mentioned in despatches' for their part in what was truly a most incredible feat of endurance and survival by any aircrew operating over the deserts during the Second World War.

CHAPTER 20

WO R. G. Faux, wireless operator – Goldfish Club

Enlisting into the RAFVR in early 1940, Faux was issued with service number 1202848. He was selected for aircrew training and qualified as a wireless operator. Faux also trained in air gunnery and would later wear the WAG (Wireless Operator Air Gunner) aircrew brevet on his uniform.

Faux's initial service took place within Bomber Command at RAF Yatesbury and Bitteswell. He received a posting to 619 Squadron at RAF Coningsby, where he joined a crew captained by Flt Lt Jones, an experienced pilot who had been awarded the DFM[117] with 106 Squadron previously.

Operations flown by WO Faux consisted of attacks upon Berlin, Munich, Nuremberg, and the important large-scale raid upon Hitler's rocket base at Peenemunde[118] on 17 August 1943. The following month saw 619 Squadron partake in a joint operation to attack the Antheor Viaduct near Cannes. This was an important coastal railway and road route between Italy and France. The viaduct was a large structure bridging two high peaks. In close proximity, there was a further section where the railway and roadway joined above a smaller solid bridge construction. Both were regarded as key targets for destruction. The renowned 617 Squadron supplied eight Lancasters, and 619 Squadron four. Faux was a crew member in Lancaster EE106, which took off at 8.06 p.m. on 16 September 1943. With such an experienced crew, confidence was high within the aircraft. In addition to the highly skilled skipper at the front, sitting in the rear gunner's position was Sgt Cartwright a DFM,[119] recipient who had previously served within 106 Squadron.

Antheor Viaduct was a difficult target to attack, a fact reflected by the squadrons chosen to be deployed by Bomber Command. Anti-aircraft guns were positioned upon the mountain terrain, providing excellent vantage points for the gunners. During the approach to the target, the Lancaster EE106 sustained significant hits from accurate anti-aircraft flak. Having

Reconnaissance photograph showing the undamaged target taken four days after WO Faux's mission.

assessed the damage, Flt Lt Jones prepared the crew for a ditching in the sea just west of central Portugal. Those words 'prepare to ditch' were not what the crew wanted to hear, but the ditching was successful, with enough time available to approach the sea in the best position possible. The emergency liferaft operated correctly, enabling the entire crew of seven to escape from the aircraft with no meaningful injuries. Even though the ditching took place at night, the navigator knew the approximate position of the stricken aircraft, and that neutral Portugal lay just due east of their position. In the morning, Portuguese fishermen sighted the life raft, and following a cautious approach, rescued the crew.

Faux and his crew,[120] FO S. Jones DFM, Sgt A. Brookes, FO Holding, Sgt G. Deschaine, Sgt C. Cook, and PO A. Cartwright DFM, all survived. The

Right: Goldfish Membership Badge.

Below: Goldfish Club Membership Card, designed by Charles Robertson.

protocol of internment[121] took place, but the entire crew were returned to the UK within a few months. After application to the Goldfish Club, Faux was sent his membership certificate and badge.

The photo reconnaissance sortie, undertaken four days after the raid, indicated no damage to the viaduct or the smaller bridge construction, which lay just east of the primary target. 617 Squadron returned to attack the viaduct on 11 November 1943. Once again, only minor damage was able to be inflicted by the nine Lancasters that took part. Undeterred, the squadron returned to the same target on 12 February 1944. Ten Lancasters dropped the 12,000 lb Tallboy bomb, again with no direct hits, and those which were in close proximity to the viaduct did not cause any serious damage. Barnes Wallis had designed the Tallboy to function in such a way that a penetration of the bomb adjacent to targets like Anthcor would suffice to cause serious structural or catastrophic damage. This particular viaduct proved to be a most difficult target to destroy, even for the amazing Barnes Wallis and 617 'Dambuster' Squadron.

Faux continued to serve within Bomber Command and completed his operational tour of duty. On completion of his war service he was awarded the 1939-45 Star, Air Crew Europe Star, and the War Medal. This combination of medals was issued to a great many members of Bomber Command, but only a select few were able to display the Goldfish Club badge alongside them.

CHAPTER 21

Flt Lt A. E. Hacking, pilot – Caterpillar & Late Arrivals Clubs; Sgt Bradley & Sgt McFarlane

On 6 September 1942, Halifax bomber W7679, piloted by PO Alan Hacking of 10 squadron, led a formation of three aircraft to bomb Heraklion airfield, Crete. The crewmembers were:

RAF Flt Lt Hacking, captain pilot
RCAF PO Turner, navigator
RAF Sgt J. Bradley, wireless operator air gunner
RAAF 404537 Flt Sgt A. E. Carson, wireless operator air gunner
RCAF Flt Sgt W J. Porritt DFM, rear gunner
RAF Sgt J. W. McFarlane, flight engineer

W7679 made its run over the target and bombed in a shallow dive, pulling out at 7,000 feet. The starboard outer engine was hit by light flak at the end of the run and petrol was seen to stream away. Shortly after, flames appeared on the outer engine, and almost at the same time, the petrol stopped streaming out. The fire continued to grow as the pilot turned south onto course. After turning, the aircraft side slipped to port, which kept the flames away from the inboard section of the wing and fuselage. At this time the tail gunner, Sgt Porritt, was mistakenly seen by other crews to bail out of the rear turret. Soon afterwards, another parachute was seen to open, and later, just before the breaking up of the starboard wing, a further three parachutes were sighted. The crew of number 3 aircraft did not see a sixth parachute, but the crew of number 2 aircraft saw a single chute before the whole aircraft broke up in the air. The aircraft crashed in flames south-east of Kastelli Pediada.

Three members of the crew, Flt Lt Hacking (RAF), Flt Sgt Carson (RAAF), and Flt Sgt Porritt (RCAF), remained in the aircraft and died in the wreckage.

10 Squadron Halifax flown by Flt Lt Hacking .

Halifax Bomber receiving her 6th Bombing Mission Symbol.

These men were later interred in the Suda Bay War Cemetery, Crete. Both Sgt Bradley and Sgt McFarlane had successfully bailed out, evaded capture, and returned to Egypt safely. They confirmed that PO Turner was the only other crew member to bail out and that he had become a prisoner of war.

Sgt J. Bradley and Sgt J. MacFarlane not only evaded capture whilst returning to allied lines, but were able to put the time to good use to support the allies, and for this they were both awarded the Military Medal. The Military Medal was rarely awarded to aircrew personnel. Only seventy-four medals were awarded during the Second World War. Sgt MacFarlane and Sgt Bradley were two of four Military Medals awarded for service in Crete. The men gained membership of the Caterpillar and Late Arrivals Clubs, and were able to wear the insignia of both.

A joint citation for 568967 Sgt J. W. MacFarlane and 1057447 Sgt J. D. Bradley was published in the *London Gazette* on 20 July 1943:

> ... These airmen were wireless operator and flight engineer, respectively, of a bomber which was shot down over Heraklion on 5th September, 1942, 3 of the crew being killed and a fourth member taken prisoner. Sergeants Bradley and MacFarlane evaded the enemy, and a fortnight later, linked up with certain British organisers, but they were not content merely to remain passive and inactive until arrangements could be made for them to be evacuated. From October 1942, until he was actually evacuated on 14th February 1943, Sergeant Bradley operated a hitherto disused W/T set and made contact with R.A.F. Headquarters, Middle East, sending much valuable information. During the period he remained cheerful in all difficulties and shared, with other members of the organisation, in the trials of hurried night moves and constant hiding necessitated by the activities of German field troops and counter-espionage agents. He also proved invaluable in making friendly contacts with local inhabitants. Sergeant Bradley assisted the organisation in every way and voluntarily became an active and enthusiastic agent. Sergeant MacFarlane proved himself equally valuable, not only assisting Sergeant Bradley but giving continual and encouraging assistance to other wireless operators ...

Of the three crew members that lost their lives on the fateful mission on 6 September 1942, PO Hacking had been eligible to become a member of the Goldfish Club for a previous incident that had taken place on 11 September 1941, when he ditched his 10 Squadron Whitley Z6867 2 miles off Flamborough Head. The crew had been engaged upon a successful raid to Warnemunde, but the return trip to RAF Leeming saw the aircraft run out of fuel. The rear gunner suffered a broken left arm in the subsequent ditching, which was the only injury across the crew of five. The life raft was safely occupied and some 2 hours later the destroyer HMS *Wolsey* rescued the crew. Flt Sgt Porritt had been awarded the DFM at the end of May 1942, shortly before his death. The citation for his award confirmed his courage in the face of the enemy:

> ... F/Sgt Porritt has displayed great skill and coolness in combat. During a daylight attack on the German battle cruisers Scharnhorst and Gnehenau, his aircraft was attacked by four Messerschmttt 109's. Using his guns most effectively, F/Sgt Porritt shot down one of the attackers in flames, probably destroyed another, and warded off the remaining two until fighter assistance arrived. In the encounter F/Sgt Porritt was wounded in the face and arms. One morning in May 1942, whilst returning from an operation over Germany, he engaged a Messerschmitt 109 from close range. Following a well-directed burst of fire, the enemy aircraft was observed to plunge vertically towards the ground, where, a few seconds later, it apparently burst into flames. On both these occasions this airman undoubtedly saved his aircraft from destruction.

CHAPTER 22

Sgt Allaway RAF, rear gunner – Late Arrivals Club

The desert campaigns provided a unique geographical situation to aviators in the Second World War. Aircraft were frequently covering great expanses of desert between operational bases and intended targets. Should reason present itself by mechanical failure or damage inflicted by enemy flak or aerial combat, compelling an aircraft to force- or crash-land into the desert, these unfortunate men were faced with very few options for survival. Walking back to reach allied lines was in many cases the only option available.

Sgt Allaway, an air gunner operating in 38 Squadron, was one of the few entitled to wear the winged-boot badge that confirmed his membership of the Late Arrivals Club. This young non-commissioned officer had volunteered to fly as aircrew at the earliest opportunity. Training for his chosen trade took place at 8 Gunnery School, Hamstead Norris, Berkshire, with continuation of training within A Flight,[122] 15 Operational Training Unit, situated not far from the Gunnery School. The OTU training took place in order to train crews for overseas operational duty in the Wellington bomber. Between 17 September and 16 October 1941, a total of thirty-three training flights were undertaken.

With a confirmed posting to operate in the Middle East, Sgt Allaway joined the ME Flight, becoming the rear gunner to a crew captained by a Sgt Webb. On 5 November 1941, the crew were allocated Wellington Z1045 and the aircraft was to be flown to Portreath and then onwards to Gibraltar. Some 2 hours into the flight, Sgt Webb was forced to return, probably due to a mechanical fault. It was not until 13 December that the same route was negotiated again, and this time the delivery flight progressed with no problem. The following day, Wellington Z1045 left Gibraltar for Malta, and then on to Fayoum, Egypt.

The crew of Wellington Z1045 joined the strength of B Flight 38 Squadron, but the aircraft itself left for another unit. Sgt Allaway got to be the regular rear gunner to a new skipper, Sgt Holdsworth, whilst Sgt Webb became his second pilot. Operations were scheduled to take place from an airstrip identified as LG09[123] at Bir Koraiyim, Egypt. The first operation was to be a lengthy one – 8 hours and 10 minutes on a night raid along the Ageila Road on 26 January 1942. The year started swiftly for Sgt Allaway, with further night raids upon Benghazi and the dropping of mines in Benghazi harbour. The dangers of flying in the Desert Air Force presented themselves to Sgt Holdsworth and his crew on 4 March, when a violent electrical storm struck near Derna. Benghazi was once more the target, but they were forced to abandon the operation due to the ferocity of the weather conditions. When operational, 38 Squadron flew from LG09; when not engaged in operations, they returned to what was known as 'base', in Shallufa, towards central Egypt. Sgt Holdsworth managed to reach LG09 after the encounter with the storm. The following day, the crew returned to base, where Wellington Z9110 was checked fully for serviceability. Bombing raids to the island of Crete and the Berka aerodrome brought a change to the Benghazi run (as it became known to the many crews who consistently attacked that target).

April 1942 commenced with some bad luck for Allaway's crew. On 2 April, when again attacking Benghazi, Wellington X9738 was struck by flak that broke a hydraulic oil pipe. Once again, Sgt Holdsworth managed to return after an 8 hour and 40 minute-flight, landing safely at LG09 without the ability to use any flaps.[124] Five nights later the crew were not so lucky. They commenced another Benghazi raid, this time flying in Wellington AD604. The squadron records identify AD604 taking off from LG09 at 10.32 p.m. on 7 April. The following entry was recorded:

> F/Sgt Holdsworth and crew aircraft 'U' did not return to LG09 from operations. However he sent his identity at 0433hrs so it is hoped that he has forced landed and is safe.

No further reference relating to AD604 can be found within the operational records. The events that took place were later explained within two documents, the first written by the commanding officer of 38 Squadron, Wg Cdr Chaplin,[125] on 15 April.

Ref: 38S/C.904/55/PI
Sir.
    Loss of Wellington Aircraft AD604 on Operations 7/8 April 1942

I have the honour to submit a report further to my signal FCA 36 dated 9 April 1942 on the loss of the above mentioned aircraft.

The aircraft took off from LG09 at 2240 hours for a raid on Benghazi. It was carrying a bomb load of 8 x 250lbs A.S. and 1 x 500lb G.P. totalling 2,500lbs and a petrol load of 750 gallons. The Captain was number 1051654 Flight Sergeant Holdsworth T.A. At 0350 hours the 'Operation Completed' signal was acknowledged by QUOTAFIYA[126] the aircraft had left the target at 0330 hours. The identification signal was received at 0433 hours. At 0500 hours the aircraft requested a QDM[127] from QUOTAFIYA which was not able to give a QDM because the strength of the aircrafts transmission was too weak. At 0523 hours another QDM was requested but the strength was still too weak. Kabrit however took a snap bearing of the aircraft 281 degrees. At 0527 hours another request for QDM was made but QUOTAFIYA stated that strength was still too weak.

Over certain areas of the Western Desert a fog had arisen. LG09 was in fog and aircraft diverted to other landing grounds. It is presumed that this aircraft either tried to make a forced landing in the fog or mistook the fog for low cloud and crashed into the ground. From the above signals information the aircraft should have been in the SIDI BARRANI area when the final request for a QDM at 0540 hours was made. There was a fresh Westerly Wind.

I have the honour to be Sir
Your Obedient Servant.

This official account was based upon little evidence bar radio communications, which at the time, were very poor. Sgt Allaway was himself able to provide a survivor's account of events, in an undated document that compiles information supplied by members of Wellington A604 crew:

Hit by flak over Benghazi which evidently did more damage than was first imagined.

Holdsworth flew back to near base when handed over to Sergeant Webb. Still approx. 4000 above cloud.

Navigator asked pilot to come through low cloud base in order to position from beacons. Cloud base 500 ft.

Flying at 500 ft. starboard engine cut and caught fire. Webb corrected the swing losing height, could not see the ground and did not realise how near they were, with the result they hit the ground unprepared.

Upon contact the aircraft broke in two. Level with the rear of the bomb bay, the front part somersaulted, tearing the front turret away and caught fire. At this time the 2nd pilot was in the pilots' seat, front and rear gunners were in their turrets, while the captain, navigator and wireless operator were in the body of the aircraft.

Sergeant Webb was dazed in the crash and found himself thrown clear of the aircraft and noticed the front gunner still in his turret only a short distance from the blazing wreckage. Although in pain he pulled the front gunner clear and then proceeded to render the same service to Sgt Allaway in the rear turret. It was impossible to give any assistance to the three N.C.O's in the blazing forepart of the plane.

At dawn having walked as best possible through the desert it was noted that a telephone line ran across the desert and although Sergeant Webb was still in considerable pain- Medical report has now revealed that he had suffered a spinal injury- He made his way to the line and was found by a linesman of the Royal Engineers at about 1400 hours that day. An ambulance was summoned and the three airmen taken to 14 Casualty Clearing Station from where they were transferred to New Zealand Hospital Mersa Matruh. Sergeants Allaway and Rothwell are now patients at 27th General Hospital and Sergeant Webb at 19th General Hospital.

The crew of Wellington AD604 was comprised of:

1051634 Flt Sgt T. A. Holdsworth, captain
1377443 Sgt J. C. Webb, 2nd pilot
928125 Sgt J. R. F. Mann, navigator
1381392 Sgt E. C. Fiorini, wireless operator
953947 Sgt A. Rothwell, front gunner
634375 Sgt S. R. Allaway, rear gunner

Sgt Allaway's flying logbook recorded the following information, as written by him:

7/4/42 – AD604 – Rear Gunner – Operations Bombed Benghazi Starboard Engine Cut and Caught Fire Crashed Landed 30 Miles South West Sidi Barrani At 0500 Contacted Maintenance Section of R. Corps of Signals After Walking Since Dawn.

Having returned to their own lines by various means, which included walking despite the injuries sustained, Sgts Allaway, Fiorini, and Webb became eligible for membership to the Late Arrivals Club. The crew members who died were later buried in the Hafaya Sollum War Cemetery, where their graves are still tended today by the Commonwealth War Graves Commission.

Sgt Allaway's injuries were significant. He was not able to resume operational duties for five months. He returned to 38 Squadron, and on 10 September 1942, he boarded a Wellington bomber once more, climbing into his rear turret for an operation to drop two parachute mines in the harbour at Mersa Matruh. Both mines were dropped in the eastern section of the harbour, making the raid successful. They returned safely after 6 hours and 35 minutes in the air. Sgt Allaway required further medical treatment for the injuries from the crash, so it was only a matter of a few weeks before he returned to England.

It was not until another year had passed that he once again took to the rear gunner's turret of an aircraft, wearing the rank of flight sergeant. It was a Warwick, a large twin-engine aeroplane, not designed to carry any bomb load. He was operating within A Flight of 280 Squadron, flying from RAF Thornaby on air-sea rescue sorties. The Warwick aircraft was able to fly long patrols over the North Sea in search of crashed aircrews who had ditched. These crews were highly likely to become eligible for membership of the Goldfish Club. Air-sea rescue sorties proved to be a difficult job, as the North Sea was a massive expanse of water, and survival conditions were not particularly high – especially in the rubber inflation rafts deployed from a ditched aircraft. The air-sea rescue squadrons were developed to locate such surviving aircrews and arrange measures to rescue the men or increase their chance of survival. The role of 280 Squadron was to locate and parachute-drop an airborne lifeboat, which was carried slung under the bomb bay doors. These rigid-build, substantial boats carried supplies and had means of propulsion by sail and engine. When dropped in close proximity to the rubber rafts, the crew were able to transfer into the airborne lifeboat. These measures saved a great many lives. Various other air-sea rescue squadrons operated in the vital role of spotting survivors and directing other rescue units to the right locations; these may well have been Walrus flying boats, or high-speed launches that operated along the United Kingdom's coast lines.

Flt Sgt Allaway spent many hours flying over the sea, wearing the badge of the winged-boot that signified membership of the Late Arrivals Club. His key role as a rear gunner was to defend the Warwick from attack by enemy aircraft. In addition, he scanned the miles of sea looking for any sign of the ditched aircraft or crews. He had survived a crash-landing in the desert, so the thought of ditching in the sea must have always been at the back of his mind. On his second sortie on the last day of January 1944, he recorded in his logbook the sighting of a dingy with four occupants. The Lindholme rigid lifeboat was dropped, parachutes operated correctly, and a successful landing on the water took place. Sometime later a high-speed launch reached the lifeboat and completed the rescue.

Another interesting event for Flt Sgt Allaway and his crew took place on 8 August the same year. The operational record book entry for the squadron quotes:

> Whilst on search at 1248 hours in position 5458N observed pyrotechnics and sighted Danish fishing vessel No.E311 with Americans on board. Aircraft signalled course to steer and dropped medical supplies and provisions which were picked up. Aircraft, when satisfied American crew on board dropped Lindholme dinghy, advised base escorting Danish fishing vessel with American crew on board. Advised by base fishing vessel getting near dangerous obstructions, halted vessel and homed HSL on booster, rescue effected at 1640 hours.

During his service in 280 Squadron, Flt Sgt Allaway had been promoted to the rank of pilot officer. Having flown a total of sixty-one air-sea rescue sorties and twelve bombing sorties at the cessation of hostilities, he had survived a grand total of 683 hours and 15 minutes of flying during his operations over the deserts of North Africa and the freezing expanses of sea from our shores.

CHAPTER 23

Flt Lt George Willerton DFC, pilot – Caterpillar & Goldfish Clubs

Flt Lt George Bertram Willerton was born in Keelby, near Grimsby, Lincolnshire, in 1917. Educated at Brigg Grammar School, he was a keen sports person and was selected to captain the school football team in 1934/35. Willerton joined the Royal Air Force Volunteer Reserve in 1939 in order to fulfill his aspirations of becoming aircrew. The recruitment was surrounded by images of the glamour and dash at that time, with officers flying assorted aircraft. In reality, however, war was imminent.

Having undertaken training and qualified as a pilot in 1940, Willerton was posted to 224 Squadron, part of Coastal Command, performing anti-submarine patrols in Hudson aircraft. Based at RAF Limavady, Northern Ireland, the squadron later moved to RAF St Eval, Cornwall, to fly patrols off Brest and to attack shipping off the Brittany coast.

On 27 January 1942 Willerton was undertaking a routine patrol over northern France when he engaged a shipping target. During the attack his aircraft was hit by anti-aircraft fire in the starboard engine. With only one engine he was able to fly the Hudson back over the English Channel, reaching south-west England, where the crew was forced to abandon the aircraft by parachute. Willerton's Irvin parachute deployed correctly, but Willerton suffered a very heavy landing on the rough ground of Dartmoor. His life had been saved by the use of the parachute, fitting the requirement to become a member of the Caterpillar Club. After receipt of the caterpillar pin, he wore it regularly; the pin suffered the loss of one amethyst eye, which Willerton never saw the need to replace.

FO Willerton continued with the squadron's work, undertaking anti-submarine sweeps and convoy patrols. A welcome interruption arrived on 25 June, when the squadron was called upon to make up the numbers for the third great 1,000-bomber raid on Bremen. Bomber Command required assistance from operational training units and Coastal Command squadrons in order to accumulate the significant aircraft numbers for these momentous raids.

Converting to the larger Liberators the following month, 224 Squadron found this aircraft much more suited to their needs. On 13 May, Willerton was the captain of a Liberator that engaged in a U-boat patrol over the Bay of Biscay. His crew that day was Sgt Hoad, Flt Lt Luke, POs Barnham and McCall, Flt Sgts White and Bell, and Sgt Garoner. In addition to the regular crew, they also had on board Lt Church, an observer from the Royal Navy. After taking off at 1 p.m. and commencing patrol, approximately 2 hours later they were attacked from all sides by five Luftwaffe JU88s. Willerton and his crew defended as best they could, but the Liberator was badly shot up, with an explosive shell striking her ammunition store and causing outbreaks of fire in the aircraft. With two engines out of action, the Liberator finally crashed into the sea. Although under water, Willerton managed to crawl through a side window to reach the surface. He spotted the aircraft's dinghy floating in the water and swam towards it. The dinghy had automatically deployed from the aircraft and inflated. Seeing Lt Church and PO Barham in the water, Willerton dragged them both into the dinghy. The three of them were the only survivors of the ditching, but Church's arm was badly broken. Barham attempted first aid, and dressed his other wounds with the basic first aid kit stored within the inflated dinghy. Tragically, Lt Church died of his injuries that night, and was buried at sea.

The following day Mrs Willerton received a telegram from the RAF advising her that her husband had been reported missing. This was followed on 16 May with receipt of a personal letter from 224 Squadron's commanding officer, reporting her husband's failure to return from operations.

Six days later, the Liberator's dinghy was spotted by an Australian Coastal Command Sunderland flying boat from 10 RAAF Squadron. The tiny dinghy was indeed fortunate to have been spotted by the vigilant crew of that aircraft which landed and picked up the survivors. Willerton and Barham were both in the last stages of exhaustion, having suffered a great deal from exposure, hunger, and thirst, and having survived on just thirty-six malted milk tablets and a bar of chocolate between them. These lifesaving rations were within the stored equipment in the dingy, but the men had been without water for the entire period. Weather conditions had deteriorated one night, with intense winds producing waves 30 or 40 feet in height.

Willerton and Barham had been in the dinghy a total of 139 hours and 45 minutes. A member of the Sunderland crew had a camera and took a picture of the two survivors in the dinghy, and once recovered they were flown to

Original photograph of
Flt Lt Willerton being rescued.

Plymouth. Tragically, PO Barham did not recover from the ordeal, and later died in hospital.

On 19 May Mrs Willerton received a telegram informing her that her husband had been rescued. FO Willerton supplied the information concerning the rescue that led to his membership of the Goldfish Club and the award of the Distinguished Flying Cross (*London Gazette*, 20 August 1943):

> Flying Officer Willerton was captain of a Liberator aircraft set on fire when attacked by five Ju.88s while on anti-submarine patrol over the Bay of Biscay. The aircraft was forced down onto the sea, but although underwater, Flying Officer Willerton managed to crawl through a side window, swim to a floating dinghy, and in a dazed condition pulled aboard two members of his crew with him, one severely wounded. Without first-aid equipment, he dressed his companion's wounds as well as he could, and then paddled the dinghy for six days before being rescued. For his outstanding courage and fortitude he is recommended for the award of the Distinguished Flying Cross.

Willerton received his DFC from the king at Buckingham Palace on 21 November 1944.

CHAPTER 24

Flt Sgt Frederick Hesketh DFM, flight engineer – Goldfish Club

Frederick Hannaford Hesketh was born in Liverpool on 24 June 1911. Tragedy struck Frederick at the age of just five, when his father, a police constable, died, having contracted pneumonia whilst on point duty. During his service in Liverpool, Frederick's father had been rewarded twice for bravery by the Liverpool and Shipwreck Society. The first incident was for stopping a runaway horse and wagon in a busy Liverpool street in 1913; the second was for a similar incident three years later. Following his father's death, Frederick and his family left Liverpool and moved to Devon, where Frederick was educated at Torquay Grammar School and South Devon Technical College. Interested in engineering, Frederick successfully gained a position with the local gas company as an engineering apprentice.

At the outbreak of the Second World War, Frederick volunteered for flying duties but was not immediately accepted. His position as a plant engineer at the gas company was judged vital for the maintenance of gas supplies. It was 1943 before he was called up for service with the RAFVR and selected for training as a flight engineer. His call up came quite unexpectedly, as Frederick was by then thirty-two years old, and the average age of under-training aircrew was just over twenty. By now the engineering experience he brought with him would have been clearly recognised as a distinct advantage for the task of flight engineer within Bomber Command.

After his initial training, and having gained the required qualifications, Frederick crewed up with PO Henry, a pilot of the Royal New Zealand Air Force, at number 1667 Conversion Unit at RAF Sandtoft. In early 1944 the crew undertook conversion upon the Handley Page Halifax bomber. Frederick was in charge of the four mighty Rolls Royce engines and all aspects of complex engineering upon the aircraft. In July 1944, having completed his training at 1 Lancaster Finishing School, RAF Helmswell,

Flt Sgt Hesketh's bombing raid on 6 July 1944 illustrating the dangers to bombers of being struck by bomb loads from above.

Frederick was posted to 12 Squadron, RAF Bomber Command, RAF Wickenby, in Lincolnshire. His first operation, on 6 July, should have been a gentle introduction, a 3-hour round trip in daylight to bomb a VI flying bomb site in Northern France. Eight aircraft took off from Wickenby; seven returned. One Lancaster had been hit by a bomb dropped from a higher altitude aircraft but managed to stagger back to England at low altitude with a Spitfire escort. The aircraft crashed at Faldingworth with the loss of three crew members.

Being struck by a bomb dropped above your own aircraft was not an uncommon threat to aircrews on bombing runs, and unfortunately it happened many times during the war, often resulting in the complete loss of an aircraft and its crew.

Frederick's second raid, on 26 July, was against one of the best defended targets in Germany, the province of Stuttgart. It proved to be a successful

Bombing V1 rocket sites in
France, July 1944.

operation for the crew, and was their first deep penetration into Germany.
On their return, the crew of Lancaster Y-York were trapped by searchlights
over Normandy and subsequently hit by flak. The mid-upper gunner was
wounded by shrapnel. The first two operations had not been simple or
uneventful for Frederick. And the very next was to provide experience of an
even great threat to bomber crews flying over Germany. Frederick's aircraft
went back to Stuttgart and was attacked three times over the target by
night-fighters. Frederick witnessed the horrors of the Luftwaffe destroying
Lancasters, but, thankfully for his crew, they returned with no casualties.

The following eight operational flights were typical of the tasks undertaken
by Bomber Command in the late summer of 1944. Short daylight raids on VI
sites in France, attacks against troop concentrations (supporting the breakout
from the Normandy beach head), the destruction of oil refineries, and two
long flights to the Baltic to destroy the port and factory areas of Stettin.

Bomber Command crews were frequently superstitious. Operation number thirteen for Frederick turned out to be a 4-hour daylight trip to a V1 rocket site at St Ricquier. The crew was slightly reassured, as the Lancaster they were flying in was their favourite, Q-Queen. On reaching the target, the predicted flak was unexpectedly accurate. The elevator trimming tab control wire was severed and the aircraft became difficult to handle. To add to concerns, the bomb release mechanism failed on the bombing run. PO Henry turned to have another try across the target, while Frederick struggled to repair the cable and free the hung-up bombs. By now the aiming point was obscured by dust and haze, and the master bomber ordered Lancaster Q to take his bomb load back to England. Setting the big aircraft back down onto the runway, with damaged controls and a 6-ton bomb load on board, would quite understandably have raised some concern for the crew. Q-Queen spent three weeks undergoing repairs. The trust imparted by the crew on their favorite Lancaster had been more than repaid. September 1944 continued with demanding operations into Europe. Frederick and his fellow crew members flew both day and night missions into northern France, Cap Gris Nez, Calais, and Le Havre. Industrial cities in Germany, including Frankfurt, Neuss, and Saarbrucken, were also targeted. The crew's confidence grew immeasurably when their favourite Lancaster Q returned from repairs.

Duisberg was to be the twenty-second operational flight for Frederick. Queenie lifted off the runway at Wickenby and started the slow climb toward the coast and North Sea. This was a 'maximum effort' daylight attack, and 12 Squadron had twenty Lancasters in the air. They were led by Wg Cdr Stockdale, who had a passenger on board, the famous war correspondent Richard Dimbleby.[128] Flying in a loose formation, the Lancasters strained for altitude, each one carrying the maximum bomb load.

Queenie got into trouble 8 miles out from the coast. The port outer engine caught fire, which quickly spread across the entire port wing. The other crews, and no doubt Richard Dimbleby, observed and reported the blazing aircraft crossing their path as PO Henry gingerly turned Queenie back towards the coast. He was carrying a 4,000 lb 'cookie' and 1,278 small incendiary bombs. At the frighteningly low altitude of 800 feet he jettisoned the entire load. The pilot must have felt his silent prayer had been answered when the blast from the exploding cookie failed to tear the aircraft wings off. Their height of 800 feet was far below the recommended minimum jettison altitude, but he had no choice. Queenie was forced to perform a ditching. The pilot and flight engineer nursed the blazing wreck down toward the sea, which was being whipped up by a 30-knot south-westerly wind. The understanding between pilot and engineer was vital at this stage if the crew were to have any chance of surviving the impact. Just 30 minutes after take-off from RAF Wickenby, and with flaps inoperative, Queenie smashed into the waves at 120 knots. The fuselage broke in half, the dinghy inflated automatically and the eight men scrambled quickly into it, as Queenie slid beneath the surface. The large survival rubber dingy manufactured by P. B. Cow had yet again provided a means of survival for aircrew ditching into the sea. They were rescued by a high-speed launch from Mablethorpe 1 hour and 30 minutes later. The successful survival of the crew by the use of the dingy had qualified them all to join as members of the Goldfish Club. Frederick and his fellow crew members would now be able to stitch the embroidered badge onto their battle dress tunics.

A short survivor's leave provided a well-earned rest for the crew, who returned to operations two weeks later. Three quick trips were undertaken to the Ruhr, nicknamed by aircrews as 'Happy Valley'.[129] The last to Düsseldorf proved to be an eventful one, with Frederick's aircraft being coned by searchlights and approached by night-fighters. That was nothing compared to the next operation on 16 November, however. It was a daylight raid, with Bomber Command and the USAAF supporting the advance towards the Rhine. The target for 12 Squadron was Duren. At 3.30 p.m., the bomber stream approached the town at 10,000 feet. Visibility was good and they flew closer to each other than was customary in order to give mutual support against fighters. Bomb doors were opened and the point of release had been almost reached when the Lancaster flying alongside Frederick erupted into a massive explosion.[130] All 6 tons of bombs detonated simultaneously, and the blast riddled Frederick's Lancaster across its length. The second petrol tank in the starboard wing was punctured and fuel streamed back along the fuselage, cascading over the tail plane, which had the potential to catch fire at any moment. The radar set blew up and caught fire, and the pilot's windscreen had been blown in; the 160-mph slipstream roared through the interior of the fuselage, with maps, charts, and equipment being destroyed by the ferocious winds. In the midst of this chaos, the starboard inner engine ground to a halt and the aircraft was bracketed by a salvo of anti-aircraft fire from a heavy flak battery below. FO Henry struggled to regain control as their Lancaster careered wildly across the path of other Lancasters in the bombing stream. With the aid of Frederick, the pilot succeeded in gaining some stability over the aircraft's altitude, bringing it back to a level flight and feathering the useless propeller. For the next 3 hours, the two men worked to keep the wreck in the air as they headed back to RAF Wickenby on three engines. They landed safely, having demonstrated another example of the teamwork that existed between pilot and flight engineer. It was a miracle that none of the crew suffered any serious injury.

Two days later Frederick was back in the air, but this was a very different task, testing a new Q-Queen aircraft. Frederick's operational tour of duty was nearing completion and he finished his remaining three raids: Aschaffenburg in late November, Karlsruhr on 5 December, and the Krupp's works at Essen on 12 December.

For his services, Frederick Hesketh was awarded the Distinguished Flying Medal. The *London Gazette* published the award on 23 March 1945 with the following entry:

> Flight Sergeant Hesketh has completed numerous operational sorties, many of them against heavily defended targets in Germany. On one occasion, shortly after taking off, an engine of the aircraft in which he was flying caught fire. As engineer he had to take instant action. Through his calmness and skill, he was able to aid his captain to such an extent that, although it was impossible to extinguish the fire, the aircraft was successfully crash-landed without injury to any member of the crew. When on another sortie, severe anti-aircraft fire rendered one engine of the aircraft unserviceable, and punctured one of the petrol tanks. Sergeant Hesketh prevented the damaged engine from catching fire and then proceeded to conserve the remaining petrol so skillfully that the aircraft was able to return to base. The sound knowledge possessed by this Flight Engineer, coupled with his courage and devotion to duty, are worthy of the highest praise.

The operational tour of duty that Frederick completed had been difficult, with luck definitely on his side on more than one occasion. The Distinguished Flying Medal and membership to the Goldfish Club served to remind him that, with every successfully completed tour of duty, there were many members of aircrew who failed to return, and very few who completed entire tours like he had.

Frederick was promoted to warrant officer and spent the remainder of the war as a flight engineer instructor. Released from the RAFVR in June 1946, he returned to the gas industry in Torquay, Devon.

CHAPTER 25

WO Norman Pawley DFM, wireless operator – Goldfish Club

Norman Jack Pawley enlisted into the Royal Air Force in July 1939. Aged just seventeen he volunteered to become aircrew. Wireless school was a challenge that he readily accepted, and his skill on the transmission keys was something that was instantly recognised.

Norman was posted into Bomber Command as a wireless operator air gunner with 15 Squadron, RAF Mildenhall, Suffolk. Operational sorties commenced in 1943, with raids in the mighty Short Stirling bombers to Dusseldorf, Krefeld, Aachen, Hamburg, and Essen. After just five operations over occupied Europe, his name appeared on a recommendation[131] for the award of the Immediate Distinguished Flying Medal. The recommendation explains the events that took place (reference AIR2/4986):

Sergeant Pawley 651401 has carried out five operational sorties totaling 26.03 hours as First Wireless Operator/ Air Gunner of Stirling aircraft. On the night of 24th/25th June 1943, Sergeant Pawley was a Wireless Operator on Stirling aircraft in Sergeant Towse's crew which was detailed to attack Wuppertal. When proceeding to the target just after crossing the Dutch coast, this aircraft was attacked by a Ju.88, the enemy being successfully destroyed. After bombing the target, the aircraft was hit five times by flak, eventually catching fire. The captain made a series of dives which eventually put the fire out but left a starboard engine u/s and damaged four petrol tanks from which petrol was lost. This left the aircraft with only 70 minutes endurance to reach England. Sergeant Pawley, the Wireless Operator/ Air Gunner of the crew, was called upon to give the maximum wireless assistance to the Navigator to provide accurate navigation in order that, if the possibility existed, the aircraft could be flown to England on what petrol remained. This he did in such a commendable manner that the aim was almost achieved. Owing to the loss of a large quantity of petrol it became apparent to the crew over the North Sea that the aircraft would have to be force-landed in the sea. Sergeant Pawley was then instructed to carry out a distress procedure with the object of obtaining assistance from the Air/ Sea Rescue Service. In doing this, his procedure was faultless and his coolness highly commendable. Having previously made contact with the D/F organisation, he realised that there was no necessity for unduly high priority for his signals, and no greater priority than 'Important' was ever used. This was done with the object of not congesting the M.F./D.F. services in the event of other aircraft also being in distress. When the crew were ordered to take up ditching stations, Sergeant Pawley remained on watch, transmitting signals in order that the D/F service could get the latest possible fix on his position and in order to identify his signals as coming from his aircraft. Only when the trailing aerial struck the water, thereby rendering further transmissions impossible, did he leave his post. When the aircraft was ditched, he was responsible for rescuing the injured Navigator and Captain of the aircraft and transferring them to the dinghy. Confident in the reception of his signals and the co-operation of the Air/ Sea Rescue Service and despite loss in the sea of all the ancillary equipment from the dinghy, he assumed command of the dinghy until an aircraft of the Air/ Sea Rescue Service located them and picked up the crew survivors. During the whole flight, the manner of the execution of his duty was an example for the whole of his crew and, during distress conditions, his courage, coolness, and devotion to duty, together with the realisation of the possibility of other aircraft being in distress, enabled the D/F Service and Air/ Sea Rescue Service to be put into action smoothly and promptly. He was responsible for the successful rescue of this crew from the sea. His coolness and courage were further revealed in the fact that, during the whole of the ditching and rescue, he retained possession of and brought ashore his confidential documents. I have no hesitation in strongly recommending this N.C.O. for the immediate award of the Distinguished Flying Medal.

Just five days after the publication of the DFM, Norman was back in the air with his skipper, Sgt Towse, to attack Essen on the night of 25 July 1943. The Stirling BK805 took off at 10.30 p.m. from the airfield at RAF Mildenhall. A BF110 night fighter, flown by Capt. Wilhelm Dormann,[132] engaged the Stirling, which resulted in the bomber crashing nearly 2 hours after take-off, at Osterwick, 14 km south-east of Ahaus.

Of the crew of seven, Sgt Towse DFM was killed, and the remaining six were taken as prisoners of war. Norman's subsequent prisoner of war MI9 debrief provides his story:

Above: WO Pawley's dingy rescue.

Left: WO Pawley's Irvin Caterpillar pin with DFM medal.

I landed in a forest on the outskirts of Essen and after burying my Mae West, parachute and harness, I set off walking. I walked for about half a mile to the edge of the forest and decided to hide until daylight when I could see the lie of the land and get my bearings.

At dawn on 27th July, I started walking in a westerly direction with the intention of getting to Eindhoven. After I had walked 20 kms, I saw an isolated cottage so I knocked on the door. The owner of the cottage asked me in and whilst he was giving me a meal – quite unknown to me – sent one of his children to fetch the police. A short while later I was arrested by a German policeman and marched down to the local village police station.

Whilst the police were telephoning the Luftwaffe authorities I asked if I could go to the lavatory. I was escorted there by a guard and once inside I climbed through the window and down the drain pipe. I then ran out through the courtyard of the police station, over a wire fence and into an orchard. I could hear voices so I ran into a tool shed and hid in a big box which looked just like a coffin. After I had been there ten minutes a German civilian came and told me to get out. He then took me across to his kitchen and pointed upstairs indicating that I was to go up there. I climbed up till I came to an attic and hid myself behind a large wardrobe in the corner. After half an hour I heard sounds of the house being searched and shortly afterwards the attic was entered and a search carried out. I was not discovered and remained standing behind the wardrobe for eight hours. At the end of that time the same German came to the attic and I managed to understand by the constant repetition of the word 'nacht' that he meant me to make my getaway that night.

At midnight I therefore walked downstairs. Luckily the front door had been left unlocked and I was able to walk out into the road. I walked all that night in a north westerly direction until 0800 hours when I hid in a field and went to sleep.

At dusk on 28th July I set off walking and after two hours I was arrested by a German soldier who was patrolling the area. I was taken to the frontier post near Bocholt where I was searched. I was then taken by car to Bocholt where I was put in a cell at the Police Station. I was kept there till the following morning when I was taken to Abwehr Headquarters and placed in solitary confinement. On the afternoon of 29th July I was taken to a local aerodrome and placed in a Luftwaffe cell. That evening I was taken by train to Dulag Luft.

Pawley was imprisoned in Dulag Luft, Oberursel I July 1943-August 1943; Stalag VIIA, Moorsburg, August 1943; and Stalag IVB, Muhlberg August

1943-April 1945, where his Camp Number was 83672. At the latter camp he started his effort to escape and return home:

> At Stalag IVB in January, 1944, I changed identity with 17611110 Private F.A.S.C. Watter R.A.O.C. for the purpose of escape.[133] I was sent on a working party in a wood factory making prefabricated houses at Chemnitz. I planned to escape with another member of the R.A.F. (P/O Davidson) who had changed identities with a South African army private.
>
> On the night of 10th January, 1944, P/O Davidson and I took the bars out of our hut in the lager. At midnight we climbed out of the window and after crossing a river got on to the main road. Our intention was to get to a railway marshaling yard in that area and jump a train going to Switzerland. We were equipped with food, maps and compasses[134] but had no civilian clothes or money.
>
> We set off walking north east to get to the marshaling yard but after two and half hours we were arrested by two German policemen and marched down to the local police station. We were then taken by car to the police station at Chemnitz where we were put in cells. The following morning we were collected by the military police and taken to the Divisional Headquarters in the Chemnitz area. Here we were briefly interrogated and sentenced to seven days solitary confinement.

Undeterred by his capture, Pawley made a second bid for freedom:

> In July, 1944 whilst on the working party at the Josef Wicks Spinnery near Chemnitz, I made another attempt to escape. This time I planned to escape with Sgt. G. Brown, R.A.F, who had changed identity with an army private. We had previously told Private Jones A.A. (Tank Corps) at the working party of our plan to escape. On the evening of 23rd July Sgt. Brown and I hid behind some bags of cement until dark. We then just walked out on the road with the intention of getting to Prague. We were not equipped with any escape aids or civilian clothes but had been given the address of a contact in Prague who would help us. We walked all night and hid during the day. We continued like this without incident for six days living on what we were able to find in the fields.
>
> On 29th July we skirted the town of Ave (in the Sudetenland) and were seen by about a dozen of the German Home Guard. Sgt. Brown and I immediately ran off in the opposite direction. But Brown unfortunately stumbled and fell and was captured. He was carrying the haversack containing our few rations

and personal kit. I managed to get away and after running for ten minutes hid under the trunk of a fallen tree. I lay there for half an hour till it was practically dark and then set off walking again. I walked all night and at 0800 hours on 30th July I slept for a couple of hours and then set off walking again. Owing to the fact that I had lost all my rations I decided that my only way was to jump a train and get to my destination as quickly as possible.

That evening at 2000 hours I came to a goods yard 10 kms north of Karlsbad. I remained hiding watching the trains shunting backwards and forwards for some time. I eventually saw one train that appeared to be heading south so I decided to board it. Whilst I was trying to climb onto the train I was seen by a couple of railway officials who accosted me and took me to the Station Master office.

I was then taken by car to Ave where I was put in a cell for one day. On 31st July I was taken by lorry back to the working party at Chemnitz. I was interrogated there and my true identity was discovered. I was then moved to Stalag IVB and put into the Punishment Compound where I was kept for two months. At the end of that period I served 17 days in cells.

Norman was liberated by Russian forces from Stalag IVB on 23 April 1945. He later made contact with American forces and was flown to England, via Brussels, arriving 31 May. Shortly after arrival, the MI9 debriefing process was undertaken; evidence secured from that report led to the award of a 'mention in dispatches'.

CHAPTER 26

WO Sidney McQuillan, wireless operator – Goldfish Club & Guinea Pig Club; Flt Lt R. Campbell

Sidney, known as 'Sid' throughout his life, was born on 9 September 1920 at Wombwell, Yorkshire. He was the only child in a family born and bred in Yorkshire, who expected him to find work in the coal pits. Despite the pressure on him to become a miner, he secured employment as a clerical clerk within the local pits. With the onset of the Second World War, and at the age of twenty, he decided to volunteer for service within the Royal Air Force. He wanted to fly, an ambition that he had harbored for a number of years. In December 1941, Sid passed the selection process for aircrew without difficulty. He was an educated and ambitious young man, two qualities that were to support him through his entire life.

Sid was selected for the position of wireless operator and began training at 4 Radio School, RAF Madley, in 1943, with the white flash upon his uniform side cap confirming his position as a student under training. Wireless operator training school hours were 8 a.m. to 6 p.m., six days a week. Most days were spent in Harwell Boxes, a contained area where students learnt Morse code, wore ear phones for the majority of the day, and learnt about radio theory. The transmitters were known as 1154 and the receiver was called the 1155. Aircrew students undertook this initial training for three months. Sid's first air experience took place on 27 June 1943, flying in a Dominie aircraft for 1 hour and 30 minutes. Between June and the end of August, Sid flew a total of 29 hours and 50 minutes. The flying logbook issued to Sid was beginning to be completed with regular entries almost on a daily basis. Between 20 September and 15 October, Sid's flying logbook recorded a further 38 hours in Anson aircraft. Various cross-country flying exercises took place, with Sid acting as the wireless operator under instruction. Training would normally run for eight months and would be completed by a Morse code and radio theory test, which, once passed, resulted in promotion to the rank

WO McQuillan, second from left, at 18 Operational Training Unit, 1943.

of sergeant. In the case of Sid, once in receipt of his promotion, he attended Number 10 Advanced Flying Unit, Dumfries, where he performed the role of second wireless operator on a number of cross-country navigation exercises. His logbook was marked, 'Very good pupil', on completion of the course. Sid was now able to wear the wireless operator's shoulder flash, as well as his half-wing brevet, neatly sewn onto his flying tunic. Aircrew other than pilots wore a brevet indicating their trade, e.g., air gunners 'AG' and navigators 'N'. During late 1943, wireless operators were wearing differing half wings. The newly adopted 'S' signaler's wing was established, replacing the old 'WOP' wireless operator variants.

As a fully qualified wireless operator, Sid was posted into 81 Operational Training Unit at RAF Ashbourne. On 21 December 1943, Sid flew in the heavy bomber Whitley aircraft for the first time. Various cross-country and testing routes were being flown by the newly qualified crews. Within his logbook Sid recorded his crew position as '1st Operator'.

On 23 December, Sid crewed with a pilot called Ralph Campbell, a Canadian skipper within the RCAF. This was the very first meeting between the two young men, and both had no idea that they would end up lifelong friends. The OTU course saw Sid fly with several skippers. Night flying sorties were undertaken in January 1944, requiring the logbook entries to be written in red ink. This custom immediately identified any operations or training conducted in darkness by all members of Bomber Command. Sid and his crew flew several high-level bombing sorties at night in the Whitley bombers, some in excess of 6 hours' duration.

That January, 81 OTU transferred from Bomber Command into 38 Group (Airborne Forces) to train pilots and crews the skill of glider towing, in readiness for the planned operations for D-Day. Twenty Horsa gliders were made available to the unit, with work also undertaken in 1665 Heavy Conversion Unit. This was the next destination for Sid, where he commenced training within the massive four-engine Stirling Bomber. February and March 1944 saw Sid fly several sorties but with an assortment of pilots. On 11 March, FO Campbell, with Sid as his wireless operator, took up a Horsa glider for a 1 hour 45 minute sortie – the start of many flights together. A crew was formed in preparation for an operational posting. Sid's flying time within his logbook had clocked up to 139 hours' daylight flying and 58 hours' night time. He was about to become operational, flying over occupied Europe.

Formed at Driffield on 7 November 1942, 196 Squadron was a night bomber squadron in 4 Group Bomber Command. The squadron moved to Witchford on 19 July 1943, flying Stirlings Mk III with 3 Group Bomber Command. On 18 November, following its move to Leicester East, 196 Squadron was transferred to 38 Group.[135] 196 Squadron had flown its last operational mission with Bomber Command on the night of 10 November.

During the remainder of the European war, 196 Squadron would carry out 'cloak and dagger' operations: Transport, glider-towing operations, and supply-dropping to resistance forces, the squadron was also deployed with drops of parachutists, and SOE[136] and SAS missions over occupied territories across Europe, frequently operating single aircrafts at very low level. Each full moon period was a busy time for SOE operations. These were highly secret operations flown at 200 or 300 feet, almost always in moonlight over the drop zones. 196 squadron became equipped with Stirling MK IVs, a version of the famous aircraft devoted to the 'cloak and dagger' operations but more vulnerable, with only one rear turret to defend itself, instead of three turrets as fitted to other Stirlings.

On 7 January 1944, 196 Squadron moved to RAF Tarrant, Rushton, and began flying night supply-drops to the French resistance. On 14 March 196 Squadron moved to RAF Keevil, along with other 38 Group squadrons.

Massed glider-towing training flights were frequently flow at the end of May, 38 Group Squadrons were fully trained and at readiness for operation 'Overlord', the D-Day invasion. The first 196 Squadron logbook entry for Sid took place on 31 March. A glider-towing sortie, the total of towing hours recorded had now reached 5 hours and 25 minutes.

The next opportunity for Sid to write in red ink was a container-dropping exercise on the night of 10 March. This was in preparation for the crew's first operational sortie on 13 June 1944. Carrying out a special duty operation 'Sunflower VII', which was a night dropping of twenty-four containers.[137] This operation was regarded as successful, with no enemy action observed and all five Stirling aircraft from 196 Squadron returned from France safely. On the last day of the month Sid and his crew conducted operation 'Townhall', another container-drop to an area near Caen, Normandy, France. Seven Stirlings delivered 168 containers and thirty panniers of various equipment and supplies. All aircraft and crews returned safely.

On 10 July 1944, Sid's Stirling lifted off the runway at 1.10 a.m. They were to deliver twenty-four containers and two packets to 'Scientist III', at a location in France. The two packages were unknown commodities; this was the only aircraft to drop on that particular drop zone during that particular night. It would appear that an average load of twelve containers would consist of:

Six Bren guns, plus 1,000 rounds per gun, with spares, and forty-eight
    empty magazines.
Thirty-six rifles with 150 rounds per gun.
Twenty-seven Sten guns, plus 300 rounds per gun, eighty magazines and
    sixteen loaders.
Five pistols, plus fifty rounds per gun.
Forty Mills grenades and detonators.
Twelve Gammon grenades with 18 lb attachments.
156 field dressings.
6,600 rounds 9mm Parabellum, with twenty empty magazines and 3,168
    rounds, 303 (with twenty empty) Bren magazines.

A typical load would be double this on each SOE drop zone. Each container had a parachute and was dropped from the bomb bay. Any packets or panniers were dropped through the escape hatch by the nominated crew member on each operation. Sid was frequently tasked with dispatching the packets and panniers through the hatch when low over the drop zone.

Drop zones were frequently identified by agents or reception units on the ground. Supplying the resistance was all low-level flying, as low as 500 feet across France, and identifying the dropping site by a signal from a solitary figure in some remote field or plateau, who used a lamp or torch. Once codes were exchanged successfully, three more lights would spring up in a line that identified the wind direction. The drop would be made from 150 to 200 feet, flying into the wind. On 18 July, a further operation was flown, identified as 'Stationer 164', a SOE contact drop. Twenty-four containers and one package were delivered. The operation was recorded as successful but the reception to the aircraft was noted as having been poor, clearly it was a dangerous task to perform. In France, significant efforts were taken by the German occupying forces to capture agents on the ground, and if possible, shoot the low flying aircraft from the sky. Evidence exists of traps being set to lure the aircraft down and deploy searchlights and flak to shoot down the vulnerable aircraft.

The friendship between the pilot, FO Campbell, and Sgt McQuillan grew as the tour of duty progressed. Despite the rank differential that prevented some social activity in the disciplined service life on station, both men frequently spent time together in the local pub. The regular crew at this time consisted of navigator FO Leadlay, air bomber FO Capes, flight engineer Sgt Dodds, and rear gunner Sgt Gladwin. August was to prove very busy for the crew. The first operation was another SOE delivery, 'Donald 64', delivered to a drop zone approximately 70 miles south-east of Paris. The rear gunner reported fighter activity shortly after crossing the coast, with one aircraft shot down. The following night the crew delivered a further twenty-four containers and one pannier to 'Jockey 28', a location situated some 40 miles south-west of Lyon.

A respite of operations over the next two days saw the crew training with fighter affiliation and further glider-towing training during the hours of darkness. Despite no operational towing, it was clear that such requirements were most likely in the near future.

On 10 August another SOE supplies-drop, coded 'Diplomat 12', took place 60 miles south-west from Nancy. The drop was not successful, with no reception or identification taking place over the drop zone, resulting in the containers not being dropped. Over Alderny island, searchlight and flak caused some concern. The Stirling landed at RAF Mildenhall as a precaution, and following rigorous checks, no damage was found. The next morning, the crew returned the aircraft to base, signed off as fit for further duties. The crews of 196 Squadron were operating in the various – and frequently changing – operationally fit aircraft. Despite no doubt having a favorite aircraft, little choice existed when selected for the operations rostered. A delivery of twenty-four containers and four packets to 'Marc 21' was required on 23 August. Three Stirlings took off no more than 30 minutes apart to deliver upon the same drop zone. The reception was good, and all deliveries took place without any incident.

That could not be said for the following operation, and a run of bad luck was about to strike Sid's crew. On 26 August, Stirling LJ836 was heading for a drop zone in Geneva. The flight engineer, Sgt Dodds, was fighting problems with the port outer engine, and when it finally failed completely, they had to return to base. Stirling LJ836 became unserviceable. The next night, operations were on again for the crew and they were rostered to fly Stirling EF311, with one other 196 Squadron aircraft, on a joint SOE delivery of forty-eight containers and six packets close to Amiens.

As FO Campbell reached the drop zone, an emergency jettison of the load took place as a result of the aircraft's port inner engine failure. At the low dropping height, such a loss in power could well have been catastrophic, but thankfully enough height was gained and the navigator worked hard to plot a direct course home. Sgt Dodds, the flight engineer, was once more fighting to regain the use of a lost engine. It would appear he was unable to feather the propeller[138] to the port inner engine, which caused serious problems to the progress of the Stirling. The port inner propeller was unable to be stabilised, and the continued wind milling[139] caused serious damage resulting in the propeller flying off and smashing into the adjacent port outer engine. The crew had reached a position some 45 miles off the south coast. Sid radioed the position of the aircraft and an emergency ditching was inevitably going to take place. With only the two starboard engines available to the pilot, it was going to require some serious skill and ability to ditch the aircraft upon the sea. That particular night provided no moon, and with no horizon visible, they were very much in the dark. Sid had issued the SOS and switched the Identification Friend or Foe (IFF) equipment to issue the distress signal. The flight engineer dumped as much fuel as possible to try and balance the aircraft.

At 2.10 a.m., and at a speed of about 100 mph, Stirling EF311 struck the water. The impact smashed the Perspex nose and water cascaded in the aircraft, sinking the front section some 5 or 6 feet under water. Sid McQuillan had not been strapped in, and the rush of water carried him straight out through the broken astro-dome situated above his position. He was deposited upon the fuselage, and saw that not far from him was a dingy that had auto-inflated the correct way up. Such was the mass of the Stirling that the fuselage settled on the surface of the sea, with the audible groaning of metal under stress producing strange noises. The skipper and then the other four crew members all joined Sid upon the airframe at a point where the nose section dipped into the sea. Having suffered a few minor injuries, together with the consumption of a mixture of fuel and sea water, the crew members climbed into the rubber dingy. A combination of luck and skill had saved them.

EF311 continued to be audible in her signs of distress, with water gradually taking her over. After several minutes the aircraft sank. The six men were now truly on their own, with darkness around them and waves increasing in size. One small advantage of survival existed, in that it was August and sea temperatures at that time of the year were more favourable.

As dawn arrived, and with a little light now enabling the captain to see his watch, he noticed that it had stopped at the point of impact upon the sea, 2.10 a.m. on 28 August 1944. This was going to be a day that they would all remember for the rest of their lives. The bomb aimer most certainly would, for it was his wife's birthday. The dinghy was being tossed about in a southerly wind, so the skipper and Sid sat on each side of the dinghy holding a rubber tarpaulin to act as a sail. This worked well, and soon they were being pushed south towards the English coast. The swallowing of fuel caused the navigator to be violently sick. With the time fast approaching 6 a.m., the effort of holding the large 8 x 2 foot-long sheet was taking its toll. Both men were straining to maintain the progress being made. After 2 hours, a small boat with two occupants was sighted, but despite shouting and waving to the men they were reluctant to approach. The survivors assumed the occupants of the small boat might have thought them to have been Luftwaffe pilots. Sid was prepared to try anything and shouted out to them in his Yorkshire accent the names of the entire Aston Villa football team. This did the trick; the small fishing boat joined them in an effort to assist. The fishermen explained how fortunate they were. It had been a narrow decision for them to go to sea as the conditions were poor. It was decided to try and return to Selsey in the fishing boat, so they boarded, but with all eight men aboard it was a tight squeeze. Within a few minutes the engine of the tiny fishing boat stopped working, and the oars were then used as the only means of progress.

At last, Selsey harbour came into sight. Sid and his fellow crew members had survived. They beached at around 8 a.m. No warmer reception could have been provided by the Sussex fishermen. The first task undertaken by the skipper was to locate the local post office. This was the only means available to telephone the base at RAF Keevil; it proved a difficult task but one that was eventually successful. Arrangements were made for the crew to be transported to RAF Tangmere, a short distance east from Selsey. An aircraft was dispatched by 196 Squadron to pick up the survivors that afternoon. The crew were immediately issued with survivors' leave, a procedure designed to recognise the endeavours and hardship associated with such experiences. Sid and this particular crew combination would never fly together again. They did all make application to become members of the Goldfish Club as a result of the ditching into the sea on 27 August 1944.

Newly promoted to the rank of flight sergeant, Sid and FO Campbell were not to fly together again for three weeks. This situation arose from the effects of the ditching upon the crew's navigator, Leadlay, and rear gunner, Gladwin. Both men were ten or more years older than the average aircrew age, at thirty-three and thirty-five respectively. Like the skipper, they were volunteers from Canada and members of the RCAF, so it was decided that both should return to Canada and be provided with honorable discharges.

Back on 196 Squadron, the old crew of Campbell, McQuillan, and Dodds required replacement crew members to become operational. At that time, the massive combined efforts connected with the operation from 17 to 23 September 1944, operation 'Market', Arnhem, were underway at RAF Keevil. With an incomplete crew they were forced to sit and watch the squadron's intense activity, and in addition, hear stories and experiences over Arnhem. This was to be a most frustrating experience, watching the following six sorties taking place. They were only able to join in on the seventh day of operations.

Market I: 17 September. 196 Squadron deployed twenty-five Stirlings towing gliders to capture three important bridges at Grave, Nijmigen, and Arnhem (196 had two tow ropes break). All the aircraft returned safe.

Market II: 18 September. 196 Squadron towed twenty-one Horsa gliders, two of which were released prematurely. All Stirlings again returned safe despite the anti-aircraft fire.

Market III: 19 September. Sixteen Stirlings took off to re-supply troops. Several Stirlings returned with flak damages, and sadly the first 196 Stirling failed to return, the crew bailed out having been struck by flak; only three survived.

Market IV: 20 September. Fifteen Stirlings for re-supply, 20 September was to be a very bad day for196 Squadron. Six aircraft never returned: Flak was more and more intense, but with great courage aircraft made very low drops for precise accuracy.

Market V: 21 September. Only ten aircraft could take off to re-supply troops engaged in Holland. Again flak was terrifying, but there were also now German fighters present, resulting in three more of 196's aircraft failing to return.

Market VI: abandoned. The weather was too poor for operations.

Market VII: 23 September. Thirteen aircraft took off, including Stirling LJ925, flown by FO Ralph Campbell for the last re-supply operations of troops by 196 Squadron. FO Campbell and Flt Sgt McQuillan's Stirling LJ925 sustained damage from light flak over Arnhem. Over the drop zone, three containers of the twenty-four being carried hung up and failed to drop, but the four large panniers were dropped successfully. Another Canadian, WO Bruce McGovern RCAF, had joined the crew as the rear gunner. The navigator's position was occupied by FO Peter Boddington RAF. LJ926 was in the air between 2.05 p.m. and 7.15 p.m. One aircraft was flak damaged and did not return.

Fifty-six glider towing missions were provided by 196, and fifty-six re-supply missions, during operation 'Market'. Twenty-five men were killed and eleven aircraft were lost due to heavy anti-aircraft fire and enemy aircraft combat. In addition to those losses were ten Royal Army Service Corp dispatchers, carried on the aircraft to enable the stores to be swiftly dropped over the tight time frame for the drop zones.

As soon as this major airborne operation had concluded, 196 Squadron prepared to be ready for other operations. All the 38 Group squadrons were redeployed on 9 October 1944, with 196 and 299 Squadron posted to RAF Wethersfield. The next operational entry made by Sid in his flying logbook was 'Draughts 6', another red ink SOE delivery on 24 October. Once more, there was no reception, which resulted in the load being returned to station.

Frequent glider-towing exercises took place during daylight, when no operations had been rostered. On 27 November eighteen containers and two packets were delivered to a venue described in the logbook as 'Operations as ordered'. This term is frequently seen in special duty squadron records. The latitude and longitude references placed the drop zone in central Norway. As 1944 drew to a close, the massive Stirling aircraft had caused the runway at Wethersfield to be in need of repair, so a move to RAF Shepherds Grove in Suffolk resolved this situation.

It was not until 14 February 1945 that Sid finally dropped bombs onto occupied Europe. The Stirling bomber had long since been removed from Bomber Command's first line of operational aircraft. There were of course exceptions, and that night in February saw 196 Squadron tasked with 'tactical bombing' of Isselburg in the Ruhr, Germany. Eighteen 500 lb bombs were carried, but only fifteen dropped, as a result of hang-ups in the bomb bay. Sid was slightly perturbed at having the Lancaster and Halifax bombers way above them on the bombing run, due to the Sterling having a significantly lower ceiling height by comparison. Danger was never far away; bombs from the higher aircraft had to pass the Stirling's en route to the target below. Despite this, spirits were high on returning to base. It had been a new and exciting experience for the crew, with a further operation rostered for 21 February.

In the days leading up to the second bombing operation, two of Sid's original crew members were struck by illness and detained in the sick bay. Thus the 21st required a real make up of 'odd bod' crew members surplus or otherwise available to fill the assorted vacant positions. The only two original members of the crew were the faithful friends, Sid McQuillan and Ralph Campbell.

That night, the Stirling LX126 took off from the Suffolk airfield carrying twenty-four 500 lb bombs. The target was identified as Rees in the Ruhr valley. Nine aircraft left 196 Squadron for the target. This was going to be a raid that would change Sid's life forever. The raid itself proved to be a 'piece of cake' the term used by aircrews indicating an uneventful operation. The return to Suffolk was uneventful, with the flight engineer confirming to the captain that the fuel load was excellent, some 400 gallons of fuel remaining, providing a large safety margin. After crossing the English coast the skipper switched on the navigation lights, as it was standing orders to do so and designed to reduce the risk of collision, with so many aircraft returning to the airfields over Central England, the wing tips and tail lights were advantageous to all in the sky.

Stirling LX126 was given permission to land, and on the approach, the runway lights were on as normal. With the undercarriage down and flaps deployed, the approach speed was reduced to approximately 135 mph. Sid's job was done and he waited for the last few minutes to tick down. With the aircraft at 600 feet altitude and no more than a minute or two away from touching down upon the runway, disaster struck from behind and on the port side, a cloud of sparks and a sequence of vibrations struck along the fuselage. The entire port side of the Stirling aircraft had received raking fire from a German intruder, and both cannon and machine gun fire had penetrated the length of the aircraft. The bomb aimer let out a scream identifying the German aircraft as a Junkers 88. Sid at the same time reported a fire within the aircraft. Fortunately, the machine gun fire had not hit any crewmember, or disabled any flying controls. The skipper made the decision to continue with the runway landing ordering the escape hatches to be opened. The presence of 400 gallons of fuel still in the tanks would have crossed his mind immediately but the order was received and the air bomber duly opened the hatch above the pilot's position, with Sid opening the astro-dome. The last time he had gone through that hatch was when they ditched in the sea.

The descent of the last few hundred feet provided enough time for the fire to take a significant hold. The pilot, navigator, bomb aimer and wireless operator were all forced by the torrent of flames to be squeezed into the cockpit area and in fact right against the skippers seat. The rear gunner was no doubt having his own problems as the fire progressed in both directions down the fuselage. Flames and fumes passed over the heads of the crew members as it tore towards the escape hatch. The control tower staff would have seen flames streaming up to 50 feet from the tail of the Stirling. At last the aircraft touched the runway, with its speed reduced as quickly as possible through the application of the brakes, unfortunately with the aircraft requiring correction, there was a delay in the crew members escaping. At this time, Sid had grabbed the fire extinguisher fixed to the fuselage. It had been an impulse action brought on by circumstances but the extinguisher was red hot from the flames and intense heat. Sid's hands were immediately seriously burnt, as the aircraft finally halted. The air bomber, Bassett, navigator, Boddington, and skipper, Campbell, immediately fell from the cockpit escape hatch, landing 22 feet below, and managed to run from the scene of devastation. Flight engineer Doug Vince and wireless operator McQuillan had chosen to run out upon the wing and jump that same 20 feet or more onto the runway below. Both of these men sustained horrific burn injuries. There was no sign of the rear gunner, WO McGovern, and nobody had heard anything from him during the entire episode.

The five surviving crew members were removed to the station hospital. WO McGovern had perished in the mid-section of the aircraft. Both Sid and Doug Vince were taken to the large RAF hospital in Ely on the following

These pages: WO McQuillan's fire ravaged Stirling.

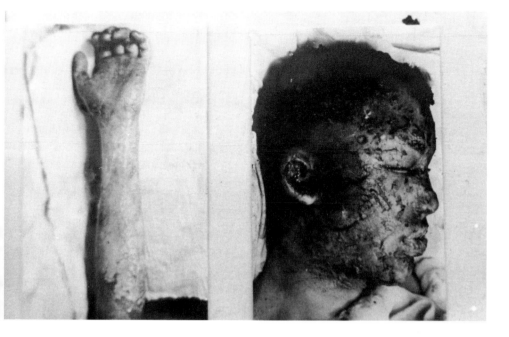

Above and right:: McQuillan's hospital photographs of burn injuries to both hands and face.

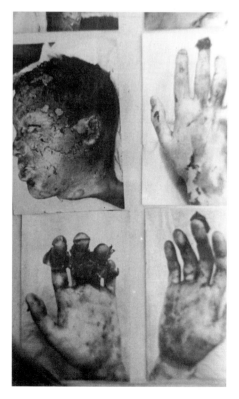

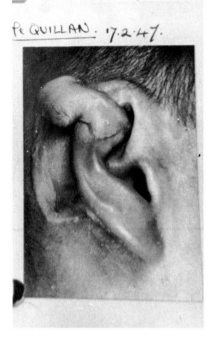

Mc QUILLAN . 17.2.47.

McQuillan's post war pedicle skin grafting.

day. The skipper, Ralph Campbell, was present when his close friend, Sid, appeared from the station hospital en route to Ely, his hands and face covered in bandages, with only two small slits open for his eyes. The journey to become a member of the Guinea Pig Club had commenced for Flt Sgt Sid McQuillan. It was a journey where bravery was compulsory, with untold pain and discomfort to be endured over months and years. Some solace would have been gained in that Doug Vince and Sid McQuillan were able to remain together. Both men were subsequently transferred from the RAF hospital at Marchwood Park to the small cottage hospital in East Grinstead, Sussex, where they were to undergo operations by the plastic surgeon Archibald McIndoe. The first thirty months after the accident saw a great many skin graft operations undertaken upon Sid, as did fellow Guinea Pig Doug Vince. Doug's skin grafts were more successful, and within a fifteen-month period he was able to return to his civilian life near Ipswich. Sid had to endure ten serious operations in East Grinstead between 1945 and '47.

Referring back to Sid's flying logbook, the last night operation entry written in red ink was made by a different hand for obvious reasons. It reads, 'Operations Bombing Rees 24 x 500 lbs. Shot up by JU88 in funnel. F.S McQuillan burned considerably. Aircraft landed in flames.'

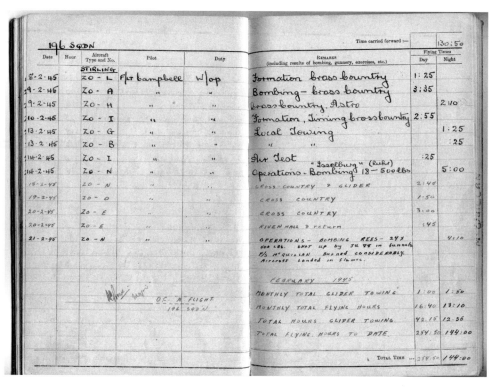

McQuillan's Flying Logbook.

Ralph Campbell survived with no injuries. He continued his tour of duty with a new crew formed around him, including one old crew member, flight engineer Ted Dodds. They were to tow gliders operationally during the Rhine crossing. Ralph was now promoted to the rank of flight lieutenant and recommended for the Distinguished Flying Cross, with a bar being added subsequently. King George VI was to present the medals at Buckingham Palace on 13 July 1945. Ralph was allowed to take two guests. An immediate enquiry to Sid McQuillan confirmed that he was between one skin graft and the next. Ralph was overjoyed that his best friend, who had endured the ditching and ensuing shooting-down episodes, could be with him. The DFC recommendation:

This officer has completed numerous sorties and has invariably displayed a high degree of courage and devotion to duty. On one occasion, in August 1944, en route to the target, engine trouble developed. Nevertheless he went on to reach the target. Whilst over the sea on the homeward flight the propeller

WO McQuillan's Guinea Pig and Goldfish Club membership badges.

Membership Card

This is to Certify that

F/Sgt. S. McQuillan

has qualified as a member of the Goldfish Club by
escaping death by the use of his Emergency Dinghy on

August 27th, 1944.

Signed

CHARLES A. ROBERTSON
Hon. Secretary

McQuillan's Goldfish Membership Card signed by the club secretary.

Guinea Pig Club members with Sid McQuillan sitting middle left.

of the defective engine flew off. It fouled a second engine, rendering it useless. The aircraft could no longer be flown but Flying Officer Campbell brought it down safely on to the sea. He displayed resolution characteristic of that which he has shown throughout his tour of duty.

Since being awarded the Distinguished Flying Cross, this officer has participated in numerous attacks against the enemy including the airborne operations against Arnhem. In March 1945 he took part in an airborne mission east of the Rhine. When setting course over base the port inner engine failed. Although the airspeed was affected, Flight Lieutenant Campbell continued his mission and by skilful flying maintained height and eventually released his glider at the correct landing zone with the minimum loss of time. His consistent good work together with his keenness and determination has set a fine example to all.

It should be noted that the recommendation makes no reference to the traumatic incident on 21 February 1945. Ralph had obtained copies of the Air Ministry photographs showing the fire destruction upon their Stirling; the rear gunner's position, where WO McGovern failed to escape, can be seen in them. The fuselage is also visible, with significant distortion caused by the heat of the fire. Sid kept his copies as evidence to his narrow escape.

Sid suffered significant trauma in his life, with the serious burns suffered in trying to save other members of his crew, and the loss of his beloved first wife in childbirth. His unborn child and wife were buried together, and it always remained his desire to be reunited with them.

Sid explored a new life and later married again, only for that union to be separated in tragic circumstances. His second wife died during a Guinea Pig reunion in Canada, whilst visiting his skipper and best friend, Ralph Campbell. Sid and Ralph did later share the experience of finding out that their ditched Stirling EF311 had been found. Divers located the aircraft resting on the sea bed, 60-70 feet below the surface in 1987. The aircraft was still essentially intact, and resting the correct way up for divers to investigate. In 1992, the RAF Sub-Aqua Association at Brize Norton undertook a dive upon EF311 to take photographs and assess the wrecked aircraft.

On 28 December 2008, Sid McQuillan passed away after lapsing into a coma. He died on the same day as his father's passing. The long-held instructions to have his ashes reunited with his first wife and child were carried out. It was the author's privilege to have known Sid.

CHAPTER 27

WO Donald Norman, wireless operator – Goldfish Club

WO Donald Norman served as a wireless operator air gunner within Coastal Command, and was based at Pembroke Docks in 228 Squadron.

Flying operations in the extraordinarily large Sunderland,[140] primarily on anti-submarine patrols, Donald and his crew were actively seeking contact with the many German U-boats operational from the U-boat pens at Brest, Bordeaux, Lorient, La Pallice, and St Nazaire in 1943. At that time, it was estimated that over 100 U-boats were constantly at sea, regularly claiming allied shipping kills. Winston Churchill had voiced his concern over the consistent losses of allied shipping, U-boats were regarded as high priority targets, which required massive efforts to both locate and destroy. The requirement for the submarines to run on the surface in order to charge their batteries provided slim opportunities of offensive action by the aircraft within Coastal Command.

On 31 May 1943, Donald was a member of FO French's crew, flying in Sunderland DD838. They became engaged in an attack upon a U-boat with another Sunderland from 10 RAAF Squadron and a Halifax from 58 Squadron. The target was in the Bay of Biscay, south-west of Brest. Although the 10 Squadron Sunderland had damaged the U-boat, it was still afloat and appeared capable of steering. FO French continued the attack, releasing four depth charges on each of his two bombing runs. U563,[141] which had sunk seven ships and damaged a further four, was sunk as a result of these final attacks by Donald's crew.

On 2 August, Donald and his crew, captained by FO Hanbury, conducted an anti-submarine patrol north-west of Finisterre in the Bay of Biscay, in JM708. In company with another Sunderland from 461 Squadron, three German destroyers were sighted in the Bay. FO Hanbury made contact with the royal navy's escort group, but whilst shadowing the destroyers, U106[142] was sighted on the surface. A combined attack by both aircraft took place; the first attack of seven depth charges was immediately followed by the second aircraft's bomb load. The total of fourteen depth charges cause the U-boat to settle stern down in the water and explode.

Donald continued with his tour of duty, flying extensive patrols in search of the elusive U-boats. Contacts were hard won, with a great many hours in the air. On 17 January 1944, whilst on a routine patrol within Sunderland JM708, a serious fire developed in the starboard inner engine. The fire extinguishers failed to quell the flames, which continued with even greater ferocity. Having managed to head towards the south-west coast on the three remaining engines, the fire damage necessitated a sudden and rough emergency landing onto the sea. One of the wing floats was torn away by the impact on the water, causing the Sunderland to tip on its side. All crew members managed to escape safely, and secured positions in the rescue dinghies. The aircraft eventually exploded at approximately 5 a.m., leaving them alone in the dawn light. Adrift in the dinghies, luck was on their side, and they were sighted and rescued at 8 a.m. by the air-sea rescue launch 144 from Tenby.[143]

Frequently, when entire crews were saved by the deployment of dinghies in circumstances like these, requests to the Goldfish Club were undertaken by the captain of the crew on a joint application. It is not known in this instance, but Donald subsequently received his membership card and badge to confirm his dramatic escape and rescue.

CHAPTER 28

Flt Sgt Maurice Bemrose, air gunner – Caterpillar Club & evader

Maurice was a worthy recipient for membership of the Caterpillar Club, not only for the act of parachuting to safety after being shot down whilst on an operation, but also for evading capture in western Europe.

Maurice was born on 1 September 1922 and brought up in Ecclesfield, West Riding, Yorkshire. Leaving school at the age of fourteen, he joined *The Star* in Sheffield as a driver's mate. Maurice became a member of the Gloops Club whilst employed with the newspaper, his first introduction to the importance of being part of a club. The aim of the club was for young people to raise money to help poor children in the Sheffield and Rotherham areas. A star membership badge was given out to all who joined, and this became one of Maurice's treasured possessions, only parting with it later in his RAF service to acknowledge the support he himself had been given by others.

In 1941, at the age of nineteen, Maurice enlisted in the RAF, and until April 1943, carried out ground crew duties at various locations. During this time, Maurice observed aircrews and decided that he wanted to become an air gunner. Following a successful selection, Maurice began training in May 1943. He passed the course with the following comment entered into his flying logbook by his commanding officer: '... a cadet who has worked hard; not lacking ability, but will need supervision ...' Maurice had clocked up 13 hours and 20 minutes of flying during the air gunnery course, with varying success in his accuracy. On one occasion, he had fired 200 rounds but achieved only five hits – 2.5 per cent. In passing his course, he achieved aircrew status and was promoted to sergeant.

In July 1943, Maurice moved onto 24 Operational Training Unit and became part of a crew, with his regular position within the aircraft as the rear gunner. Together with his new crew, they undertook training at Long

Marston. The crew passed through the operational training unit, moving on to 1659 Conversion Unit at Topcliffe, where they converted to Halifax bombers. At the beginning of October 1943, Maurice and his crew were finally posted to Leeming to join the operational 429 squadron, part of the 6 Royal Canadian Air Force (RCAF) group which had just begun to operate with Halifax bombers. The new crew joined B Flight, but during their first month with the squadron, they recorded few flights, with Maurice clocking up only 6 hours and 59 minutes, and all in daylight. Bomber Command operations over Europe were sparse towards the latter part of 1943, primarily due to bad weather.

On 18 November, the 'Battle of Berlin' began. Four hundred and forty Lancasters were dispatched by bomber command. Few German fighters sighted. Berlin was completely cloud-covered and path finder marking and bombing were both carried out blindly. Bomber Command was unable to make an assessment of the results. Alongside this operation, a major diversionary raid was taking place on Mannheim and Ludwigshafen by 395 aircraft – 248 Halifaxes, 114 Stirlings, and 33 Lancasters – of numbers 3, 4, 6, and 8 Groups. For reasons unknown, although Maurice's crew were involved in the operation, Maurice was not with them. His place was taken by another air gunner, Sgt. O. J. Davis. For the diversionary raid, the German fighters successfully engaged the bomber force and twenty-three aircraft – twelve Halifaxes, nine Stirlings, and two Lancasters – were lost (5.8 per cent of the force). Cloud had been present over the target area and much of the bombing was scattered. One of the aircraft to be lost held Maurice's crew. Of the seven men on board, skipper Flt Sgt Smith and Sgt Crawford were killed, Sgt Morris died from wounds two days later, and the remaining four were captured and taken as prisoners of war. The separation from an operational crew by a single crew member occurred frequently, primarily due to illness.

With the loss of his crew, Maurice was posted to 1666 Conversion Unit at Wombleton in the Vale of York on 1 December 1943. As a more experienced air gunner, he was selected to join the crew of FO McRobie. On this crew, his position was that of Mid-Upper Gunner. Maurice now had a total of 150 hours flying recorded in his flying logbook. With the new year of 1944 having arrived, and having spent a short period on a conversion unit to Lancasters, the crew were posted to 426 RCAF Squadron, part of 6 Group and named the 'Thunderbird' Squadron, based at Lynton-on-Ouse. Over the next few months, Maurice and his fellow crewmembers were involved with mainly night-time operations over Europe:

During January 1944, Maurice attacked the German manufacturing town of Brunswick, Berlin. For this raid, 6 Group were asked to supply 147 aircraft. Sixteen crews went from 426 Squadron. Maurice made the following comments into his logbook: '... 55 lost. Searchlights, flak and fighters. Not a bad trip ...' Records confirmed that enemy fighters got into the bomber streams and a total of fifty-seven aircraft were lost, 8.8 per cent of the strength. On 19 January, 426 Squadron sent thirteen Lancaster's to Leipzig, Germany. The bombers were under almost constant attack on their flight to this industrial city. Seventy-eight of the 823 aircraft sent to Leipzig were lost – a devastating night for Bomber Command.

Maurice and his crew gained some rest for a few weeks, with operations commencing once more on 20 February – this time to Stuttgart. Schweinfurt was the next operation just four days later. This was Bomber Command's first attack on Schweinfurt, where Germany's main ball-bearing factories were based.

The railway marshalling yards at Le-Mans were selected for 6 March 1944. The raid was designed to cripple the transportation network prior to the planned invasion in June. Maurice's aircraft was one of fourteen from Thunderbird Squadron involved in the raid. Operational records confirm that the bombing damaged the rolling stock and yards extensively with no loss of aircraft. Stuttgart was attacked on 15 March. Maurice's crew, together with thirteen others from 426 Squadron, reached the target without incident, however fierce fighting took place over Stuttgard. Maurice entered a comment into his logbook for this raid: '... Attacked by fighters over target ...' Two of the fourteen crews from Thunderbird Squadron were lost.

Frankfurt was the location for operations on 18 and 22 March. The crew were lucky to return from the last excursion, as their aircraft was struck by flak between the starboard engines when they were over the target.

Berlin was once again the target on the night of 24 March. This was the eighteenth, and last, time for 426 Squadron to take part in the bombing raids over Berlin. Winds in excess of 100 mph caused many crews to go off track when crossing into Germany. Ten aircraft from 426 Squadron managed to reach Berlin and release their bombs, returning to England safely. Others were less fortunate, with seventy aircraft lost of the 811 that took part.

As the year progressed towards the build-up to the planned D-Day operations – although aircrews were not aware of what was to take place – operations diverted away from Germany to targets in France. The Battle of Berlin had ended, with the war moving towards the Normandy campaign. There was a slow start to operations in April, hampered by persistent rain and fog. This gave the opportunity for training and lectures by visiting speakers on escape techniques and interrogation of prisoners of war. Little did Maurice realise how useful this training would be over the coming months.

Maurice and his fellow crew members resumed operations once the weather cleared. On 10 April, his aircraft was one of ten to form part of the 163-strong force attacking the marshalling yards at Laon, 130 km north-east of Paris. This was to be 426 Squadron's 1000th operational sortie. A further night-time operation took place on 18 April, causing significant damage to the Noisy-Le-Sec railway yards, 10 km north-east of Paris, with their exploding delayed action bombs severely hampering repairs.

During the month of April, the conversion to Halifax Mk III bombers took place. Operations continued over France during the month of May. On the 19th, Maurice's pilot, Flt Lt I. M. McRobie, was promoted to squadron leader and took over as A Flight commander. On the 27th, a scheduled operation took place to attack an army camp at Bourg-Leopold, near Antwerp. Deployed were 17, 426 squadron Halifaxes, one crew being Maurice's and piloted by Sqd Ldr McRobie. The target area had clear skies and there was a contingency of ineffective German night fighters. All 17,426 aircraft returned safely to England, but were diverted to airfields across the country due to bad weather. At Westcott, Buckinghamshire, Halifax NA510/OW 'E', piloted by Sqn Ldr McRobie, had brake failure on landing, this caused some damage to the aircraft. The crew and aircraft were able to return to base the following day with repairs carried out, and a much-needed stand down from operations was put in place.

Operations continued during early June 1944, with further attacks taking place to support the D-Day landings. The objective for the crew was to knock out as many railway bridges at Coutances in Normandy, France, as possible. The bombings were unrelenting over the next few days, with constant attack on railway junctions. On 12 June, the crew of Halifax NA510 reached their planned destination, the Cambrai railway junction. This was to be the twenty-fourth sortie for Maurice. As they proceeded on the bombing run, an enemy JU88 attacked and inflicted fatal damage on the aircraft. The decision was taken to abandon the Lancaster; the crew were instructed to bail out. This was the moment Maurice entrusted his life to his Irving parachute, and became eligible to join the Caterpillar Club. Operation squadron records for this sortie showed that nothing had been heard of Maurice's aircraft since take off.

Although Maurice became eligible to join the Caterpillar Club following his bailing out of the aircraft, he could not have done so without surviving in enemy territory and returning back to England. So many dangerous situations could have prevented this from happening. The events that took place after he successfully landed serve as testament to the tremendous support and heroics from the resistance movement to protect the Allied airmen and help them to evade the enemy during the war. It was to be three months before Maurice returned to England. Maurice completed a MI9 report, detailing what took place during the flight, bailing out, and his time in France:

… We took off in a Halifax Mark III from Linton-on-Ouse at 1015 hrs on 12 Jun 44. On the bombing run we were shot down by a JU.88. The first thing I knew, there was a large fire in the port wing. I informed the skipper, who gave the order to prepare to abandon aircraft. I bailed out and landed in a field of cauliflowers about 100 yards from the main road to CAMBRAI. I buried my parachute in the field and started walking parallel with the main road. I walked about two miles in a westerly direction, and buried my Mae West in a wheat field. Eventually I came to a small wood and rested here until daylight. I started walking again and after an hour or so came to another wood, where I remained for the rest of the day.

About 2100 hrs I started walking again. I met a French boy and girl who took me to a small hut in a field. The boy stayed with me and the girl went to her home in the village, returning with some civilian clothes. By this time it was getting dark so I walked with them to the village of VAUX-VRAUCOURT where I stayed with their parents until the following night. These people put me in touch with the French Resistance (F.F.I). A member of this organisation took me by bicycle to ECOUST where I stayed in the cemetery for eight days. A Captain of the F.F.I. brought me food every day. After I had been here three days, I met my rear gunner F/O D. Murray R.C.A.F. On the 22 July, we were taken by car to the village of SALLAUMINES. A lady came with us in the car. She was a member of the underground movement and was looking after 21 allied airmen in hiding in the area. We stayed in a grocery shop in the village for two weeks. About 5 August, the lady came to see us and said we must leave as the people in the village were gossiping.

That night about 2100 hrs, we were taken to the village of BILLY MONTIGNY and stayed in a house next door to the lady who was helping us. Four days later, we moved back to our former billet in SALLAUMINES, and remained here until the British arrived on the 4 September. From the time the British arrived until I was able to return to the U.K. we helped the F.F.I. to round up Germans who were hiding in woods in the area…

Flt Sgt Bemrose, mid upper
gunner, leaning against Daniel
Murray's rear turret.

Maurice had been one of the fortunate airmen to be helped by a M. and
Mme Heller, who hid twenty-one allied airmen during the war. They took
in their first two English airmen in January 1944, entrusted to Mme Heller
by an organisation that could not hide them. During March of the same
year, two more came seeking help. From then on, every month, she helped
more airmen, reaching a total of twenty-one in the July. At the time of
the liberation, sixteen airmen were still in her care, sheltered within the
neighbouring communities, the five others having reached allied lines.

Mme Heller undertook many tasks to keep the airmen safe. She herself
went by car to fetch the airmen in various areas, occupied by increasing
numbers of Germans, within an approximate radius of 40 km. Frequently,
the airmen were very poorly dressed, so Mme Heller improvised in order
to provide them with sufficient clothes. The airmen only went out of their
safe houses in the dark of night. As soon as someone outside the host family
became aware of an allied airman's presence in someone's home, the airman
was moved to another address.

Flt Sgt Bemrose's false identity card used in his evasion in France.

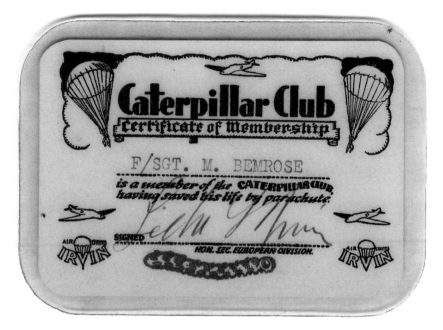

Flt Sgt Bemrose's caterpillar membership card.

Mme Heller contributed to putting in place an organisation of 400 resistance workers in the region. In direct contact with intelligence agents, she often gave them information on munitions stores, torpedo emplacements, troop movements, command posts, etc. Her devotion spread everywhere; she even succeeded in taking food to Russian prisoners in hospital.

On liberation day in Billy-Montigny, France, where she lived, Mme Heller went round to her hidden airmen where they were staying. From the window of his house, the bastien commandant addressed the crowds. Their cheers became delirious when the sixteen allied airmen appeared with Mme Heller. She, and many others like her, risked their lives to enable airmen like Maurice to return safely to England and become a member of the Caterpillar Club.

Maurice did not have many possessions when he was liberated. He had, however, kept his Gloops Club badge with him throughout his service, and it was this he gave to a colonel of the resistance movement to say thank you for the help he had been given.

Maurice applied to join the Caterpillar Club on 10 January 1945:

NO.1505087 F/SGT M. BEMROSE

NO. 1 SERGEANTS' MESS
WEST CAMP
R.A.F. STATION
CRANWELL
JAN 10TH 1945   SLEAFORD, LINCS.

TELEPHONE: SLEAFORD 300 EXTN. 186

Dear Sir

On the night of June 12/13th 1944 whilst on a bombing mission over enemy territory I was unfortunate enough to get shot down in combat with enemy fighters and had to bail out whilst over enemy occupied territory. As I used an Irvin Shute, I would very much like to become a member of your Caterpillar club and also to express my appreciation to you and your staff for your good work which has saved so many lives. Would you please be so kind as to send me a list of particulars required to become a member of your club. My navigator who was with me on the occasion is already a member of your club. His name is F/Sgt now P/O A H Hammond and this statement can be confirmed by the commanding officer of 426 Squadron R.C.A.F. 6 Group, RAF station Lynton-on-Ouse, Yorkshire, England.

Hoping to hear from you in the near future.
I remain sir, yours sincerely
M Bemrose

Maurice received a response from the Caterpillar Club, dated 19 February 1945:

Dear F/Sgt Bemrose

Many thanks for your letter of January 10th, and I am terribly sorry that it has not been possible to reply sooner.

I am indeed glad that you were able to save your life with an Irvin Shute and am very pleased to welcome you as a member of the club. Hearty congratulations on your return to this country.

I have pleasure in sending you your membership card with our best wishes, and your caterpillar pin will follow as soon as received.

Wishing you the best of luck. I am
Yours sincerely
Leslie L. Irvin

Maurice's story appeared in *The Star*, which detailed his escape and that he had given his Gloops Club badge to the free French colonel who helped him during his evasion. A young 'Glooper' wrote to the newspaper's editor asking him to forward her silver Gloops badge to Flt Sgt Bemrose. She hoped the badge, which had been worn by her mother when she was a little girl, 'would bring him all the good luck he so richly deserved'.

The Gloops Club had a renowned following across Sheffield. In June 1942, the club awarded the 'Distinguished Conduct Silver Star' to Howard Nelson, Derek Lee, and Lewis Tomlinson, three schoolboys, who had been camping on the moors when they sighted three men acting suspiciously amongst the rocks. The men were observed and recognised as escaped Italian prisoners of war; two of the boys kept observations on the three Italians, whilst the third escaped back to his cycle and rode to the nearest house to contact the police. Sometime later, having convinced the police of the story, they arrived at the rocks and entered a cave where the three prisoners of war were subsequently arrested.

Maurice was to keep his Gloops Club engraved star-shaped badge, alongside his Caterpillar pin, with him throughout his life.

CHAPTER 29

Sgt E. Dash, air gunner – Guinea Pig Club; Sgt R. Hawksworth

Tragic flying accidents frequently took the lives of so many young men whilst undertaking training, prior to an operational posting.

Sgt E. D. Dash was one of the many who reached the point of qualification where he was ready to be posted onto an operational squadron. Having completed the initial training like all volunteers within the RAF, he commenced his chosen trade of air gunner training at 10 Air Gunnery School at Castle Kennedy in June 1944.

Air gunners faced the shortest training schedule. In normal circumstances, there was swift progression through the air gunner school, followed by a posting onto an operational training unit. Often, a heavy conversion unit would follow before being posted operationally, which entailed operating as a complete crew upon the large multi-engine heavy-bomber aircraft. The timeframe for training to become an operational air gunner rarely exceeded five or six months.

Many aircrew volunteers never achieved the objective to fly operational sorties. Pilot training was obviously intensive, as was the progress of qualifying to be a navigator. The formation of various trades within a bomber – air gunner, bomb aimer, flight engineer, navigator, and pilot – took place within the operational training units. Here, all the trades required to operate a bomber joined together, a selection process made purely by consent between the men themselves. This process was what led towards such strength of bonding and camaraderie between operational crews in Bomber Command.

Sgt Dash was posted to an operational training unit, flying from Edgehill and Chipping Warden, in October 1944. Flying in Wellington bombers, he joined what he hoped would be his regular crew. In common with standard training, OTU crews were tested and trained to the best levels possible – a

Above: Sgt Dash having been promoted to Flt Sgt but still being supported by walking stick.

Left: Sgt Dash on his wedding day with his injuries clearly visible.

favoured method being the nickel raid. Nickel raids were not always soft runs, however, and there were many instances where novice crews failed to return from such operations, with night fighters' searchlights and flak both known to take their toll. Operational training units were frequently called upon by Bomber Command to supply additional crews in support of mass raids upon Germany, and these novice crews made up the numbers to achieve the first 1000 aircraft raids.

Sgt Dash had completed a total of thirty sorties whilst training with the Wellington. Now fully qualified and part of an effective crew, he engaged on one of his final training flights in early 1945. Unfortunately, tragedy struck as the Wellington aircraft hit high-tension power cables and burst into flames in the ensuing crash. Sgt Dash received serious burn injuries but survived.

The East Grinstead hospital burns unit was by this time fully established, with proven results with aircrew burn casualties. Sgt Dash was immediately identified as requiring the services of the skilled medical staff at the hospital. The subsequent operations performed by Sir Archibald McIndoe provided him with his membership to the Guinea Pig Club.

Though unable to swap stories of flying Spitfires or bombing raids over Germany, his fellow Guinea Pigs still recognised the personal price Sgt Dash had paid in the war. Cpl Panton of the Women's Auxiliary Air Force had been his love and sweetheart prior to the crash incident. After his treatment at East Grinstead Hospital they were married. Sgt Dash's name sits forever within the infamous register of this most exclusive club.

Another person on that exclusive list of Guinea Pigs was Sgt John Hawksworth, also an air gunner whose life was forever changed by high-tension power cables. John was being flown in a Lysander aircraft by Flt Lt Paul Jenkins, operating in the role of anti-aircraft calibration duties with 116 Squadron. It was a support squadron, providing aircraft to assist the anti-aircraft batteries in calibrating their radar equipment. The squadron was formed from 1 Anti-Aircraft Calibration Flight on 17 February 1941, and operated the Westland Lysander, best known for its use in the clandestine role of dropping off agents in occupied France. The squadron's role was to fly its aircraft across the hundreds of anti-aircraft batteries spread across the United Kingdom, to make sure that their height predictors were properly calibrated, and therefore accurate. As a result, the squadron was dispersed around an unusually large number of airfields in an attempt to cover the country's defense structure. The air gunner's role in the Lysander also entailed operating the wireless, with communications being a vital role in the tasks undertaken.

At midday on 6 August 1942, Lysander L4795 was flying over Howden, Yorkshire, near Knedlington.[144] The pilot was extremely low, reducing to the height of the field crops, when he saw some high-tension electric cables ahead. With insufficient height or power, the Lysander flew into the cables, crashing across the open field and coming to rest in a ditch. As the aircraft was torn apart, the pilot was thrown clear of the tumbling wreckage. John was secured by his harness and remained inside what was left of the cockpit structure, hanging upside down with serious injuries. Aviation fuel was strewn about, but by good fortune it had not ignited. The crash had been seen by a farm worker, who went to John's assistance. Due to his inverted position, the weight of his body upon the quick release harness buckle was problematic to operate, but through sheer determination, and with only one hand available, John managed to operate the buckle and fell from the harness. Further assistance arrived from other locals, who managed to remove John to a location where the village doctor assisted with his injuries prior to removal to the nearest military hospital. The pilot Paul Jenkins had been killed in the crash.[145] John was assessed and confirmed as having a fractured skull, crushed right hand (resulting in an initial amputation), a seriously damaged left leg (dislocated at the hip with torn flesh), and both knees lacerated, in addition to his face. These injuries resulted in John's later admittance into East Grinstead, and subsequent surgery by McIndoe on the amputated wrist, where his thumb digit was miraculously saved.

John Hawkworth's case is a fine example of the reconstructive surgery to serious trauma injuries undertaken at Queen Victoria Hospital. As a member of the Guinea Pig Club, John retrained his left hand in the art of painting, and in addition, he was able to gain post-war employment as a lithograph artist. The saving of his thumb upon his right hand proved to be a most important factor for the rest of his life. In 1999, John wrote an account of his story, which was published in the Guinea Pig Club magazine.[146]

Westland Lysander serial number L4674 built within the same consigment as Hawksworth's Lysander.

CHAPTER 30

Sub Lt Henry David Whelpton, Fleet Air Arm pilot – GQ Club

The Royal Navy operated its own 'air force' during the Second World War, primarily to provide her ships with protection from enemy airborne strikes. Offensive aerial operations were also undertaken. HMS *Illustrious* was an aircraft carrier that was commissioned and constructed by Vickers Armstrong in Barrow between 1937 and '39. The aircraft carrier became one of the most modern and efficient of her time, fully equipped to deploy an arsenal of aircraft from her deck.

HMS *Illustrious* served in the Mediterranean, deploying Swordfish aircraft upon the Italian fleet at Taranto, and later protecting the vital convoys to the besieged island of Malta. Severely damaged by axis aerial attacks in 1941, HMS *Illustrious* was subjected to several repairs and refits. In 1944, she joined the eastern fleet in the Indian Ocean. On board were approximately forty aircraft, which included a number of F4U Corsairs, one of the most powerful fighters to have flown in the Second World War. Manufactured in the United States, this aircraft was in production throughout the years 1942-52, and was regarded as a robust and sturdy aerial fighting platform, used by many squadrons and allied air forces. The unique 'gull wing' structure identified the Corsair immediately. The pilot was sat well back from the Pratt and Whitney Double Wasp engine, which presented the Fleet Air Arm pilots with serious visibility challenges when landing on the aircraft carriers. That said, many pilots' lives were saved from serious crashes upon the landing decks, as the solid Corsair could withstand serious damage, which enabled rescue parties to successfully recover pilots from what might well have been fatal circumstances.

Sub Lt Henry David Whelpton was a fully qualified Corsair pilot, with considerable flying experience, having survived three accidents during his service – the first of which was whilst taxing his Corsair JT195, no doubt negotiating the difficult visibility issues from his cockpit. He was part of the pilot compliment upon HMS *Illustrious*, having joined 1830 Squadron and embarked at Colombo, Ceylon, in May 1944. Whelpton later took part in the Fleet Air Arm raid upon Sourabaya,[147] with a further fifteen Corsairs and sixteen Avengers.[148] On 21 June, an attack took place on Port Blair in the Andamans. Whelpton carried out the attack in company with six other aircraft, strafing the Japanese airfields. The allied fleet were constantly seeking contact with Japanese cruisers thought to be in proximity of Trincomalee, Ceylon. Between 24 June and 8 July, Whelpton flew every day in an effort to sight the Japanese navy. His second flying accident occurred on 20 July; he applied the brakes too early when landing Corsair JT283, causing damage to the propeller.

The allied fleet comprised of the battleships *Queen Elizabeth*, *Valiant*, *Richelieu* (French), and *Renown*. Accompanied by seven cruisers and ten destroyers, the carriers *Illustrious* and *Victorious* departed Trincomalee on 22 July for a major raid against Sumatra. The Fleet Air Arm engaged a compliment of eighty-four aircraft to protect the fleet and attack Sabang airfields on the 24th. Whelpton attacked the airfield, with fierce anti-aircraft fire present, but luckily no losses were incurred. Several Japanese aircraft were destroyed on the ground. The radar station was also attacked from the air, as the fleet bombarded the harbour from the sea. Attacking the same target the following day, Whelpton and twelve other Corsair pilots were directed by radar to intercept Japanese aircraft approaching Sabang. In an aerial battle that followed, six Japanese fighters were shot down. These were recorded as the first carrier-operated Corsair combat claims for the Fleet Air Arm. Sub Lt Whelpton shot down a 'Zeke' or Japanese 'Zero' fighter aircraft at 6.15 p.m. on 25 July.

The offensive against Sumatra was a massive undertaking, and it was quite remarkable that no Fleet Air Arm losses occurred. Life became less exciting for Whelpton, who undertook domestic flying training, including the essential deck landings. When flying Corsair JT345 on the last day of July, he made a heavy landing that damaged his aircraft. The crew flights on HMS *Illustrious* were adjusted in November and he was teamed up with Lt Retallick, Sub Lt Facer, and Sub-Lt Quigg.[149]

In late December, the carriers HMS *Illustrious*, *Indomitable*, *Indefatigable*, and *Victorious* were all tasked with attacks upon the oilfields at Palambang, Sumatra. In January 1945, Whelpton's Corsair was able to deliver accurate bomb loads onto his targets, with the Pratt and Whitney engine producing a specific whistle when the aircraft dived towards its intended target. The

Japanese made reference to the Corsair as 'whistling death'. The targets at Palambang were producing up to half of the Japanese oil requirements, and at least two thirds of the aviation fuel requirements for her air force, making it a target of the utmost importance. The courage of allied pilots engaged in operations upon these targets was recognised in the post-raid analysis of the attacks. Twelve aircraft failed to reach the carrier's decks, each one being forced to ditch into the sea. From those aircraft, ten crews were rescued but two were lost without trace. These appear to be high numbers of ditchings, but aircrews were resilient in their efforts to avoid capture by the Japanese at almost any cost.[150] On 29 January 1945, Whelpton was required for a further attack, this time upon another refinery within Palambang. In addition to Whelpton, HMS *Illustrious* supplied twelve Corsairs for attacks upon Japanese aerodromes; the objective was to suppress the numbers of Japanese fighters called to defend the refineries. A further sixteen Corsairs and twelve Avenger aircraft attacked the refinery. Similar compliments were deployed from the other aircraft carriers. The Japanese air force managed to defend the intended target areas with some efficiency, and in addition, the defensive balloon cables and flak all presented difficult conditions for the allied pilots. Whelpton sustained a massive hydraulic failure to his Corsair JT539, and was forced to bail out from the cockpit, where he fell away and deployed his GQ parachute. His life was saved, but over the two days of operations allied aircraft losses had reached a total of forty-one. Direct enemy action had accounted for sixteen allied aircraft, with twelve aircraft forced to ditch in various circumstances. The dangers of deck landings were highlighted by fourteen crashes upon the aircraft carriers. Within the casualty statistics was a fellow Corsair pilot, Sub-Lt E. J. Baxter, Royal New Zealand Navy. He managed to escape by parachute, but was unable to avoid being captured by the Japanese. Suffering the same fate was an Avenger crew of Sub-Lt K. M. Burrenston, Sub-Lt W. E. Lintern, and Petty Officer McRae, forced to ditch into the river. The crew of another Avenger aircraft – Sub-Lt J. Burns, Sub-Lt D. Roebuck, and Petty Officer Barker – survived, but became prisoners of war. All these men suffered in the Japanese prisoner of war system, with allied pilots and aircrews frequently subjected to inhumane treatment. All seven men were eventually executed.[151]

Whelpton had managed to return to HMS *Illustrious*, which undertook repairs in Sydney, Australia. The task of replacing the carrier's central drive shaft took many weeks to complete. Whelpton continued with his tour of operational flying, during which time he applied for membership to the GQ Club. His gold lapel badge was precisely engraved with 'Sqn Lt (A) HD

Above and below: GQ parachute badge.

Whelpton 29 Jan 1945' and the numbers '411', indicating the issued number of the badge. When compared to the significant numbers of Caterpillar pins issued by Irvin, it becomes easy to recognise the rarity of the GQ numbered membership badges or lapel pins. Each individual badge also carries a hallmark, in the case of Whelpton's it is 'Birmingham 1945', and the initials 'JRG & S', identifying the badge as being manufactured by J. R. Gaunt & Sons.

CHAPTER 31

Sgt Patrick Drown, pilot – Goldfish Club; Flt Sgt D. Norton

Charles Robertson, secretary of the Goldfish Club, would have opened a letter from Sgt Patrick A. Drown in December 1944, no doubt with a smile of irony when he saw the applicant's name. Patrick's application confirmed that he had avoided death by drowning, and therefore was eligible for membership to the Goldfish Club.

Patrick had been a long-serving member of the Air Training Corp, 335 Unit 2nd Plymouth Squadron. At the first opportunity he volunteered for service, and following a period in training, he qualified as a fighter pilot and was posted into a Bristol Beaufighter Squadron in the Mediterranean theatre of operations. This twin-engine aircraft was crewed by two personnel. Patrick's navigator was Flt Sgt D. A. Norton. On 15 August 1944 they were to suffer an unexpected engine failure, resulting in a ditching into the sea. The Beaufighter was a sturdy and robust airframe, so Patrick managed to perform a classic ditching that caused no injuries to the crew. The aircraft had a wingspan of just over 57 feet, sufficient to support the aircraft on the water's surface. In this instance the crew were able to escape into a dinghy with safety.

Flt Sgt Norton had sufficient time during the events that unfolded to transmit the location of the Beaufighter on the wireless. Rescue attempts were expected to be fairly swift and successful in these circumstances, however the tiny dingy was still a very small item to find in a large expanse of water. On this occasion it was a local civilian fishing boat that came to their aid.

Flt Sgt Norton and Sgt Drown posted off their joint application to the manufacturers of the rubber dinghy. Addressed to the Goldfish Club, and for the attention of Hon Secretary C. A. Robertson, Beehive Works, Honeypot Lane, Stanmore, Middlesex.

Charles replied on 16 December 1944 as follows.

F/Sgt D A NORTON
108 Copthall Road
Handsworth
Birmingham

Dear F/Sgt Norton.

Very many thanks for your letter of the 5th inst applying for membership of the Goldfish Club on behalf of yourself and Sgt Drown. You will be pleased to hear that you have been enrolled as life members, and I enclose herewith your badges.

The official membership cards have been sent to the processors for enclosure in the waterproof case, but I hope to have these back during the next two or three weeks, when I will send them along.

May I offer my congratulations on your escape. I hope you were none the worse for the experience when picked up.

Would you be good enough to ask Sgt Drown to let me have his home address in connection with post-war activities of the club.

Compliments of the season.

Charles posted the membership card to 1586686 Sgt P. A. Drown, Sergeants Mess, RAF Station, Castle Camps, Cambridgeshire, at the close of December 1944. Patrick Drown remained a member of the Goldfish Club during his post-war duties as a police officer, eventually retiring in the rank of Inspector.

Flt Lt Dennis Derby DFC, pilot – Caterpillar Club; Maj. Gen. Horace Birks, Brig. Cecil Timmis, Maj. Gen. Henry Foote VC & Maj. Gen. Noel Napier-Clavering

Dennis Derby was born at Ruislip, Middlesex, in 1918, the elder brother to Kenneth and sister Eileen. Educated at East Sheen County School, his first job was as an articles clerk at a local solicitor's practice.

Dennis joined the Royal Air Force Volunteer Reserve in 1940. He commenced training at Initial Training Wing, Scarborough, between December 1941 and April '42. Dennis received his aircrew posting to Canada, 19 Elementary Flying Training School, Manitoba. He was transported to Canada on the steamship *Letitia*.[152]

In October 1942 Dennis was classed as an 'above average student pilot' by his instructor. Whilst in Canada, he received news that his sister had joined the Women's Auxiliary Air Force, and his brother had been accepted within the RAFVR as a student pilot. Dennis was promoted to pilot officer as he progressed through his training, serving at the reconnaissance school on Prince Edward Island, and then 32 Operational Training Unit at Patricia Bay.

Returning to England, Dennis undertook further training at an OTU in Cumbria. The final part of training required Dennis to locate a navigator. Dennis was posted onto an operational squadron flying the Bristol Beaufighter.[153] PO John Manners, a recently trained navigator, was looking for a pilot. They became instant friends and commenced what was to be an eventful and successful team, flying together in the exciting Beaufighters in 39 Squadron, which operated from Alghero, Sardinia.

It was April 1944 when Dennis Derby and John Manners, both now promoted to the rank of flying officer, commenced operational flying. After several practice rocket attacks, striking targets replicating shipping or ground force transportations, they were ready for operational sorties.

Caterpillar recipient Flt Lt Derby with his navigator, PO John Manners, April 1944. They were to shoot down a JU88 on their first operation the day after this picture was taken.

John Manners, in correspondence with the author, provided details of their time at Alghero and the most unexpected events surrounding the very first sortie they were charged with:

> When we arrived there was no room for us in the mess, the Commanding Officer kindly cleared out his office which was a four wheeled box trailer with side door and rear windows for us. Den and I slept in this, within a yard or two of the sea.
>
> Den and I were briefed to patrol in our Beaufighter N for Nuts along the Mediterranean coast of Spain keeping our eyes peeled for enemy reconnaissance aircraft believed to use that route after spying on our Middle East convoys. It was our first sortie, in company with one other Beau flown by Pilot Officer White, I was slightly worried about the navigation and arriving exactly on spot and keeping on station during what was to be a long time, then getting back to base with minimum errors. Any thoughts of sighting an enemy aircraft seemed very remote to me.
>
> Leaving base we set off as low as possible for the 300 mile flight to reach the patrol area. 39 Squadron proudly credited itself with flying lower than anyone

else, it helped in many ways, easily enabling targets to be sighted and avoided radar detection. We had not been on patrol long when we spotted an aircraft about a mile away. Keeping as low as possible we set off in pursuit, closing rapidly it became obvious that the aircraft had spotted us, our quarry started to gain distance from us. Den opened the taps to maximum, the Beaufighter responded and we started to gain a little. The quarry was a Ju88, it was a straight race and I reminded Den that the Beau should only be used on full power for no more than ten minutes. Den opened fire with the 20mm cannon at the extreme range having just crossed the coast. It occurred to me that the JU88 had rear facing guns and that we were directly behind, pieces of the enemy aircraft started to come away and falling directly towards us, we pulled away. The JU88 had a smoking engine and it flew directly into the ground and disintegrated. I used my camera and took several photographs of these events.

We returned to the coast and Den requested a course to base. He told me he had been injured and asked me to join him. I gave the course and scrambled over the main spar to reach him, I was able to stand behind his seat on what was his escape hatch. He looked quite sick and worried he might pass out at any moment, the only way I would be able to take control would be to lean over and fly on stick and throttle only. My few sessions in the link trainer and a couple of experiments on leaning over the pilot suddenly appeared woefully inadequate. I cut open Den's battledress and placed a dressing on his wound. His face and arms were suffering minor wounds from the shattered Perspex window shattered by the Ju88's returning fire. Another bullet had gone through the rudder cable and also through Den's boot causing another flesh wound.[154] The front cowling to one of the engines also received a bullet which luckily struck nothing important.

Den's condition improved enough for me to return to my station and check our position. In due course we met our headland off Alghero four hours after we had departed. Den was whipped away to hospital while I went to debriefing. Den was in the number 15 American Field hospital for some time and it was to be three weeks before we flew again.

The above sortie took place on 1 May 1944. Regarded by Dennis as his first operational sortie, he was recommended by the air vice-marshall of the Mediterranean Allied Coastal Air Force for the immediate award of the Distinguished Flying Cross. The recommendation was dated 21 May 1944, and four days later the Air Marshall Royal Air Force, Mediterranean and Middle East approved the award.

The DFC was awarded in two distinctly different ways, as an immediate and non-immediate award. The immediate award nearly always related to

The Junkers JU88 shot down on the 1 May 1944.

Photograph showing the crash location of the shot down JU88.

Flt Lt Derby's DFC medal group, with the bullet recovered from his flying boot.

an act of courage, the non-immediate award tended to indicate devotion to duty and courage whilst flying in active operations against the enemy.

Dennis and John resumed operations, completing many successful attacks upon merchant vessels and transportation targets. On 13 October 1944, events unfolded involving the loss of a Beaufighter into the sea. The two men set course on an armed shipping strike between Khalkis and Volos, Greece. Sqn Ldr Payne and Flt Sgt Potts were forced to ditch as a result of engine trouble and the propeller failing to feather properly. Dennis arrived and immediately recognised the signs of a large oil patch where the Beaufighter had recently sunk; the sea was fairly calm and the dingy was immediately located. Difficulty was experienced in contacting any base station on the radio, however a Warwick air-sea rescue aircraft was eventually homed onto the area, and a flying boat later undertook a landing and rescued the crew. John took several photographs during their time spent protecting the dingy. The ditching happened at 11.34 a.m. and the rescue was completed at 3.42 p.m. Sqn Ldr Payne had apparently sustained the usual deep cut over the

Flt Lt Derby's sighting of a rubber dinghy, with a visible oil patch from the ditched aircraft.

eye inflicted by the gun sight, a common injury to any pilot when ditching a Beaufighter.

A move to 272 Squadron came in late 1944, where once again operations continued in the Beaufighter, operating within a detachment of the squadron strength at Foggia and Falconara in Italy. The successful combination of Derby and Manners added to the accumulation of operations attacking the familiar shipping targets and identified targets on the mainland. On 20 November 1944, truck concentrations at Novska, Yugoslavia, were attacked with rockets and cannons. A petrol or ammunition truck exploded unexpectedly, with a massive force (probably by Dennis' strike); the following Beaufighter was almost consumed by the fireball and returned covered in debris. John Manners had once again captured the event with his camera, and the pilot concerned was able to keep the evidence of his narrow escape. The impressive calculations of one enemy aircraft destroyed; seven coasters and schooners sunk; fourteen merchant vessels attacked and four sunk; ten barracks, warehouses, and stores destroyed; two Speerbrechers[155] damaged; one landing craft damaged; one liner [156] destroyed; two railway engines destroyed; and twenty-eight other targets attacked had all been recorded in the crew's flying logbooks.

Dennis Derby, having been rested from operations, was posted to the Communications Flight of the Allied Balkan Air Force. Flying the Expeditor aircraft, he was engaged on many transit flights, carrying important personalities across the Mediterranean theatre. The Balkan Air Force was part of the Mediterranean Allied Air Force; it operated in direct support of the partisan forces across the Balkans, in particular those under command of Mar. Tito in Yugoslavia.

On 19 September 1945, Dennis was required to fly the unit's Hudson aircraft serial FK674 from Naples to Berlin. The passengers were Maj. Gen. Birks, Brig. Foote, Brig. Napier, Brig. Timmis, and an aide, L. Cpl Fisher. Two officers with special military expertise, and one recipient of the Victoria Cross, were amongst this senior group of personnel.

Maj. Gen. Horace Leslie Birks (1897-1985):

1940	General Staff Officer, 17th Amoured Division (North Africa)
1940-41	Second in Command, 4th Amoured Brigade (North Africa)
1941-42	Commanding Officer, 11th Amoured Brigade
1942	Commanding Officer, 11th Tank Brigade
1943-44	General Officer Commanding, 10th Amoured Division (Middle East/North Africa)
1944	Major General, Royal Amoured Corps, Central Mediterranean Force

Brig. Cecil William Murray Timmis (1904-81):

1943-44	Commanding Officer, 2nd Special Service Brigade (Italy
1944-45	Commanding Officer, 2nd Commando Brigade (Yugoslavia/Italy)

Maj. Gen. Henry Robert Bowreman Foote VC (1904-93):

1941-42	General Staff Officer, 1 10th Amoured Division
1942	Commanding Officer, 7th Royal Tank Regiment
1944	General Staff Officer, 1 Allied Armies Italy
1945	Deputy Commanding Officer, 9th Amoured Brigade
1945-47	Brigadier, Royal Amoured Corps Middle East Command

Maj. Gen. Noel Warren Napier-Clavering (1888-1964):

Derby and Manners standing
alongside their Beaufighter's
propeller.

1937-39   Assistant Adjutant & Quartermaster-General, 4th Infantry
          Division
1939-40   Chief Administration Officer, British Troops in Egypt
1940-42   Deputy Adjutant General, Middle East Command
1942-45   Head of the British Military Mission to Egypt

The Hudson experienced unexpected poor weather conditions, resulting in
icing, which caused Dennis to turn back over Munich. Shortly after this,
however, the Hudson experienced a double engine failure. The passengers
were required to make an emergency jump from the aircraft, followed by the
crew. The brigadiers and the major general were all wearing the observer's
type of Irvin parachutes. Dennis ensured the passengers and crew departed
his aircraft safely. Locking the control column in the cockpit to provide
a stable exit for himself, he leapt from the Hudson, pulling his parachute
ripcord. The occupants from the aircraft all landed safely, approximately 5
miles east of Innesbruk.

Eventually Dennis and his crew returned to the Communication
Flight base. The officer commanding subsequently placed his personal

signature to a letter directed to Irvin. It was Flt Lts Derby's application to join the Caterpillar Club, on 15 October 1945. The letter advised of the circumstances and passenger details. The individual parachute identification records applicable to his important passengers were included, indicating that they should likewise receive membership.[157]

Dennis Derby DFC died in 1968. His navigator, John Manners, wrote in 1993:

> I know we made a good team with great faith in each other. Den was considered an excellent shot with both cannon and rockets and I coped reasonably well. I am sure it would have been a lifelong friendship, but our contact was severed on Den's sudden death.

CHAPTER 33

Flt Sgt John Stearn DFM, air gunner – Goldfish Club

John Francis Stearn achieved his personal ambition to fly within Bomber Command during the closing years of the war. He trained successfully as an air gunner, and subsequently flew a significantly high number of operations. He was recognised for his ability and later served within 156 Squadron as a member of the path finder force, where he completed a second tour of operations. The role of pathfinding, marking the targets and later controlling the bomber stream of aircraft, was well-established by late 1944, and proven to achieve good results for the command. Many daylight raids on specific targets had been recently undertaken by 156 Squadron, supporting the allied push from the D-Day landings.

Numerous key operations took place during John's extended operational tour of duty. One of specific note occurred after D-Day, on 26 August 1944. His captain, Flt Lt Etchells, lifted the crew's Lancaster PB302 off the runway at RAF Upwood at 8:21 p.m. Bomber Command dispatched a total of 372 Lancasters to attack the German naval base of Kiel. Attacked several times previously, this important target was very well defended and additionally equipped with smoke generators capable of producing massive quantities of smoke, which prevented or frustrated the path finders.

The raid to Kiel was a return to standard night raid operations undertaken by the squadron. The crew reached the target area when they were immediately attacked by a JU88 Luftwaffe night fighter. That engagement caused some severe damage to the aircraft, however the Lancaster was still airworthy and they pressed on to the objective, found and marked the target, and continued to stay in the area to direct the attack until the last bomber had left. This duty was only undertaken by the 'master' or 'deputy' bomber crew. As the crew left the target area, they were once again attacked by a night fighter, which caused further damage and resulted in a loss of power

156 Squadron Lancaster.

with one engine. Returning to RAF Upwood would now be impossible. The attacking fighter was destroyed by the rear gunner during the aerial combat. It was quickly realised that they could only keep their aircraft in the air for a short duration, so they headed out to sea. Losing height all the time, Lancaster PB302 eventually ditched in the North Sea, 10 miles from the German coast. The Lancaster was one of seventeen aircraft that failed to return from the raid upon Kiel.

John and his crew all managed to escape safely from the floating Lancaster and climbed into the large auto-inflated dingy that was by then tethered to the wing. It was 48 hours later that, adrift in the dinghy, Flt Lt Etchells and his crew were sighted by a Danish fishing boat, returning to its home port in Denmark. The fishermen were persuaded to head for England, where they were eventually escorted into Grimsby Harbour by a RAF air-sea rescue boat. The crew returned to their base five days after leaving, and fellow crews were amazed to hear their story of survival. Rapid applications to the Goldfish Club followed. Applications for membership frequently included praise for the manufacturers at P. B. Cow, outlining the events and performance of the dinghies that had saved their lives. In this instance, it appears that the ditching drill, equipment, and careful designs incorporated within the Lancaster's manufacture all led to this crew's successful rescue.

John Stearn not only joined the Goldfish Club, but was rewarded with the Distinguished Flying Medal in December 1944. The following details were extracted from official records:

> Flt. Sgt. Stearn has completed 44 operational sorties, 35 of which have been with the P.F.F. Some of the targets have been heavily defended areas in Germany, including 7 on Berlin. This N.C.O. is a keen and determined Gunner, and his vigilance and efficiency has on many occasions been contributory to successful evasions of enemy aircraft. During combats with the enemy he has proved himself to be a cool and courageous Gunner and has been a valuable asset to his crew. He has set a high standard of devotion to duty.

One further badge was awarded to John on 6 September 1944, by Air Vice-Mar. Bennett. The letter advising him of the award reads as follows:

> Headquarters
> Path Finder Force
> Royal Air Force
> To
> 960576 Flight Sergeant Stearn J F
> Award of Path Finder Force Badge
> You have today qualified for the award of the Path Finder Force Badge and are entitled to wear the badge as long as you remain in the Path Finder Force.
> You will not be entitled to wear the Badge after you leave the Path Finder Force without a further written authority from me entitling you to do so.
> [Bennett signature]
> Air-Commodore, Commanding, Path Finder Force.

The 'path finder eagle' was authorised to be worn on the left breast pocket. This small eagle immediately identified to all crews that the wearer was a qualified member of the path finder force. Flt Sgt Stearn (960576) later added the 1935 Star, Air Crew Europe Star, Defence and War Medals to his DFM.

CHAPTER 34

Sgt Raymond Brooke, navigator – Guinea Pig Club

Raymond Brooke was involved in one of the most tragic air disasters to have occurred during the Second World War. Having successfully completed his aircrew training as a navigator in Canada, Raymond returned to the UK, where he was placed in the RAF Aircrew Holding Unit, Kirkham, Lancashire.

Holding units provided temporary accommodation for various pools of aircrew, all fully trained and awaiting operational postings. At Kirkham friendship groups were made that frequently saw visits to the nearby local café, The Snack Shack, in Freckleton village. The café had a strong reputation for excellence, which was handed down by departing airmen to the newly arrived. It was the place to go for an excellent breakfast and general refreshments.

Situated not far away was the United States Army Air Force base at Warton. The Snack Shack was nearly always occupied by American servicemen, with lesser numbers of British and Commonwealth aircrew.

On 23 August 1944, Raymond Brooke and three fellow RAF friends from the holding unit were all off duty. During the morning an intense storm blew up quite unexpectedly. Caught in the terrible downpour, the four RAF men ran for The Snack Shack. The weather conditions meant several villagers and American servicemen had also taken shelter there.

During the storm, and in the air, were two American B24 bombers, known to the RAF as Liberators. They had taken off from Warton on air test flights. Warton was primarily a repair and modification facility, with aircraft constantly arriving and departing the base, which was extensive in size. The violent and sudden storm conditions caused the flight control to recall the aircraft, requesting them to land as soon as possible. Within minutes the storms intensity grew; thunder, lightning, and ferocious winds

The Snack Shack in Freckleton. The proprietors, staff and customers from the RAF, RAAF and USAAF. (*Philip Kaufmann*)

struck the entire area. The returning aircraft were unable to land. Courses to fly north in order to escape the weather were agreed, but tragedy was about to strike the village of Freckleton.

At 10.45 a.m., Raymond Brooke and his crew mates were ordering tea in The Snack Shack, and discussing the storm. The good news that Paris had been liberated by the allied forces was in general discussion. Victory in Europe was becoming a realistic thought, along with a desire to receive their anticipated postings into operational squadrons.

At that time, one of the Liberators, having aborted the attempt to land at the airfield, struck a tree with a wing-tip, and in doing so the same wing then struck a building. After a short distance, the aircraft, having partly demolished three houses, crashed into The Snack Shack. In addition, the aircraft struck the Holy Trinity School, which suffered the destruction of its infant wing, whilst being occupied by young children. Ruptured aviation fuel ignited and spewed across the entire crash scene, causing total devastation.

American rescue personnel from the airfield were swiftly on the scene. This prompt response enabled seven young children and one teacher to be rescued from the school. However, with serious injuries sustained, four of these children and the teacher subsequently died. In total, thirty-eight children and two adults lost their lives in the Holy Trinity School. Only three children survived the tragedy.

In The Snack Shack, fifteen people were killed instantly. Three people were rescued from the carnage, but later lost their lives as a result of the injuries sustained. Raymond Brooke was seriously injured, with the burning fuel inflicting horrific wounds to his right leg, face, and both hands. All the rescued survivors were raced to the American airfield, where emergency hospital facilities were present. It is without question that the initial treatment for his significant burn injuries led to his survival. His fellow RAF aircrew, Sgts Cannell, Bateson, and Bell, all died the following day as a result of the injuries they had sustained. Sgt Newton had lost his life in the initial crash.

The total death toll reached sixty-one, forty-five of whom were civilians. Freckleton had suffered a terrible tragedy. Raymond was later transferred to East Grinstead Hospital, where his burn injuries were treated and painful reconstructive surgery took place. Raymond was operated upon by McIndoe, enabling him to join the Guinea Pig Club. He endured many operations, primarily upon his hands and face. Whilst recovering after one such operation, he managed to hear the name of Bill Foxley mentioned. Raymond had met Bill during their initial training days in 1942, where they had been good friends. Despite the bandages and communication problems for Raymond, the nurses confirmed that Bill was a patient on the ward and recovering from similar reconstructive surgery. The two men managed to communicate and enjoy each other's company, despite their situation.

Bill had been admitted to the hospital in East Grinstead having suffered terrible burns to his hands and face. Whilst on a training exercise on 16 March 1944, his Wellington bomber had crashed immediately after take-off from Castle Donington. He escaped the crash unscathed but, hearing the shouts of a trapped comrade, went back into the aircraft despite an intense fire within the fuselage. He managed to drag his wireless operator free, but suffered severe burns in the process. Sadly his heroic actions and personal sacrifice were not rewarded, as his wireless operator, Sgt Tony Rowley, died shortly afterwards. The tail gunner, Sgt Ernest Small, also died as a result of his injuries the following day.

Archibald McIndoe undertook almost thirty operations to rebuild his face, including procedures to give him a new nose and to build up what was left of his hands. The Guinea Pig Club itself bonded the friendship of Bill and Raymond, which remained with them for the rest of their lives.

In Westminster Abbey, the Civilian War Dead Roll of Honour records the names of the forty-five men, women, and children who lost their lives when the B24 Liberator bomber fell upon the village of Freckleton.

Royal Air Force Escaping Society (RAFES); Sgt W. Bilton – Caterpillar Club & evader

The Royal Air Forces Escaping Society adopted the Latin motto 'Solvitur ambulando' (solved by walking). The society was created to foster continued friendship between escapers, evaders, and their helpers. Air Chief Mar. Sir Basil Embry was the president of the RAFES from its formation in 1946. In 1963, the chairman, Oliver Philpot MC DFC,[158] provided the following account of the purpose of the RAFES:

> Everybody has heard of the RAF, most people have heard of escaping activities, but why a society, and why is it registered as a Charity under the War Charities Act of 1940.
>
> To begin with we are not only talking about the RAF, but about all air forces, and air crews incorporated in it during the 1939-1945 War. Secondly we take the broad meaning of the word escape to cover both those of us who escaped from prison camps, and those who evaded capture altogether after stepping out of their crashed aeroplanes. Every man however, to be a member of the RAFES had to reach the UK, allied or neutral territory during the war.
>
> The escapers whom I mentioned were frequently helped on their way home by all sorts of people, civilians, some peasants some businessmen; others were priests and nurses, housewives and girls, bakers and boys. The significant thing was the risk, death for the helpers, but only prison camp for the escaper. Those helpers were often caught. Mme Guiho's son was shot in Brittany for helping before her eyes. Other helpers had their husbands snatched away in police vans for ever. It did not matter where they were, whether in France or Greece, Belgium or Holland, Luxembourg or Poland the same terrible rules applied. The British authorities got in touch after the war with those helpers who survived, and formed proper records. The escapers and evaders joined the Society which was formed in 1945 by Lord Portal at the end of

The Royal Air Force Escaping Society.

his five year period as Chief of Air Staff. He became the society's first president.

The society members chase around and by appeals, raffles or lectures raise money which is carefully kept against the needs of helpers, many individual members are often still personally in touch. Our secretary Mrs B Johnstone has one standing instruction as regards the society's monthly executive meetings. That is 'Helping helpers' Monsieur 'X' in the Ardennes will be cold this winter £15 or £20 for coal. The two old Mesdemoiselles 'Y' are permanently bed ridden in hospital in Belgium … so a parcel goes to them.

All of us in the society think of this all the time, but we are always finding that people have just not thought about those helpers, several thousand in number.

Of the Royal and Commonwealth Air Forces aircrew, 2,803 members who were shot down during the Second World War managed either to escape from captivity, or in the majority of cases, to evade capture. In many cases their eventual return to allied territory was by clandestine means. In escaping or evading, they forced the enemy to devote scarce resources to stopping them. They also gave heart to the allied forces operating over enemy territory;

Sgt William (Brian) Bilton of 10
Squadron in flying gear. (*James Caws*)

aircrew knew it was possible to get back. Escapers and evaders were almost
always reliant on the goodwill of ordinary people – extraordinarily brave
people – in the countries under Fascist control. These helpers risked torture
and death for the help they gave, and their families faced deportation to
concentration camps. Many thousands suffered because they aided allied
aircrew.

The RAFES published the following account to all members in the 1964
progress report:

'Helpers we have helped'
The Three Malard Sisters.

Three sisters, Lucie, Marie and Yvonne Malard lived in the remote little hamlet
of St. Aubin, Morbihan, France, and sheltered Sgt. Brian Bilton in 1943 when
his plane crashed and he bailed out in their area.

Sgt Bilton had been serving in 10 Squadron. His Halifax Mk II aircraft had
taken off on a raid to attack the Dunlop rubber factory at Montlucon in central
France. By strange coincidence, within the crew, both the pilot and navigator

RAF 10 Squadron crew with Sgt Bilton standing far left. 10 Squadron frequently painted good luck mascots on their aircraft; this Halifax has made forty-one operations.

Sgt Bilton's crew with their ground crew. The crews Halifax is typical of a series 1 special modification type of 1943.

were named Dunlop. 209 Halifax bombers were engaged upon the raid to
Montlucon. By extreme bad luck, Brian Belton's aircraft was one of only two
that failed to return from what had been a most successful operation. Their
Halifax crashed at Ecorcei France. Three crew members escaped successfully
by parachute; Sgt Bilton, Sgt Lewis and PO Stapley. The four remaining crew
members had apparently been unable to escape from the falling aircraft
and were killed in the subsequent crash. The Commonwealth War Graves
Commission now tends their graves at the Churchyard in Ecorcei.[159] Sgt Lewis
and PO Stapley were captured, becoming prisoners of war. Sgt Bilton with
an injured ankle hampering his escape was eventually given sanctuary by the
Malard sisters at their farm in St Aubin. For ten weeks he was kept hidden in
their house while his ankle mended. During this time he tried to teach Lucie
English, and gave a helping hand with a cow that was calving, going outside
only at night when it was relatively safe. While he was under the Malard's roof
he learned of a radio in the attic, which kept regularly in touch with London,
and of nocturnal visits from the local resistance, who hid parachuted supplies
on the Malard's property and distributed it in their lorries. During this time
many villagers thought the Malard's were engaged in black market operations
and were envious of the money the sisters were imagined to be piling up. After
the allied invasion, the retreating Germans looted the village and the elder
brother in the Malard family was shot. The three sisters then in their thirties
were left to carry on farming and running the village shop without male help
and advice. The award of French, American and British Certificates and medals
for their war work aroused some envy; they lost the right to run the Post
Office, while the trade of their shop declined. Slowly their financial situation
deteriorated and a Government re-arrangement of local agricultural holdings
resulted in an absence of income from the land, just as they had invested in
a tractor on hire purchase. They were forced into bankruptcy; resulting in
the sale of their property at a farcical price. An article in a French newspaper
about the serious situation which these helpers were in was sent to the RAFES
Society. Mr Brian Bilton was alerted at his farm in Hampshire. With an English
speaking French journalist he flew to Paris and drove to St. Aubin. He brought
encouragement and support to the sisters and a substantial cheque from the
society. The ensuing publicity brought the sisters an opportunity long denied,
to appeal against the forced sale. When the hubbub of publicity died down
and the sisters were awaiting the legal proceedings, jealousies and feelings of
hostility were revived. The RAFES telegraphed the Prefect of Police and sent
him reasons for protection. The Co Operation of the Air Attaché at the French
Embassy in London was also invited. It may well be that the Malard's legal

Right: Sgt Bilton meeting the Malard sisters, Lucie, Marie and Yvonne in 1963.

Below: Sgt Bilton standing outside of the Malard sisters' store in St Aubin.

proceedings will drag on indefinitely, but if Home Office permission can be obtained, and their case is over in time for the beginning of the strawberry season, the Malard's great wish to leave France for ever and spend the rest of their days in England may be realised.

On Mr Bilton's return to England, the Hampshire farmer published an article called 'The War is Over'. He harboured a strong personal desire to publish the plight of those that assisted in saving his life (W. H. B. Bilton, 5 October 1963):

Twenty years ago this September I was a member of the crew of a Halifax bomber attached to 10 Squadron Bomber Command and stationed near York. I had returned from leave on the 14th September 1942 and that evening we were sent to bomb a rubber works at Montlucon in Southern France. On crossing the French coast about 1a.m. our aircraft was hit by coastal defences, one of the four engines caught fire, this was quickly put out and we continued on our mission. Twenty minutes later a second engine caught fire and the pilot gave the order to 'bail out' this I did. It was like daylight as I floated down to earth by the light of the 'Harvest Moon'. I hit the ground with a thud, gathered my parachute together and on looking round found myself in the midst of a herd of 'black and whites'. The aircraft was now burning fiercely some distance away. I made for the cover of some trees, where I hid my parachute and began to walk across the fields in the opposite direction to the blazing aircraft. I continued walking, crossing a stream in case of German tracker dogs, and keeping clear of any roads. It was almost dawn when I hid myself in the middle of a thick hedge; my ankle was badly sprained on landing so I decided to remain hidden until dusk. This gave me ample time to think, from my position it was apparent I was close to a busy road, close to a flock of sheep and close to some women potato picking. It was almost dark when I emerged from the hedge. I found my ankle very swollen and painful as I hobbled across the fields towards the sheep. In the far corner of the field by the shepherds hut I met my first 'French friend', a boy about 16 who was shortly joined by his father who had brought his son's supper this he shared with me, as in broken French and with the help of a map which he produced from the hut I explained who I was. The boy's father disappeared and returned some time later with another man in a van, who I found out later to be a haulage contractor. He took me to his house; I was given a hot bath, some food and put to bed. I slept for 24 hours. I stayed here for 10 days, was given civilian clothes, false identity papers and an assurance I was 'on the road to escape', together with the sad news that two of my crew were taken prisoner by the Germans and four were killed in the aircraft. One night my friend drove me to Rouen, I stayed a few days there, and then by train I went to Paris. From Paris to Le Man and Rennes eventually arriving at St. Aubin near Plumelee in North West France. It was here that I stayed hidden with some American aircrew for ten weeks, being looked after by three sisters and their aged mother. I left these good people about the 20th December and made my way with a Frenchman who was being sought by the Gestapo by car (which ran off the road at night and was pushed back on by some German soldiers) to a house on the cliffs on the French coast almost opposite Southampton. I was joined here by a British Intelligence Officer who informed me we were awaiting a radio message, a boat would pick us up and we should be in England for our Christmas dinner. This however was not to be, the radio message was received on Christmas Eve. At midnight we quietly made our way to the beach under the cliff. Shortly afterwards I heard the throb of a motor boat's engines, my British friend heard them too and by means of the radio telephone which he carried on his back, called the captain and requested him to 'cut' his motors. Within seconds the German searchlights came into action across the bay, the guns opened up and with a roar the boat disappeared in a sheet of spray out to sea. We could do no more than hurry back to the house on the cliff, we had fortunately dug a large hole under the floor boards in the front room as a precaution, but fortunately no search was made. Within 48 hours I left this house and with help made my way back to Paris and then via Lyon, Toulouse to Perpignan at the foot of the Pyrenees, this journey took five weeks. It took me two days to walk over the Pyrenees into Spain, a short rest and then to Barcelona by cattle truck attached to a goods train to Madrid where I contacted the British Consul. Arrangements were then made for me to get to Gibraltar, and on the night of the 14th February 1943, I left in a Boston aircraft and flew back to England. I recently heard through the R.A.F. Escaping Society that the three sisters who have a small farm, and general store in the village were in trouble, at the beginning of September I went back to St. Aubin to see them.[160] I was shocked to find after twenty years that these gallant ladies holders of an English citation, French and American medals, who were driven from their home by the Germans, had a brother tortured and killed, had a secret radio transmitter in their attic and arms parachuted into their fields during the war, had for the past ten years been persecuted and victimised by the villagers and are now bankrupt and have to leave their farm. Not only myself but hundreds of allied airmen owe much to the farming people of France. What better place to hide than a barn, a loft, a straw rick with a false middle and extra food for those in

Left: Sgt Bilton's farming experience being utilised with one of the cows belonging to the sisters.

Below: Sitting in the farmhouse kitchen where sanctuary had been provided for Sgt Bilton in 1943. The three brave sisters enjoying his company twenty years later.

the cities who were hiding us on our way back? Our Escape Society is doing all it can to help them. My story is not the only 'Escape Story', about 700 British Airmen were helped and our Escape Society of 67 Portland Place, London is continually being called upon to help the people who helped us then. Old age, bad health through the treatment some received in the concentration camps makes it necessary for them to appeal to us. Should the readers of the Farmers weekly on reading my story wish to make a small contribution for these gallant folk, I am sure all would be most thankful.

As a result of the publication, several donations were received from readers, and even more importantly, two generous and interesting offers were volunteered. One was a free rental of a cottage, some land around it, and four months' paid work annually on a fruit farm, from a strawberry grower in Hampshire. The other was an offer to help the sisters, with a regular grant of money from a reader in Surrey.

From research undertaken, the Malard sisters never realised their dreams. They remained in France, supported as best possible by the RAF Escaping Society. With the passing of time, the society itself was disbanded on 17 September 1995. The laying up of its flag standard took place in Lincoln Cathedral. The last society president was Air Chief Mar. Sir Lewis Hodges.

Postscript

Flight publication, April 1943:

> Few decisions of the Air Council can have had more far-reaching effects on the moral, economy of man-power and operating efficiency of the Royal Air Force than the adoption of the Irvin Airchute for flying personnel.

Irvin Air Chutes Caterpillar Club
Advertisement, 1939.

Appendices

Appendix 1: RAF Combined Flying Suit and Harnessuit

Irvin had designed and manufactured a combined pattern flying suit, which evolved from the very early Sidcot flying suit – the all-in-one rubberised linen overall that facilitated a chest or backpack parachute. This design later included large flotation collars or life preservers; the concept was to save space in the tight-fitting cockpits and aircraft within the Royal Air Force. Both Irvin and GQ received contracts to manufacture these Sidcots for the Air Ministry during the mid-1930s.

When the Air Ministry committed to the Boulton Paul P82 Defiant aircraft in 1937, the aircraft was uniquely designed with a power-operated air gunner's turret. The air gunner, situated immediately behind the pilot, required a specific parachute assembly to escape from the tight fitting canopy. In 1938, the short-sleeved, short-legged flying suit pattern was developed. The GQ Co. produced this combined flying harnessuit specially for the Defiant rear gunners. Incorporated in the design was provision for the clip-on seat- or chest-type parachute packs. Manufactured in drab olive-coloured robust cotton, and referred to as the 'GQ parasuit', the detachable stole was the inflatable bladder to act as a life preserver, which required oral inflation. The Defiant fighter proved to be a disappointment – the concept of a fighter being well armed in that fashion proved to be unfounded. In addition, the GQ suit itself was not as successful as hoped. It was produced in limited quantities and superseded by the Irvin harnessuit in 1940.

The Irvin combined pattern suit or harnessuit was manufactured and used across most commands of the RAF from 1940. Once more comprising of heavy cotton, with no arms or legs, the CO_2 cartridge inflating life-preserver bladder was incorporated in the design. The full webbing parachute harness

Left: A GQ early suit.

Below: A Czechoslovakian bomber crew wearing Irvin combined suits, 1940.

was beneath the outer garment. This particular garment is easily identified by the long twin zippers and the front parachute clips, which are clearly identifiable. Despite its improvements, the harnessuit was never a popular item, and the vast majority of aircrew preferred to wear the seat-pack and observer-type harnesses and the individual Mae West life preservers.

The photograph produced by the Air Ministry (*c.* 1940) shows a Czechoslovak bomber crew wearing the Irvin combined flying suit on their way to the aircraft. Most men are carrying the chest-type parachute, which clipped onto the clips that can be seen attached to the webbing stitched across each shoulder.

Appendix 2: RAF Life Preserver

Introduced in 1932, the life preserver was a simply designed over-garment, constructed with internal flotation bags that required the wearer to inflate via a mouth tube. Many iconic pictures of fighter pilots flying in the Battle of Britain are shown wearing this early variant of life preserver.

The voluptuous actress of the time, Mae West, led to this life preserver's nickname. No doubt when semi-inflated and worn across the chest area, it was easy to understand the correlation suggested by the young men of the time.

These early life preservers were manufactured in rather drab colours. It became common for an application of bright paint to be applied in order to assist with visual recognition. In effect, the early garment was no more than a strong cotton waistcoat, secured by three large buttons and webbing tape ties. The collar area was accessible to install the inflation pads and the inflatable rubber bellows.

A marked improvement took place with the development and issue of the 1941 life preserver. This life preserver was known simply as the '1941 Mae West'. Constructed of bright yellow cotton, it was fitted with self-inflating activation devices that initiated a carbon dioxide cylinder to instantly inflate the inner bellows. The wearer was provided with better securing straps that held the preserver in the primary position required to support the man in the water. Earlier life preservers had been difficult to secure, resulting in great difficulties for the wearer to support himself in the water.

As development progressed, additional pockets or pouches were designed to carry water-colouring die packs, an ingenious method to stain the sea around the survivors with fluorescein, a brown powder that quickly turned

A 1941 Mae West life
jacket.

Pilots in Mae West life
jackets.

the water a vivid and fluorescent green. There were also the personal battery
torch lights, manufactured by Easco, and known as the 'Eascolyte' life jacket
lamp. These additional aids were developed as a result of valuable lessons
learnt from operational use. Pilots and crews reported the great difficulty
in assisting a man from the water into an inflated dingy whilst wearing the
life preserver. The waterlogged uniform created significant extra weight, and
combined with the swell of the sea, it was almost impossible to pull a man
over the inflated rim. As a result of the feedback to the manufacturers in
1942, two heavy-duty webbing straps or handles were fitted to the front of

the Mae West, which provided the means to lift a man from the sea and into the dingy.

Charles Robertson at P. B. Cow was in an ideal position to hear of suggestions raised from aircrews, and the Goldfish Club assisted in the continual development of life preservers within the Royal Air Force during the Second World War. P. B. Cow was just one of a number of producers of life preservers to the Air Ministry.

Appendix 3: RAF Seat-pack Parachute Assembly

This was the most commonly used parachute by pilots during the Second World War. Referred to as the 'pilot's parachute', the wide canvas strapping combined shoulder, waist, and leg straps, which all met at the single point quick release box. Most of the metal fittings were produced in forged stainless steel.

The combined assembly of harness, parachute, and dinghy pack all fitted as comfortably as possible within the empty bucket of the pilot's seat. This parachute assembly was worn by pilots throughout the entire operational flight, and in effect, it was the seat in which they sat upon – as such, frequently left within the aircraft. The pilot wearing his Mae West would simply fasten his harness around himself as he settled in his cockpit.

The 24-foot diameter parachute was deployed from its pack by pulling the large d-shaped ring, which was positioned within easy reach and close proximity to the quick release box. The ring would be pulled across the chest area by the wearer's right hand; the parachute would then stream from the pack behind the wearer.

Appendix 4: RAF Observer Parachute Assembly

Manufactured by Irvin, this harness had a similar arrangement of webbing straps to the pilot's seat type.

The personal harness was worn at all times whilst in the air. With no parachute attached, crew members were able to move about with significantly less restriction. The parachute pack would be stowed and accessible at all times. Fitted with metal loops, it was simple to clip the parachute pack onto the harness hooks. This Irvin assembly was well liked by the vast majority of aircrews, and in emergency situations, the parachute could be attached

Left: The 1940 parachute assembly.

Below: The Sutton harness release.

with no regard to its position. Either way up, the d-ring or ripcord could be pulled by the left or right hand.

The observer parachute assembly became the most commonly used harness used by aircrews across all commands of the Royal Air Force. The key to that success was the method of simply attaching the parachute pack onto the two chest-mounted fasteners. The parachute pack itself was a rectangular-shaped brown-coloured canvas envelope, fitted with four carrying handles – one to each side – and closed centrally, secured with a flap and three metal clips. The metal d-ring ripcord directly connected to the parachute canopy, normally located in a fabric pocket. Fitted to the reverse are a pair of metal buckles with spring clips for attaching onto the hooks fitted to the observer's parachute assembly harness. Once attached, the parachute sits upon the wearer's chest, but when deployed, the harness strapping becomes detached by the stitching, to rise from the wearers shoulders.

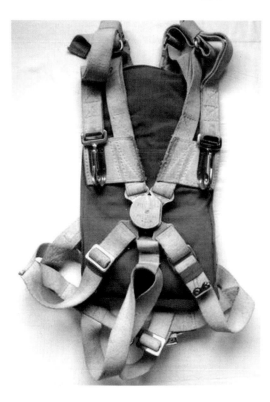

The Irvin observer harness.

The observer parachute.

The bomber crew parachute.

Appendix 5: RAF Backpack Parachute Assembly

The backpack parachute assembly was specifically designed for aircrews within Bomber Command, and in particular, for Lancaster and Halifax aircrews. The perceived benefit of bomber crews wearing a complete harness and parachute assembly proved unfounded when applied practically.

The webbing harness and parachute were combined similarly to the pilot's parachute assembly. The quick-release box was larger as it accommodated six fixing points; this factor alone appears to have made the wearer critical of the design.

Due to its cumbersome and restrictive nature, it was not popular with the crews it was specifically designed for, or indeed any other aircrews across the various commands. This parachute assembly was produced in far lesser quantities than any other parachute of its time.

Appendix 6: RAF K-Type Dinghy Pack

The single man k-type dinghy was tightly compressed and folded into an outer heavy canvas material pack. The cover had a stitched multi-lingual label to ensure instructions were clear to the various exiled pilots serving within the Royal Air Force. Internal pockets held survival equipment. This design proved to be ideal for operational deployment across the entire allied air forces.

Fighter command pilots sat upon the dinghy pack, which was attached to the actual parachute pack. The webbing straps terminated at a metal coupling that connected the dingy to the complete assembly.

Later developments enabled multi-crewed aircraft within other commands the opportunity to hold personal k-type dingy packs. These were simply stowed alongside the observer-type parachute packs and attached by secure clip fasteners. This facility proved to back up the standard large-crew dinghy-support structure already in place. The k-type dingy packs were responsible for saving further lives with Bomber Command.

Appendix 7: Irvin Clothing for Aircrews

The Irvin jacket, designed by the parachute pioneer Leslie Irvin, was tested, assessed, and approved by the Air Ministry. Simply referred to as an 'Irvin', it was ordered in significant numbers, with production contracted out to many manufacturers. The Irvin jacket was issued in slightly differing forms to the Royal Air Force and Commonwealth aircrews during the Second World War.

The first examples went into production in 1931, and were manufactured with undivided one-piece body panels that required only the minimum of necessary seams. Although this facilitated easier assembly, it consumed much greater quantities of material. Irvin jackets constructed in that fashion are now referred to as 'Battle of Britain issue'. The early fighter pilots were all issued with this iconic design of jacket.

With the demand for jackets increasing, a more economic method of manufacture was devised. It was decided that the earlier pattern should be divided into smaller panels of sheepskin, resulting in better use of the materials, but with increased numbers of stitched seams. Coastal Command and Fleet Air Arm crews were issued with an Irvin that had a modified full hood, designed to provide additional protection in cases of having ditched into the sea. The hood was yellow as an aid to being spotted by rescue crews.

As time progressed, and with demand continuing to increase, even greater measures were taken to reduce any waste of the valuable sheepskins. Jackets were produced with additional panels, with increased seams, creating almost

The late Irvin
jacket.

patchwork results. Despite the leather jackets, bomber crews still suffered
from the intense cold, in particular the exposed air gunners. Electrical
heating elements were fitted underneath the external seams, enabling the
crewmember to plug in the suit so it remained warm. The Irvin has become
an item that strongly associates the pilots and aircrews of the Second World
War to that period in aviation history.

The lesser-known Irvin trousers were produced at the same time, and
were designed as one-piece, slip-over, thermal insulated trousers. When
worn with the jacket, the dual sheepskin outer garments provided some
protection from the freezing temperatures at high altitudes. The trousers
were complete with fitted braces to enable easy dressing. The legs were fitted
with separating zips running the full length of each leg, a design crucial
to allow easy removal to treat any wounds. These trousers were also fitted
with electrical elements that ran down both legs, enabling the wearer to gain
constant warmth at high altitudes.

Unlike their parachutes, the Irvin jacket had been completely phased out
by the Royal Air Force by the 1950s. The illustration shows a typical late-
Second World War Irvin with the multiple panel being almost a patchwork
construction.

Appendix 8: Mk I Spitfire Pilot (*c.* 1940), 602 City of Glasgow Squadron

The pilot climbing into the cockpit of his early period Spitfire is wearing the Irvin jacket with its collar pulled upwards. These collars were fitted with an elasticated strap that held it in place. Behind the jacket collar can be seen the Mae West life preserver. The RAF seat-pack parachute is shown hanging below the harness assembly. The pilot would sit upon the parachute and strap himself into the cockpit with the separate harness. In any emergency exit from the aircraft, only the separate harness needed to be opened; fighter pilots frequently adopted the practice of inverting the aircraft and simply falling from the cockpit once the harness buckle was opened.

When hostilities with Germany began, 602 Squadron commenced operations from RAF Drem. On 16 October 1939, the squadron attempted to intercept the first air raid by German bombers on Britain – twelve Junkers JU88 attacking naval shipping near the Forth Bridge. Spitfires from 603 Squadron, based at RAF Turnhouse near Edinburgh, joined the fight and claimed the first kill: a JU88 that hit the sea off Port Seton. A second JU88 was engaged and shot down by 602 Squadron off the Fife village of Crail. This engagement over Scotland marked the first enemy aircraft to be shot

Mk I Spitfire pilot.

down by the Royal Air Force over Britain during the Second World War. The winter of 1940 was a severe one, no doubt the reason why the pilot in this photograph was wearing the full extent of clothing available to him at that time.

Appendix 9: Mk II Spitfire Pilot Wearing the Seat-pack Parachute Assembly.

This spitfire pilot can be seen wearing the complete parachute assembly. Of particular interest is the d-ring ripcord affixed to the webbing structure, which is the direct link to the parachute. Although it looks rather cumbersome in the photograph, once settled within the seat of the cockpit the assembly was practical and no doubt reassuring for the wearer. The d-ring ripcord was partially enclosed within a cloth pouch to protect from unintended deployments. The d-type oxygen mask and b-type flying helmet complete this early period operational pilot's flying equipment.

This particular Spitfire aircraft was the first of two Spitfires donated by Halifax in Yorkshire, identified by the name 'Halifax' painted below the

Mk II Spitfire pilot.

cockpit. This Mk II aircraft carried the identification lettering of P8093, and saw service with 226 Squadron during early 1941. It subsequently served within 123 Squadron and engaged upon convoy protection sorties in Scotland.

In 1942, as a result of a flying accident, Spitfire P8093 was deployed for service at an operational training unit. On 26 June, after a further flying accident, the Spitfire was assessed as damaged beyond repair, and scrapped. Obviously this process involved the recovery of component parts that were capable of re-use, whilst the remainder was re-constituted in various metal recovery processes.

Appendix 10: 609 Squadron Spitfire W3117 (*c.* 1941)

Sgt Thomas Rigler, looking a lot older than his thirty-two years, is seen examining his Spitfire, which had sustained damage during an aerial combat over the summer of 1941. He still has his Mae West life preserver on, which appears to have been painted with what may have been a silver finish. The pouch, which has been roughly stitched to the cotton and has no paint finish,

Sgt Rigler wearing a Mae West life jacket.

would have been used to hold a torch or lamp assembly. The self-inflating tube used to blow air into the bellows is clearly seen on the opposite side, bent double and retained in its own pouch.

Sgt Rigler is wearing the iconic fighter pilot's silk scarf around his neck. This was actually a very important item that allowed consistent head movements to watch the sky above and behind, whilst not causing his neck to become sore, as his sergeant's tunic was made from very rough and coarse material.

Sgt Rigler was posted to 609 Squadron in February 1941. He swiftly made an impression, and claimed two victories during his first engagement with the Luftwaffe. Within the following five weeks, an additional five enemy aircraft were shot down or damaged by him. This photograph is thought to have been taken after the events over Dunkirk on 22 June, when his Spitfire returned suffering from damage. He was awarded the DFM towards the end of 1941, then commissioned as an officer but seriously wounded in 1942. Once recovered, he was further rewarded with the DFC in 1945.

Appendix 11: 609 Squadron Pilot's Press Photograph

Sgt Thomas Rigler is once more seen wearing his Mae West life preserver in this posed photograph, taken during the summer of 1941.

Standing immediately behind, leaning against the fuselage of the Spitfire, is Flt Lt Paul Richie. His Mae West has been personalised by the painting of his name down the side of the cotton fabric surface. A bright-coloured lanyard is affixed above the upper button fastening.

Paul Richie was already an 'ace' pilot when he joined 609 Squadron. During the Battle of France he had destroyed several enemy aircraft. Richie was an early member of the Caterpillar Club, having parachuted to safety on 11 May 1940. On 19 May, having engaged and shot down three Luftwaffe bombers, he sustained serious injuries from returning fire. Forced to make an emergency landing, he was unable to continue flying. Although he was awarded the DFC towards the end of 1940 for his actions over France, it was little compensation for his inability to continue operations during the Battle of Britain

Flt Lt Richie and Sgt Thomas Rigler were both gifted pilots, whose service within 609 Squadron combined to account for twelve enemy aircraft destroyed, in addition to nine probably destroyed or damaged, along with other combats where enemy aircraft were shared between a number of

609 Squadron pilots.

pilots. Famous for their squadron mascots, 609 Squadron posed in this publicity photograph with a goat and two dogs. Sgt Rigler is seen holding what is clearly a young puppy.

Both Rigler and Richie endured serious combat injuries, but thankfully survived the Second World War.

Appendix 12: GQ Club – 'A height of only 300 feet'

RAF
Somewhere – in – England

Dear Sir

I am in grateful receipt of your letter of November 20th and the enclosed gold badge, which as you say, is a memento of the occasion, and to me a highly prised one.

I owe my life to the reliability of your parachutes. Please accept my deepest thanks.

I believe you are acquainted with the circumstances of the jump and the height of the abandoning aircraft … I have nothing but praise for the performance of the chute and most certainly no criticism. The ripcord was pulled immediately and I was clear of the aircraft, at a height I believe of about 300 ft. Two witnesses have confirmed this height. There was no great jerk when the parachute opened, although I recall I had the harness very slack about my body. Furthermore, it opened in time otherwise I would not have the pleasure of writing this letter.

In a few words, Sir, I could wish for no better safety than flying with a GQ parachute.

I remain, Sir,
Your Obedient Servant

Highly significant is the tribute to the GQ parachute expressed in this letter – a convincing testimony to the GQ equipment (*Flight* magazine, October 1944).

Appendix 13: GQ Club

RAF
Somewhere – in – England

Dear Sirs.

I bailed out at approximately 2,500 feet, but as I lost consciousness for a short time, I cannot tell you the sensation after I had pulled the ripcord. However I was floating very safely down to the sea when I recovered consciousness.

I should like to comment on the extreme efficiency of my parachute whereby my life was saved. I am very grateful for the work of your company, and I know that should I ever have to bail out again with one of your parachutes, I can be assured of a safe landing.

Yours faithfully.

A flying man's demands upon his safety equipment are necessarily varied, often unique, and sometimes fantastic, as this letter graphically testifies. Yet GQ parachutes that perform so notably under abnormal wartime conditions were fashioned to meet just such demands. Should you have occasion to bail out anywhere, anytime, using GQ equipment you automatically qualify for membership to the GQ Club. Drop a line to the Parachute Co. Ltd, Stadium Works, Woking, Surrey, when applying for your gold badge and certificate. Give the following information: full name, rank and service number, date of authenticated emergency descent, and number and type of GQ parachute. Send a confirmatory letter from the squadron intelligence officer, squadron or flight commander, or officer in charge of the squadron parachute section.

Appendix 14: Ditching Instructions, Avro Lancaster Bomber Crew

Pilot: warns wireless operator to take up ditching position, then re-establishes intercom with air bomber and navigator. Lowers flaps to 25 degrees and turns into final approach position according to state of sea, switching on landing lamp if ditching at night. Warns crew, 'Brace for ditching' and disconnects intercom.

Navigator wireless operator and flight engineer: brace for impact with hands behind neck, backs against the main-spar, and feet against the flapjack.

Bomb aimer, mid-upper and rear gunner: take up ditching positions with arms around each other's necks, and brace feet

Pilot: secures harness and braces feet against rudder bar.

Evacuation of aircraft.

Pilot: climbs out through roof hatch and inflates Mae West, then crawls over the top of the fuselage and drops down onto starboard wing.

Navigator: climbs out through mid-ditching exit with his satchel and lifeline (handed to navigator by wireless operator) and climbs onto starboard wing

Wireless operator: holds lifeline and climbs out through mid-ditching exit and climbs down onto starboard wing

Flight engineer: operates manual dinghy release and follows wireless operator through mid-ditching exit; climbs down onto starboard wing.

Mid-upper gunner: collects emergency packs, numbers four and seven.

Rear gunner: operates rear dinghy manual release, holds lifeline, and crawls along top of fuselage; climbs down onto starboard wing.

Bomb aimer: follows rear gunner.

Navigator: holds dinghy steady whilst wireless operator climbs aboard and applies leak stoppers where necessary. Navigator then climbs in and assists wireless operator.

Rear gunner: steps into dinghy.

Bomb aimer: climbs onto starboard wing and holds lifeline.

Flight engineer: climbs onto starboard wing and stands with pilot, then collects emergency packs from mid-upper gunner.

Mid-upper gunner: hands radio and kite assembly to pilot.

Bomb aimer: climbs into dinghy.

Flight engineer: hands emergency packs to rear gunner and climbs into dinghy.

Flight engineer and rear gunner: haul in the emergency stowage pack from the sea and stow.

Pilot: hands radio to rear gunner and climbs into dinghy with kite assembly over his shoulder.

Mid-upper gunner: last to climb into dinghy, enabling cast off from aircraft.

RAF aircrew in late-type dingy launching a kite.

Endnotes

Introduction

1. Reginald Foster Dagnall was born in London in 1888. In 1920 he formed the company RFD Ltd, designing and manufacturing pneumatic dinghies and barrage balloons. He died on 16 November 1942. The company later amalgamated with the Beaufort Co. and became RFD Beaufort.

2. Silkworm is the common name for the silk-producing larvae of several species of moth. The larva is not a worm at all, but a caterpillar. The adult moths are extinct in the wild but are reared in large numbers by the silk industry. The silkworm feeds mainly on the leaves of the mulberry tree.

3. Formed by Lord Portal in 1945. Members included RAF escapers and evaders, and those who assisted them. A large proportion of RAF evaders parachuted from distressed aircraft into occupied territory.

4. Oflag is an abbreviation of *Offizier Lager*. These camps were for officers only.

5. Stalag is an abbreviation for *Stammlager*. These camps were for enlisted men.

6. Stalag Luft camps were for airmen.

7. During the night 24/25 March 1944, seventy-six allied airmen escaped from Stalag Luft III Sagan. Seventy-three prisoners were quickly recaptured; on orders from Berlin fifty were then executed by the Gestapo. Of the remainder, four were later recaptured and sent to Sachsenhausen Concentration Camp, two to Colditz, one imprisoned in Berlin, and another to the Stalag Luft camp, Barth on the Baltic coast. Fifteen were returned to Stalag Luft III, and three who evaded capture eventually reached England.

8. J. B. Haywards, PoW nominal register, 1990.

9. McCook field was the army air service's experimental test field.

10. Walter Lees joined the Caterpillar Club on the 13 May 1924. He was flying a second-hand German First World War aircraft, which, for no particular reason, developed serious control problems immediately after take-off. He managed to make a circle and head into the field for landing, but the instant he throttled back, the plane went completely out of control. He knew he had to use the chute but did not have enough altitude to jump; he slid up in the seat, pulled the ripcord, and let

the chute pull him out of the cockpit. He was so low that his side hit the ground on the first swing of the chute and he sustained a leg and hip injury that caused him considerable trouble the rest of his life. The plane crashed and was badly wrecked less than 100 feet from where he landed.

11. Stanley Switlik was born in Poland on 4 December 1890. He died in the USA on 4 March 1981

12. Michael C. Dilts, Vice President Switlik Parachute Co.

13. Aircraft identified as HE111 in After the Battle publication, *The Battle of Britain Then and Now.*

14. Shores, Christopher and Williams, Clive, *Aces High.*

15. P. B. Cow & Co. originated in 1826. The founder, Mr Cow, was a great inventor and innovator, not only in rubber. He wrote a book *Cow on Boats*, with illustrations of amphibious vehicles, landing craft, and buoyancy aids. Trials took place during the Boar War. By 1938 the company director commenced looking for military contracts and acquired a trial order for gas masks. Further orders immediately flooded in and within three months the firm was employing additional staff, all on piecework. Meanwhile the head office was experimenting with several other wartime requirements – out of which came the production of dinghies and other survival equipment deployed in the Second World War.

16. Vaughan-Thomas established a reputation as one of the BBC's most respected correspondents. In 1943 he volunteered to participate in a bombing raid to Berlin in order to report from within a Lancaster.

17. Fleet Air Arm pilots and aircrew.

18. Mae West was born on 17 August 1893 and died on 22 November 1980. She was an American actress, playwright, screenwriter, and sex symbol.

19. The Gloster Gladiator was the RAF's last biplane fighter to be produced. It appeared at a time when monoplanes like the Hurricane were already eclipsing biplanes, and yet the Gladiator achieved fame in the hands of skilled pilots, fighting some of the most dramatic battles of the early war years. When Italy entered the war in June 1940, Gladiators were serving with 80 Squadron in Egypt. The Gladiator proved a fairly even match for the Fiat CR.42 and was successful in helping repel the Italian invasion of Egypt and defeating Italian forces in East Africa.

20. Harold Gillies pioneered early developments in plastic surgery, but his work during the First World War went largely unnoticed. He was a major influence on his cousin, Archibald McIndoe, who advanced plastic surgery techniques still further during the Second World War.

21. Founded as a cottage hospital in 1863, the Queen Victoria Hospital was built on its current site during the 1930s. The hospital became a specialist burns unit headed by Archibald McIndoe during the Second World War.

22. Self-sealing tanks were constructed with multiple layers of rubber and reinforcing fabrics, vulcanised rubber and untreated natural rubber, able to absorb fluid and expand when wet. When a fuel tank is punctured, the fuel will seep into the layers, causing the swelling of the untreated layer, thus sealing the puncture. The Sorbo Co., famous for its pre-war rubber ball manufacturing, was engaged in self-sealing laminating construction and development throughout the Second World War.

23. Anniversary Reunion held at Felbridge Hotel, East Grinstead.
24. The Handley Page Hampden, a British twin-engine medium bomber of the Royal Air Force serving in the Second World War. Because of its cramped crew conditions, it was known as the 'Flying Suitcase'. The Hampden was retired from Bomber Command service in late 1942.
25. Commander of the Order of the British Empire.
26. Editor of the Guinea Pig Club magazine. Jack Toper was of great assistance to the author in many respects.

Chapter 1: Taking to the Sea

27. Arthur Travers Harris, born in 1892 in Cheltenham. He went to boarding school in England and then settled in Rhodesia. At the outbreak of the First World War he returned to England and joined the Royal Flying Corps. Harris later became a squadron leader in the newly formed RAF, serving in India and the Middle East. He returned to England at the outbreak of the Second World War in early 1942, taking over as commander-in-chief of Bomber Command. Heavy losses of bombers on daytime raids at the time caused Harris to implement a new and more efficient bombing strategy.
28. Whistles were attached to the Mae West life preservers by a cord. Early issue were metal chromes, but in extreme cold conditions the metal surface froze to the airmens' lips. Later variants were designed and constructed of a light-coloured plastic.

Chapter 2: Taking to the Silk

29. The de Havilland DH9A, known as the 'Ninak', was developed as a medium bomber. It was produced in 1918 and saw limited service in the First World War, before going on to form the backbone of the Royal Air Force's post-war colonial bombing force.
30. SOE: the most secret dropping of agents by parachute across occupied Europe.
31. Sterkrade, Germany, was an allied bombing target for the oil campaign of the Second World War.
32. German defensive anti-aircraft fire.
33. The point where the pilot maintains a constant and predicted course on approach to the target.
34. 494 Lancaster bombers took part in this raid. German night fighters intercepted the bombers over France and shot down thirty-nine Lancasters, representing a combined total of 312 allied aircrew personnel who failed to return. The bright moonlight had assisted the Luftwaffe night fighters in achieving these statistics.

Chapter 3: Flt Lt Paul Libert, Spitfire pilot – Caterpillar Club

35. Belgium preliminary insignia for pilots.
36. Belgium full pilot's wings.
37. The Westland Whirlwind was the first twin-engine fighter to enter RAF service.

When it appeared it was faster at low altitude than any single-seat fighter and armed with four 20 mm cannons, yet only two squadrons were ever equipped with the Whirlwind.

38. 349 Squadron were the second Belgium squadron to be formed within the RAF. This squadron flew Spitfires, presented by the Belgian Congo Fighter Fund, each aircraft bearing the name of prominent districts, towns, or personalities.

39. Ramrod fighter escort duties to bombers.

40. Intelligence reports indicated Hitler's forces were using it as a base to strategise attacks on England. It was later identified as housing troops operating the V1 launch sites.

41. When fitted with bombs, Typhoon ground attack aircraft became known as 'Bombphoon'.

42. Camille Gutt was responsible for saving the Belgian franc before and after the Second World War. Before the war, he saved the Belgian currency by secretly transferring the gold reserves of the Belgian National Bank out of Nazi reach. After the war, he was able to stabilise the Belgian franc and forestall inflation, with what is still known as the 'Gutt Operation'.

43. De Breteuil, Paris, used for a prison during the French Revolution and for Luftwaffe headquarters during the Second World War.

44. The term 'Dulag Luft' was short for Durchgangslager der Luftwaffe, or 'Transit camp of the Luftwaffe'.

45. Prisoners were frequently offered medication in exchange for information.

Chapter 4: PO William Fullerton DFM – Caterpillar Club

46. Millions of leaflets were dropped by the RAF. All were produced by the PWE (Political Warfare Executive) for propaganda purposes. Leaflet-dropping sorties were referred to as 'nickel raids'.

47. A method of doing away with rod or cable control linkages, typically linking actuator and control by hydraulic means and most commonly used in propeller pitch control gear.

48. Taylor, *Operation Millenium: Bomber Harris's raid on Cologne, May 1942*.

Chapter 5: Sqn Ldr Barcroft Mathers DFC, navigator – Caterpillar Club & PoW

49. In 1932, the Westland Wallace was put into production for the Royal Air Force. Three years later, Westland designed an improved version fitted with a more powerful engine and the then-novel idea of an enclosed canopy over both crew positions. This offered greater comfort for the crew and improved the rear gunner's aim by protecting him from the slipstream. This was a significant development leading towards future fighter aircraft development.

50. Razzles were small pellets of phosphorus inserted between pieces of celluloid. They were transported in water containers for release over the target areas, designed to burst into flame and start fires as they dried out on the ground. There were a small number of operations by 10 and 77 Squadrons dropping these devices between July and November 1940.

51. It was not until the winter of 1943/early 1944 that Bomber Command commenced concentrated raids upon Berlin, referred to as the 'Battle of Berlin'. Berlin always represented a dangerous 650 miles or more harrowing experience for the bomber crews dispatched to the 'Big City', as they called it.

52. Correspondence with the author, 2007. Al Trotter DFC DFM: 23 February 1923 to 18 August 2011.

53. Daylight operations by Bomber Command were required to be written in green ink. Night operations were recorded in red ink. Training duties or other duties were written in black ink.

54. Taken from a newspaper cutting in Barcroft's personal account, as sent to his parents in Australia.

55. FW (*Flugzeugfuehrer*) Erwin Egelar Stab 14/NJG1 was later shot down in air combat on 19/20 October 1944 (Dr Theo Boiten).

56. Marlag Nord was situated 30 miles south-west of Hamburg and 10 miles north of Bremen. It was a camp created for the confinement of naval and merchant marine prisoners of war.

57. Darmstadt suffered significantly from air raids conducted by the RAF. It must be presumed the hostile reaction imposed upon Sqn Ldr Mathers was as a result of those experiences upon the residents.

Chapter 6: Flt Lt Philip Anscombe DFM AFC, pilot – GQ Club

58. The British Hawker Hind was a Royal Air Force light bomber of the interwar years produced by Hawker Aircraft. It was developed from the Hawker Hart day-bomber introduced in 1931. The Bristol Blenheim replaced the Hind at the beginning of the Second World War.

59. Chorley, *OTU Bomber Command Losses*, vol. 7, p. 191.

60. GQ membership badges are all identified by the sequential numbering.

Chapter 7: Wg Cdr William Douglas DFC & bar, pilot – Guinea Pig Club

61. This incident entitled both pilots to apply for membership to one or other of the GQ or Caterpillar Clubs. No evidence exists to ascertain if that took place.

62. Formed on 1 June 1943, 2nd Tactical Air Force Army Co-operation Command. It took units from both Fighter Command and Bomber Command in order to form a force capable of supporting the Army in the field.

Chapter 9: Flt Lt Cedric Stone DFM, Spitfire pilot – Caterpillar Club

63. The name of Parnall was associated with the development of a range of aircraft in the interwar years. During the Second World War they specifically produced gun turrets to Archie Frazer-Nash's design until the war ended.

64. RAF Hornchurch was situated on the outskirts of East London. The Thames estuary acted as a funnel for attacking German aircraft, flying in a westerly direction after locating the estuary, which took them directly into London. 'Barrow Deep' is the Thames estuary area.

65. This merchant vessel carried many troops and personnel (approximately 5,000) to the Middle East area of conflict during the war. For this voyage, she joined a convoy made up of twenty-seven ships with escorts of royal navy battleships and aircraft carriers.

66. Nichols Debono., aircraftsman 1st class, RAFVR, from Qormi, Malta.

67. Alwyn Harold Sands, flight sergeant, RAAF, from Manly, New South Wales, Australia.

68. Derek Harland Ward DFC and bar, a Second World War New Zealand flying ace. Credited with six kills, one shared destroyed, one probable, and four damaged against the Luftwaffe. Sqn Ldr Ward was shot down and killed by the German ace Hans-Joachim Marseille on 16 June 1942.

69. Hans-Joachim Marseille, 13 December 1919 to 30 September '42. One of the best Luftwaffe fighter pilots of the Second World War, Marseille claimed all but seven of his 158 victories against the British Commonwealth's Desert Air Force over North Africa. Seventeen aircraft were shot down by him in one day. (Toliver, *Fighter Aces of the Luftwaffe*.)

70. War service was to be counted as 'double'. The requirement for this award was ten years efficient service in the Auxiliary and Volunteer Air Service.

Chapter 10: Sqn Ldr Terence Carr DFC AFC, pilot – Goldfish Club rescuer; PO Dunn, Sgt Savill, Sgt Gibbons, Sgt Allen & Sgt Riley

71. 230 Squadron were to experience the delivery of the first Short Sunderland flying boat, an aircraft that made a strong impact upon the air force and went on to serve throughout the Second World War.

72. An entire chapter is devoted to this remarkable rescue by Masters in his popular wartime book, *So Few*.

Chapter 11: Flt Lt George Dove CGM DFM, air gunner – Guinea Pig Club

73. James MacCoubrey was, from the outbreak of hostilities, serving as a sergeant pilot within 10 Squadron. After nine months operational flying, he was rested and posted for instructor duties at 19 Operational Training Unit, Kinloss. On 18 February 1941, the Whitley aircraft in which he was captain suffered engine failure on approach to Forres, crashing on the aerodrome boundary. Five of the crew died in the wreckage; Sgts Lawley and MacCoubrey were rescued but seriously burned. Three days later, MacCoubrey died of his extensive burns.

74. Aircraft crashed into high ground 5 miles NNW of Alston, Cumberland.

Chapter 12: Sqn Ldr Jack Purcell BEM, air gunner – Goldfish Club

75. Augustus Rodney Gibbes DSO DFC and bar, RAAF (commissioned RAF), was killed in action 1943, when he was shot down and crashed into the sea during his third operational tour of duty. He is commemorated on the Malta Memorial.

76. Wg Cdr Holder received the DSO in October 1942. The recommendation, from official sources, states: 'Wing Commander Holder took over the command of 218

Squadron on 1.1.42. Since taking over operational command of 218 Squadron he has carried out 14 sorties including a successful daylight attack on Lubeck in which he led his squadron. His courage, coolness and ability as Squadron Commander is outstanding. The esprit de corps of his squadron and the confidence his crews have in his ability and leadership, his keenness for operations does not effect the administration of his squadron and with his organising ability he has always managed to maintain a high serviceability with his Sterling aircraft. I have no hesitation in recommending him for an award of the D.S.O.'

77. On the night of 25 April, 218 Squadron was given a special assignment to strike the Skoda works at Pilsen, Czechoslovakia. A small force of six bombers was allocated to the low-level attack, which was carried out at just 1,500 feet.

78. A return visit was ordered for this target during the first week of May. Sqn Ldr Arthur Waite Oldroyd added an immediate DFC to his AFC during this particular raid; his aircraft was subjected to damage by flak and night fighters.

79. Regarded as a gallantry award and referred to as an MID, this was signified by the wearing of a bronze oak leaf emblem stitched onto the medal ribbon or worn directly upon the uniform itself.

Chapter 13: Sgt Woolston, pilot – Goldfish Club; Sgt McKay, Sgt Chandler & Sgt Wood

80. Sgt Woolston's sickness, exacerbated the dehydration of his body, explained these symptoms.

Chapter 14: Sqn Ldr George Davies DSO MID, pilot – Caterpillar Club

81. William Arthur Fullerton DFM, 58 Squadron, Bomber Command – account within this publication.

82. Reference identity sequence written in squadron operational record book, details of sortie.

83. PO Davies received recognition for night photographic work on 6/7 July during inclement weather.

84. Sgt Neil Stockdale from Huddersfield, aged twenty-six, was buried in Driffield Cemetery.

85. Sgt Colin Campbell Scott RAAF, aged twenty-three, from Victoria, Australia.

86. Air Mar. Sir Hugh Sidney Porter Walmsley KCB KCIE CBE MC DFC was a senior commander in the Royal Air Force during and after the Second World War.

87. Hamish Mahaddie DSO DFC AFC was responsible for many developments into the path finder force within Bomber Command. His crew were due to receive a combined eleven decorations at Buckingham Palace in 1943, however after the crew's first operation without him, they failed to return from that sortie.

88. Recognised within the RAF as PFF.

89. I am indebted to Oliver Clutton-Brook, who allowed me to quote from his 16 January 1990 interview with the late George Davies.

90. TI path finder force reference to target indicators, coloured flares used to control the main bombing force.

91. The MI9 PoW questionnaire compiled by Davies on 11 May 1945 advises his capture at 6 a.m. on 15 July 1944.
92. Date of registration at the interrogation centre was 24 July 1944.

Chapter 15: Sgt Philip Felton, navigator – Goldfish Club; Sqn Ldr Harrison-Broadley

93. Sqn Ldr John Harrison-Broadley DFC; born 14 October 1920, died 13 November 1983.
94. Stuart Carl Thompson, Caterpillar Club member, bailed out at 4,000 feet over Belgium and evaded capture (1940).
95. Stuart Thompson was killed in the Avro York MW205, which crashed near Cairo on 20 November 1946, in transit to the UK.
96. Stuart Thompson escaped over the mountains with two others, covering 200 miles and reaching allied lines in sixteen days of walking.

Chapter 16: Flt Lt Gordon Bennett, pilot – Late Arrivals Club

97. The term 'zero feet' was used to indicate the requirement to attack at the lowest height possible.
98. Axis alliance, Axis nations, Axis countries, or just the Axis, was a reference to the alliance of forces fighting the allies during the Second World War. In this context, the Italian forces were fighting alongside the German forces in North Africa.
99. 72 Operational Training Unit, based at Nanyuki in March 1942, trained light bomber crews under tropical conditions. Flying Blenheims, Bostons, and Avro Anson aircraft as part of AHQ East Africa.

Chapter 17: Sqn Ldr Leonard Pipkin DFC & bar, pilot – Caterpillar Club & evader; Sqn Ldr Saxelby, 'Great Escape' participant

100. This is now Blackpool Airport.
101. After initial reticence by high command within the RAF, Polish squadrons did evolve and came to operate within all commands of the RAF.
102. Clive King Saxelby CBE DFC AFC later became a PoW in Stalag Luft III, where he played a leading role in the planning and organisation of the 'Great Escape'. Know as 'Big Sax', he was automatically selected to be in the first 100 men to leave the escape tunnel. Allocated position eighty-one, he about to leave the tunnel when it was discovered – just as escaper seventy-eight exited to the woods.
103. Sgt C. E. Benstead, later buried in the Jonkerbos War Cemetery in Nijmegen.
104. Research via the Dutch Association of Allied Aircrew Helpers, W. J. M. Willemsen, 1999.

Chapter 18: FO Patrick Flynn DFC, pilot – Caterpillar & Goldfish Clubs

105. The 'Arnold Scheme' commenced in 1941, taking the name of Gen. 'Hap' Arnold. USAAC (United States Army Air Corps) was based in the SEACTC (South-east

Air Corps Training Centre) area. The scheme's aim was to train 4,000 British and USAAC pilots. The last intake of student pilots took place in early 1943.

106. RAF Tangmere near Chichester, Sussex. SOE Lysander aircraft flew from this airfield delivering and collecting agents across France. It was also a front line fighter airfield during the Battle of Britain.

107. Edward Selwyn Moulton-Barrett: born 1895, commissioned RAF 1918, retired 1946 as wing commander.

108. Focker-Wulf FW200 Condor: long-range armed reconnaissance aircraft capable of operating for 15 hours in the air.

109. Convoy code lettering SL, West Africa to Great Britain.

110. Goldfish Club membership by use of a Mae West resulted in the card being endorsed accordingly.

111. There were nine combat catapult launches in total; eight aircraft and one pilot were lost. Eight German aircraft were destroyed and one damaged. Twelve of the thirty-five CAM ships had been sunk while sailing on 170 round-trip voyages.

Chapter 19: Flt Sgt Raymond Warwick – Late Arrivals Club; PO Hare & PO Chappell

112. Geodetic construction of the aircrafts fuselage comprised of six main metalwork frames; once constructed, the fabric was stretched over the entire structure of the aircraft.

113. As supplied to the author by the family in 1999.

114. Sgt R. Smith, 37 Squadron, in correspondence: 'The story went around that the Italian vehicle they attempted to steal from had Italian soldiers sleeping in the back, the fugitive crew were forced to scatter.' Sgt Smith took part on the same raid over Tobruk.

115. Salt marsh depression in the western desert of Egypt, covering 7,500 square miles and 400 feet below sea level. Very soft sand made it virtually impassable to vehicles. The depression protected the left flank of the allied armies before and during the second battle of El Alamein in 1942. It was consistently used as a navigation point for allied aircrews.

116. The Military Medal was only awarded on five occasions during the Second World War to members of the RAAF.

Chapter 20: WO R. G. Faux, wireless operator – Goldfish Club

117. Stanley Ernest Joseph Jones – DFM awarded having completed thirty-four operations during his first tour of duty.

118. *Heeresversuchsanstalt Peenemünde* (Army Research Center), today simply known as *Peenemünde*.

119. Albert William Edward Cartwright – DFM awarded having completed thirty-six operations during his first tour of duty.

120. FO Holding joined 617 Squadron, but died in a flying accident in January 1944. He was killed in Lancaster ED918, one of the surviving aircraft from the famous Dambuster raids of May 1943.

121. Portugal was a neutral country during the Second World War. There was some allegiance towards the allies, however. Faux and his crew were interned as required to comply with their neutrality, but this was foreshortened, allowing them to return to the UK.

Chapter 22: Sgt Allaway RAF, rear gunner

122. Two flights normally existed, identified by the lettering 'A' and 'B'.
123. Desert landing strips were very basic affairs. Identification was by LG (landing ground) and numbering.
124. The broken hydraulic system rendered the wing flaps inoperable, and without flaps the aircraft was denied additional reduction in landing speed.
125. Wg Cdr Chaplin DSO DFC had worked with Barnes Wallis, developing the flying magnetic mine detonation device that was fitted to Wellington aircraft. He received personal congratulations from Winston Churchill for his work.
126. LG20 Quotafiya I, LG104 Quotafiya II, LG21 Quotafiya III, western desert landing grounds.
127. Requesting magnetic course to steer with zero wind to reach a specific location.

Chapter 24: Flt Sgt Frederick Hesketh DFM, flight engineer

128. Richard Dimbleby was born in Richmond-upon-Thames, London, on 25 May 1913. He married in 1937 and had four children. He commenced his career working for the family newspaper, the *Richmond and Twickenham Times*. He joined the BBC as one of the first radio news reporters in 1936, and accompanied the British Expeditionary Force to France as the first BBC war correspondent in 1939. He reported from front line in Middle East, East Africa, the western desert, and Greece, in 1939-42. He also flew on twenty missions with RAF Bomber Command and was the first reporter to enter Belsen concentration camp. After the Second World War became the foremost commentator on state occasions, and presenter of the BBC's *Panorama*, 1955-63. He was awarded OBE 1945 and CBE 1959. He died in London on 22 December 1965.
129. The Ruhr valley was the exact opposite of happiness, which is how the reference came about.
130. The term 'scarecrow' was used by aircrews for such massive explosions; it was thought that special ordinance or weapons capable of such devastation were being used by the Germans (though this was later refuted).

Chapter 25: WO Norman Pawley DFM, wireless operator

131. *London Gazette*, 20 July 1943. 651401 Sgt Norman Jack Pawley, 15 Squadron, jointly listed with 1316716 Sgt W. Towse, 15 Squadron.
132. Wilhelm Dormann had shot down 14 aircraft when he himself was shot down by an RAF Bristol Beaufighter of 141 Squadron on the 17 August 1943. Dormanns radar operator Friedrich Schmalscheidt was killed when his parachute failed to operate correctly, Dormann suffered serious head injuries and burns as he bailed

out, he never flew operationally again.

133. Prisoners above the rank of Corporal and all RAF POW's were not allowed to undertake work details. This prevented any escape attempts whilst on work parties. In addition it prevented reconnaissance for possible escape attempts under planning. Identity exchanges were agreed by mutual consent.

134. Escape attempts were authorised by the respective camp 'escape committee'. The supply of escape compasses, maps and supplies were allocated to authorised escape attempts.

Chapter 26: WO Sidney McQuillan, wireless operator – Goldfish Club & Guinea Pig Club; Flt Lt R. Campbell

135. RAF, Second world War, 38 Group squadrons: 161, 190, 196, 295, 296, 297, 298, 299, 570, 620, and 644.

136. Special Operations Executive officially formed by Prime Minister Winston Churchill and Minister of Economic Warfare Hugh Dalton in 1940. Instructed to aid local resistance movements, it was ordered by Churchill to 'set Europe ablaze'. Its mission was to encourage and facilitate espionage, sabotage, and reconnaissance behind enemy lines.

137. Stores were usually parachuted in cylindrical containers, known as a c-type; 69 inches long, and when fully loaded, could weigh up to 224 lb. The h-type was the same size overall, but could be broken down into five smaller sections. This made it easier to carry and conceal, but impossible to transport long loads such as rifles.

138. The changing of pitch or angle of the blade into the air, feathering is usually done when there has been an engine failure in flight. It is done by turning the prop blades at right angles to the line of flight, to reduce drag and to stop the engine from sustaining serious mechanical damage.

139. The rotation of a propeller by the force of air, acting with no power from the engine.

Chapter 27: WO Donald Norman, wireless operator – Goldfish Club

140. Short Sunderland was one of the most widely used flying boats throughout the Second World War. Significant developments evolved from its deployments against U-boats. Crewed by eleven men, this massive aircraft was built by the Short Brothers in Belfast.

141. U563 was launched early 1941. A type VIIC submarine, these were the workhorses of the German U-boat force in the Second World War, with boats of this type being built throughout.

142. U106 was launched in 1940.

143. High speed launch 144 was built by British Power Boat Co. in 1940. It was a Mk II 63-feet long launch referred to as a 'Whaleback'-type due to the distinctive curve design to the deck. HSL144 was replaced by the Mk III design in 1943.

Chapter 29: Sgt E. Dash, air gunner – Guinea Pig Club; Sgt R. Hawksworth

144. Knedlington is a small hamlet located in the East Riding of Yorkshire, and forms part of the civil parish of Asselby. It is situated approximately 1 mile west of the market town of Howden.

145. Paul Jenkins was buried in Kirkby Wharfe Cemetery, near RAF Church Fenton, Yorkshire. His twin brother, also a pilot in the RAF, had been killed two years previously on 16 June 1940, whilst serving with 223 Squadron in North Africa. PO M. T. Jenkins was flying Wellesley aircraft L2694 when shot down by flak. Jenkins and his crew member Dixon are commemorated on the Alamein Memorial, as their bodies were never recovered. The Jenkins twins had been born on Malta, which was first bombed on 11 June 1940, after Italy's entry into the Second World War.

146. J. Toper, Guinea Pig Club.

Chapter 30: Sub Lt Henry David Whelpton, Fleet Air Arm pilot – GQ Club

147. Sourabaya Java, Japanese naval dry-dock installations.

148. Grumman Avenger was an American aircraft used by the royal navy's Fleet Air Arm, where it was initially known as the 'Tarpon'; this name was later discontinued and the Avenger name was consistently used throughout the war.

149. Sub-Lt B. D. Quigg also claimed a zero during the engagement on 25 July 1944.

150. The Japanese established three prisoner of war camps in the area of Palambang. In May 1944, the commander of the Soengei Geru Camp ignored pleas by the ranking prisoner of war British naval surgeon to build isolation wards to prevent the spread of dysentery. As a result, the disease spread throughout the camp, causing significant additional suffering and loss of life.

151. The Royal New Zealand Navy published (1956): 'Execution by Japanese of Fleet Air Arm officers Sub-Lt (A) J. K. Haberfield, RNZNVR, of HMS *Indomitable*, and Sub-Lt (A) E. J. Baxter, RNZNVR, of HMS *Illustrious*, were shot down on 26 January 1945 during an attack on the oil refineries at Palembang, Sumatra. They were captured by the Japanese and, in February 1945, sent to Singapore where they were placed in Outram Road gaol. At the end of July 1945 they were executed, together with seven other Fleet Air Arm pilots. There was no trial before the execution of the prisoners. The two Japanese particularly concerned were Captain Toshio Kataoka, who was the senior officer, and a Captain Ikeda. These men committed suicide. Kataoka, in a will made before his suicide, said: "We took nine prisoners from Outram Road in a lorry to the beach at the northernmost end of Changi and executed them with Japanese swords. The bodies were put in a boat prepared beforehand and sunk in the sea with weights attached. Now that the responsibility must be borne out publicly, I hereby pay for my deeds with suicide."'

Chapter 32: Flt Lt Dennis Derby DFC, pilot – Caterpillar Club; Maj. Gen. Horace Birks, Brig. Cecil Timmis, Maj. Gen. Henry Foote VC & Maj. Gen. Noel Napier-Clavering

152. SS *Letitia* was an ocean-going liner, built initially for service with the shipping firm Anchor-Donaldson Ltd. Requisitioned at the start of the Second World War. The *Letitia* served as an armed merchant cruiser, later withdrawn from that service in 1941 to become a troop ship. She was badly damaged in 1943, becoming a hospital ship in Canada. SS *Letitia* was returned to civilian service in 1946.
153. Referred to as the 'Beau' by aircrews, a long-range heavy fighter, this aircraft had a long career and served in almost all theatres of war in the Second World War – first as a night fighter, then as a fighter bomber, eventually replacing the Beaufort as a torpedo bomber.
154. This bullet was recovered from the pilot's seat and kept by Dennis Derby as a personal good luck charm.
155. Freighter or minesweeper class of vessel.
156. On 8 September 1944, the Italian liner *Rex* was hit by 123 rockets launched by RAF aircraft. She burned for four days, then rolled onto the port side, and sank in shallow water. This attack prevented the liner from being deployed as a blockship by the Germans for Trieste Harbour.
157. Irvin Caterpillar Club records confirm the applications.

Chapter 35: Royal Air Force Escaping Society (RAFES); Sgt W. Bilton – Caterpillar Club & evader

158. Oliver Lawrence Spurling Philpot MC DFC (6 March 1913 to 6 May '93) was a Second World War RAF pilot, best known for being one of the three men to successfully escape from Stalag Luft III in what became known as 'The Wooden Horse'. Philpot experienced ditching in the sea and surviving two days exposure in a dinghy before being rescued by the German navy. It has not been possible to establish if he applied for membership to the Goldfish Club.
159. Ecorcei is a village 44 km east of Argentan and 6 km south-west of Laigle. The cemetery holds twelve Commonwealth war graves from the Second World War.
160. Brian Bilton visited the farmhouse, staying with the sisters and assisting on the farm. Photographs of this visit were kindly provided by the family, and in particular, Mr James Caw, who also confirmed the existence of Sgt Bilton's Caterpillar Club membership.

Bibliography

Bishop, E., *McIndoes Army* (Grubb Street)
Carter, N. and C., *The DFC and How It Was Won* (Savannah)
Chorley, W. R., *Bomber Command Losses* (Midland Counties)
Clutton-Brock, O., *Massacre over the Marne* (PSL Publishing)
Halley, J., *Squadrons of the RAF & Commonwealth* (Air Britain)
Matron, M., *Honour the Air Forces* (Token)
Middlebrook, M. and Everitt, C., *Bomber Command War Diaries* (Viking)
Tavender, I., *The DFM Register for the Second World War* (Savannah)
Wynn, K., *Men of the Battle of Britain* (Gliddon)

RAF Flying Training & Support Units (Air Britain)
The Battle of Britain Then and Now (After the Battle)
The Blitz Then and Now (After the Battle)

National Archives recommendations for honours and awards, under the terms of the Open Government Licence.